Mewati Rebellion of 1857

Aijaz Ahmad

Originals
Delhi-110052

Published 2017

ISBN 10: 81-8454-153-8
ISBN 13: 978-81-8454-153-3

Published By
Originals
(an imprint of Low Price Publications)
A-6, Nimri Commercial Centre,
Near Ashok Vihar Phase-IV,
Delhi-110052
Phones: 011-27302453
e-mail: info@Lppindia.com
Website: www.Lppindia.com

Printed At:
D K Fine Art Press P Ltd.
Delhi-110052

PRINTED IN INDIA

In the Memory of my Father
Late Shafaat Mohammad
who will always survive in our hearts

Preface

This work "Mewati Rebellion of 1857" is an attempt to understand the role of the people of Mewat region, including the districts Mewat, Gurgaon, Palwal, Faridabad, Rewari and Mahendragarh, in the Rebellion of 1857. Rebellion of 1857 is, although, considered to be the most written event of the world history, but still many of its dimensions seem to be enveloped in confusion and elusiveness, and the role of the Mewatis is one of them. The main focus of this research is to analyze the role of Mewati people during the Rebellion of 1857 in qualitative and quantitative terms through content analysis. Being close to Delhi, their role in the Mewat region and other parts of Haryana, Punjab, Rajasthan, Uttar Pradesh and Madhya Pradesh, in crucial phase of 1857-58, was much important. In the lack of appropriate attention towards this forgotten community, their role in the Rebellion still left for proper research and writing.

The Rebellion of 1857 was such an event, which had various aspects and outlook that it is very difficult to come to a decisive conclusion, particularly in identifying its character even today. In order to put the ideology on an open platform, the scholars are divided into different schools of thought. The British historiography or imperialist school of thought continuously stressed on its mutinous character right from its beginning. They claim that the revolt was a mutiny of the Sepoys while ignoring the grievances of the local people and their mass level participation in the Rebellion. It followed a long-standing debate over its nature and character. During the Rebellion, the political thinkers Benjamin Disraeli claimed the Rebellion as national revolt and on the same time the world fame philosopher Karl Marx characterized it a popular insurrection. Sir Syed Ahmad Khan also blamed the policies of the British Government for this general insurrection. After a long gap, the theory of Disraeli was revived by Vinayak Damodar Savarkar in 1909, by calling the Rebellion as war of independence.

During the uprising centenary celebrations in 1957, there started a re-examination of the same question of nature of the Rebellion. Surendranath Sen wrote an official history that concluded, carefully and with admirable restraint, that it was a war of independence, which assumed a national scope. Subsequently, the Marxist historians began to write the history of the Rebellion keeping in view the problems and participation of the common people. S.B. Chaudhuri, Eric Stokes, Rudgrangshu Mukherjee, Gautam Bhadra and Tapti Roy gave much stress to the peasants and common people's participation in the Rebellion by raising the subaltern theory.

In the most recent study, during the celebrations of the 150th anniversary of the Rebellion in 2007, the religious factor was given much importance by the social scientists. William Dalrymple was the main propagator of this theory. By searching hundreds of letters of the revolutionaries and other discourses, he concluded that most of these documents bear the religion-based problems, which compelled the Sepoys and other people to rise against the British. He pronounced that the Rebellion of 1857 was a sort of fundamentalist religious war, a *Jihad.*

Mewat region was one of those places, where the Rebellion took a popular character due to the mass level involvement of the rural population or peasantry. The narration of the Mewati scholars and Mewati history writers also testifies the same thesis. Unfortunately, no trained historian of the Rebellion has touched the most sensitive area of Mewat in the suburb of Delhi. The Mewati history writing is generally indigenous, based on the stories told by the Mirasis or bards or Jagga of Mewat. These Mirasis inherit the history of the region from last many hundred years. The Mewati scholars are continuously writing their texts based on these indigenous sources which are the best oral history ever maintained by any group of the people. Their history writings are in Urdu and Hindi and deploy an impassioned language with slight exaggeration. Their work depicts the viewpoint of the person deeply loyal to their community. They have also documented the primary and secondary sources with proper scrutiny. There is abundance of local hyperbolic narrations, which generally deviate from documenting the chronological events and other true stories. They are writing history with a mission by claiming a past and using it for the furtherance of their future.

The Rebellion of 1857 was undoubtedly a marker for the Mewati people to prove their nationalist credentials, and claim their own space in the freedom struggle and the history of a nation in the making. By this, the Mewatis also seek to win acceptance from the wider society by creating and legitimising a space for themselves within the nationalist narratives. The Mewati scholars also reveal a deep impassioned plea to recognise their heroes of the Rebellion of 1857, who were often illiterate and left no written records. Folk songs, oral narratives and myths also thus become the basis of these accounts.

This work is a humble process in writing the history of Mewati people and the participation of the great Mewati community in the Rebellion of 1857. Both the written records and oral narratives are used with much care and scrutiny. The interviews of the Mewati people and Mirasis are also quoted with a slight hypothesis. In this work, the role of the Mewati revolutionaries, their retribution and loss of property have been mentioned prominently.

There is a long list of the Mewati heroes, both amongst the military and civilians, whose patriotism and involvements in the first war of independence have been highlighted in this text. The remarkable role of the Mewatis beyond the Mewat region, who fought against the British until their last breath, also has been mentioned prominently and enlisted in the martyrs of the Rebellion of 1857. Their actions were as noble, and their endurance was as great, though their valorous deeds have not been so obviously recorded and needs further research in this regard. All their names and involvements in the Revolt of 1857, it has been my endeavour to indelibly preserve.

I have covered the whole work in the seven small chapters, and enveloped all aspects related to the theme and events in chronological orders. In the first chapter, I have given the details of the glorious past of the Mewatis, right from the Muslim invasion in India to the Rebellion of 1857. The radiant and patriotic history of the Mewati people enabled them to participate in the Rebellion of 1857 and subsequently highlight the heroic deeds of their heroes. The rebellion of 1857 placed the Mewati people on the position of identity markers. The patriotic role of their forefathers honoured the entire Mewati community and boosted this marginalized community in their everyday struggle for dignity and self-respect.

In the second chapter, I have discussed the nature and causes of Mewati Rebellion of 1857. While discussing the different schools of thought regarding the nature of the Rebellion, I have given much stress on the role of the subalterns, their grievances, and their hatred against the British. The distinctive grievances of the Mewati peasantry such as heavy taxation; annexation of the princely state Firozpur Jhirka; British interference in their social traditions and religious matters has been discussed in detail. The martial background of the Mewati community and de-industrialisation policy of the British also has been given the proper coverage under the causes of the Mewati Rebellion.

The third chapter of this work covers the beginning and progress of the Rebellion. It starts with the attack of the revolutionaries on Gurgaon on the same day when they rushed the Delhi on 11th of May, 1857. In this chapter, it has been discussed that how the traditional armed peasantry of Mewat successfully occupied the entire Mewat region and fought against the British officers like William Ford, Captain Nixon and Mark Thornhill at different fronts in Gurgaon, Mewat, Mathura, Kosi and Hodal. Both the civilian and military Mewati revolutionaries forced William Ford, the Deputy Commissioner of Gurgaon to flee for Delhi.

When the mutiny erupted by the Sepoys of Meerut on 10th May 1857, it snowballed into the national war on the next day when the rebellious Sepoys reached in Delhi and enthroned the last Mughal Bahadur Shah Zafar as the Emperor of Hindustan. The Mewat region, which is now the part of the districts of Mewat, Palwal, Gurgaon, Faridabad, Narnaul, Rewari, Mahendragarh,

Alwar, Bharatpur and Mathura, affected a lot by the Rebellion of 1857. Right from the chiefs to the lowest man over here was unhappy with the rule and policies adopted by British East India Company. Following the Sepoys and other revolutionaries of different parts of north India, the neighbouring region of Mewat also burnt in the fire of Rebellion against the British regime. In this war, everybody of all classes participated, from noble to the peasant.

The village level and inter-village panchayats took leading part in the Rebellion of 1857, and sooner or later the whole of Mewat came under these panchayats and the chaudharies of their respective villages. They established rule of the people in Mewat under Emperor Bahadur Shah Zafar. The independent rule functioned independently for more than six months until the British succeeded in gaining back the whole of Mewat by November, 1857.

The Meo revolutionaries fight against the British, and their loyalists has been discussed in detail. The establishment of their rule in the entire region of Mewat and loot and plunder of the Government property has furthermore been covered in this chapter. In this chapter, I have tried to show that apart from the peasantry of Mewat, the Meo religious class in alliance with the Wahabis of Frontier fighters fought in Mewat region and also in Delhi against the British. The motivation of the religious class of Mewat for fighting against the British was successful in the whole Mewat region. This factor sentimentally aroused the people of Mewat against the British, irrespective of their race and caste. The fight of the Meo revolutionaries against Jaipur resident Major Eden has been also discussed in full details as I could find from different sources.

The fourth chapter covers the role of Mewati revolutionaries beyond the region of Mewat. The state and city wise details of Mewati fight against the British have been given in this chapter. It is well known that the Meos better known as Mewatis reside in different parts of north and central India. Naturally, they had the same martial background as of the Meos of Mewat. They all rose against the British, whether they were peasantry, artisans or

Sepoys in the services of the British Government and in the princely contingents. Their efforts definitely provided strength to the other revolutionaries and prolonged the Rebellion.

The fifth chapter deals some untoward incidents in Mewat, which certainly shows no doubt of their patriotism but the gradual rift and predatory martial character of the Mewati community. It exposes their mutual animosity, fight to each other on petty grounds and even lawlessness in the absence of the regular British Government. Unfortunately, the incidents which were happened between Meos versus Meos, Meos versus Khanzadas, Meos versus Jats and Rajputs, Meos versus Ahirs, undoubtedly weakened the revolutionary solidarity and power. It provided fair chance to the British and other loyalists to regain their power in Mewat region. It naturally caused a setback to the national movement started by the brave Mewatis for their self-respect and freedom of their country. Notwithstanding, the uncountable sacrifices of the Mewatis, these gradual rifts caused the loss of men and property and even their independence.

In the sixth chapter, I have discussed the suppression of the Rebellion in Mewat after recapture of Delhi by the British forces in alliance with the forces of the princely states. From Delhi, many forces were dispatched to Mewat under various officers like Brigadier Showers, Wigram Clifford, Lieutenant H. Grant, Captain Drummond, Captain Ramsay, Mr. Macpherson and Colonel Gerrard. The heroic role of the Mewati revolutionaries in different battles such as battles of Raiseena (Alipur), Rupraka, Ghasera, Mahu, Narnaul (Nasibpur), etc., has been discussed in detail. All these battles completely suppressed the Mewati people and reduced them tenancy and starvation. In the last, the famine of 1860-61 also has been discussed in detail, which further deteriorated the position the community and consequently, compelled them to beg for their livelihood.

After failure of the Rebellion, the people of Mewat faced great hardships in comparison to the other regions of Haryana. The victorious British government brought severe punishment for the whole Mewat region. All prominent leaders and general people who were suspected as the revolutionaries on whom the British could lay their hands were severely punished. Frequent failure of crops and occurrence of famines added to the distress of the peasantry. The money-lenders charged exorbitant rates of interest, and the peasantry was heavily in debt. After years of retribution and wiping out the traces of all the revolutionary marks from Mewat, the British authorities were awakened about the duties of the ruler. As a first step to check the irregularities of the money lenders, the British Government passed the orders in 1863 for proper maintenance of accounts.

The seventh or the last one is the conclusive chapter in which I have given my own opinion regarding the Mewati Rebellion of 1857. I have mentioned all and every possible reason of Mewati participation and thrown light on the sacrifices of their lives and property. While discussing the patriotism of the Mewati community I have a lot of hopes from the government to provide the due share to the martial community of the Meos and proper development to the region.

By writing the inspirational history of this kind and highlighting the bravery, sacrifice, and patriotism, my sole purpose is to aware the readers about this unique predatory community, which still bears aborigine culture and traditions. Keeping in view of the paramount importance of linking Mewatis with nationalist narrative, my only purpose is to stimulate and highlight the Mewati nationalism and their patriotic sentiments. My aim is to clear the misconceptions and negative ideology regarding the Mewati people which have been wrongly developed in the minds of the people. This work is a humble process to provide dignity to the Meos or Mewatis as a whole to remind the readers about their patriotic role during the Rebellion of 1857. I hope this work would firmly assert the role of the Mewatis in the freedom struggle and bound the government to give them the opportunity to serve the nation through both the military and administrative departments.

As I have mentioned in the paragraphs of this preface, I have covered almost all aspects in writing the role of Mewatis in the Rebellion of 1857, and tried my level best in documenting the events based on historical facts, narration of the bards and some hypothetical imaginations. I am conscious that there must be many imperfections and errors in this work and without any hesitations, I feel sorry for those mistakes. As the research never ends, I invite the scholars to research on this topic and join hands with me in highlighting the role of the Mewatis which deliberately ignored by trained historians. I am sure that this work would be successful in inviting the attention of the social scientists and historians of India and abroad.

The completion of this work has been my grand aim and in order to achieve this end I have often examined and compared the works of other writers and tried bridge the gap wherever I find the necessity. Besides all this, there has been the long and wearisome labour of going through many lengthy contemporary texts and tedious travel to access the important libraries at various places. However, the challenges goaded my will power to complete the task. The theme of the text, Rebellion of 1857, was very important for me as it stands as beacon light of incipient Indian nationalism, and served as a perennial source of inspiration for freedom struggle.

In completing this task, I have accessed various libraries such as Mehru Memorial Museum and Library, New Delhi; National Archive, New Delhi; Academy of Haryana History and Culture Gurgaon; Maulana azad Library Aligarh; YMD College Library, Nuh. The works of Cunningham, Channing, Kay & Malleson, Charles Ball, Savarkar, Sir Syed Ahmad Khan, Eric Stokes, Ibbetson, Cave-Browne, etc. helped me a lot in completing this work. I also consulted and took the interviews of various scholars, bards or Mirasis, Jaggas of Mewat, which definitely proved the great aid to my work.

In fulfilling this sacred trust, I owe my hearty thanks to all those who have afforded me their kindly aid. Firstly, I thank to Chaudhary Zakir Husain, Professor K.C. Yadav, Professor Ali Athar, Mr. Syed Mohammad Javed, Mr. Wahid Ali, Dr. Waseem Raja, Mr. Mazharul Haq, Mr. Zulfiqar Ahmad, Dr. Mushtaq Ahmad and Dr. Jagdish Prashad Yadav for encouraging me to further and perpetuate this important record. I also thank to my other friends and colleagues, who have furnished me with valuable information and details of personal experience, not otherwise obtainable. Lastly, I have been desirous to mention the names of my family members, Imrana Anjum, Lubna, Iram, Anam and Sadaf for their constant support and encouragement in completing this important work.

Dr. Aijaz Ahmad
Associate Professor in History
Yasin Meo Degree College, Nuh, Mewat

Contents

1

Historical Perspective of Mewat

Before discussing the details of the Rebellion, there is a need of introducing the region of Mewat and its people by highlighting its short history. A brief chronology of events can provide the changing relationship between rulers of Delhi and the Mewati rulers and people. It would also introduce the martial historical background, including chivalry and patriotism along with their retribution and destruction.

The loosely defined area of Mewat never remained constant and changed its boundaries from time to time. The Mewat region located within the triangle formed by Delhi, Agra and Jaipur. It is a cultural region rather than an administrative unit. Beginning approximately 64 km south-west of Delhi, its fluctuating boundaries are now estimated to extend 112 kilometers north to south and 80 kilometers west to east between latitude of 26 and 30 degrees north and longitude of 76 degrees east. As it was a mountainous area with jungles large enough, the rulers of Delhi used to go there for tiger hunting.

At the very beginning the term Mewat was firstly heard in the historical narrations around 1194, when Hemraj, the brother of Prithviraj Chauhan, was enthroned at the throne of Ajmer. After the attack of Ruknuddin Hamza, Hemraj took refuge in the hills of Mewat. Undoubtedly, the Mewatis would have supported him in his fight against the Muslims. Eventually, Hemraj was defeated by Aibak. On his shameful defeat, Hemraj mounted a funeral pyre and perished in the flames.[1]

During the Delhi Sultanate, Mewat was a small kingdom with its capital at Kotila. In the Mughal period, the Mewat was divided into different administrative units or Sircars. In the British period, the Mewat region was divided into many parts; Gurgaon district under British, Bharatpur under Jats and Alwar under Narukas. The other parts of Mewat was also divided under several local principalities, such as Tijara and Tapukara under George Thomas[2]; Firozpur Jhirka under Nawab Ahmad Baksh Khan; Ghasera under Badgujar Hathi Singh and Bahadur Singh; Rewari under the Rao Tej Singh; Bahora under Rao Ram Baksh; Shahjahanpur under Harnarain Haldia; Jharsa under Begam Samru,[3] Hodal under Mohammad Khan Afridi; Palwal under Nawab Murtaza Khan; Hathin under Faizullah Beg; Gurgaon under Hakim Abdul Haq; Pataudi under Faiz Talab Khan; Jhajjar, Dadri, Kanaud, Narnaul and Bawal were under Nawab Nizabat Ali Khan; Rewari and Sohna were under Rao Tej Singh as Istamrari land, etc. However, before the Rebellion of 1857 most of the Jagirs were confiscated and annexed in the British Empire.[4]

The Gurgaon district came under British rule in 1803, In order to administer the region the head-quarters of the civil officers of the district were established at Bharawas near Rewari. After some time when the Bharawas force was transferred to Nasirabad, the civil officers were also removed to another place, the Gurgaon, near Delhi. Up to that time the district was in the direct charge of the Delhi Resident; but in 1819, Mr. Cavendish received charge of the Gurgaon district with the title of Principal Assistant Commissioner of the Southern Division. In 1832, this title was changed to that of Collector and Magistrate.[5]

The Gurgaon district, which covered the larger part of the Mewat region, was under the direct control of the Bengal Government, right from its occupation by the British Government on 30th December 1803. The Government administered the area through a resident under the direct supervision of the Governor General in Council. After the formation of a new province North-Western Province in 1834, by the Charter Act of 1833, this region came under the new province. Apart from Gurgaon, the neighbouring districts of Rohtak, Panipat, Hisar and Delhi were also part of the same province under a new unit called Delhi Division. After the termination of the Rebellion of 1857, the

Gurgaon district, including Mewat region were transferred to the Punjab Province.[6]

In 1947, at the time of the independence of India, the area of Mewat lay in three political units- two princely states, Bharatpur and Alwar of Rajputana, and the district of Gurgaon in the province of Punjab. Now an area has been selected within the Mewat cultural region and named as Mewat district by Haryana Government. It was carved out from erstwhile Gurgaon and Faridabad districts and came into existence on 4th April 2005 as the 20th district of Haryana. The newly constituted district comprises three sub-divisions such as Nuh, Firozpur Jhirka and Hathin. The district headquarter is located at Nuh. The district comprises six blocks namely Nuh, Tauru, Nagina, Firozpur Jhirka, Punhana, and Hathin.

However, before establishing the principality of Mewat by the Mewatis, the salient point of the history of Mewat region was troublesome as quoted by the Persian and British historians. Ibbetson writes that the Meo was a highly composite tribe found in the hill country of Gurgaon, Alwar and Bharatpur also scattered over the Delhi district and the Bawal nizamat of Nabha. The Meos have given their name to the Mewat. They are all Mohammadan, though, as will be seen presently, their religion is of a very impure type. Powlett's ads in the description Ibbetson that the Meos are now all Musalmans in name; but their village deities are the same as those of Hindu Zamindars. They keep, too, several Hindu festivals. Thus, the Holi is with Meos a season of rough play, and is considered as important a festival as the Muharram, Eid, and Shabibarat; and they likewise observe the Janam Ashtmi, Dashehra, and Diwali. They often keep Brahmin priests to write the *pili chithi*, or note fixing the date of a marriage. They call themselves by Hindu names; with the exception of 'Ram' and 'Singh' is a frequent affix, though not so common as 'Khan'.[7]

Ibbetson writes that the Meos were composed of four Rajpoot stocks, Tanwar from Delhi, Jaduns from Mathura, Kachhwahas from Jaipur and Chauhans from Ajmer. As the time passed they divided themselves into several Gotras and Pals. Presently, the Meos are divided into twelve Pals and fifty Gotras.[8]

To the Mohammadan historians, the Meos appear to be unknown by that name, but the Mewatis. Powlett has very deeply described that the mass of the population of Mewat are called Meos; they are Musalmans, and claim to be of Rajput extraction. They must not, however, be confounded with the Mewati chiefs of the Persian historians, who were, probably, the representatives of the ancient Lords of Mewat. In fact, the expression 'Mewati' usually refers to the ruling class, while 'Meo' designates the lower orders.[9]

In this work, wherever the term Mewati was used, it denoted to all the inhabitants of Mewat irrespective of their race, class and religion and more predominantly to the Meos. However, for the regions beyond Mewat, the term Mewati has been generally used for those who belonged to Mewat or the Muslim Meos who were living different areas of the country. The Meos originally belonging from Media kingdom of ancient Europe were migrated to Sindh and subsequently in the present Mewat region, which is known by their name. They were the martial community, relied on the strength of their hill retreats, plundered the country far and wide whenever the central authority was from any cause temporarily weakened.

The Meos began to convert into Islamic fold from the time of the invasion of Mahmud Ghaznavi. His relative Sayyed Salar Masud Ghazi[10] reached the Mewat region in 1032, and through his preaching, converted many of the Meos to Islam. According to the local traditions, before the invasion of Mohammad Ghauri, the Rai Pithora of Ajmer was annoyed of the conversion of the Meos to Islam, employed the Badgujars to harass them and thus compelled them to reconvert to Hinduism. However, subsequently, Miran Sayyed Husain Khung Sawar[11] came to Mewat and motivated the conversion into Islam.[12]

At the time of Balban, the repeated raids were made on Mewat region due to the warlike and notorious habits of its inhabitants. Ibbetson while branding the Meos a notorious and troublesome to the governments also praises them a lot. He says that the Meos are by nature very hospitable, serving their guests with better food than they eat themselves, generally giving them rice, sugar, ghee, etc.[13]

The rulers of Delhi faced a lot from the turbulence of the Mewatis. In retaliation, the rulers of Delhi adopted severe measures, from time to time, to repress them. No authority tried to eradicate the reasons of their unrest but crushed then brutally whenever they rose against Delhi. However, the turbulence of the Mewatis was due to the heavy taxation of the central authority without assessing the barren lands as well as by neglecting their financial positions.

The British rulers, during their rule in India, also were not having cordial experiences with the Meos or Mewatis. A British scholar Charles Aitchison writes about this community that, "In the south of Gurgaon the Meos or Mewatis, believed by some to represent the original non-Aryan inhabitants of the country, predominate. These are predatory races, thieves and cattle-lifters, the turbulent people, who were ever a thorn in the side of the Muhammadan Government and have given much trouble to ourselves. Nevertheless, three-fourths of the population of the Delhi Territory belongs to honest and industrious agricultural tribes. The flower of the peasantry is the Jat. Not a few of the villages can trace their pedigree back for more than a thousand years and, amid all the revolutions of time and changes of dynasties, have preserved written annals of their history from a time when William the Conqueror had not yet landed on the shores of England."[14]

The term Mewat (Mendipatti) and its history in India was first mentioned by Chand Bardai in his Prithvi Raj Raso. He says that Mahesh, Lord of Mewat (Mendipatti) paid homage to Bisaldeo Chauhan of Ajmer in Samvat 821 (A.D. 764), and afterwards his descendant 'Mangal' was conquered by the famous Pirthvi Raj of Delhi. Mangal and Pirthvi Raj were married to two sisters, who were daughters of the Dahima Rajput, Chief of Bayana.[15]

During the Delhi Sultanate, the first Muslim ruler, who invaded the Mewat region, was Sultan Iltutmish (1211-36). He built a great mosque of Chaunsat Khamba at Kaman, out of Hindu materials, the pillars alone numbering about two hundred. During the weak reigns of his successors, Mewat was left undisturbed until 1256, when the rebel Kutlugh Khwaja sought refuge in Mewat with the Rana Ran Pal. Ulugh Khan (Balban), the active minister of Nasiruddin Mahmud Shah, invaded the country and forced the rebel to fly. The Mewatis, due to their rebellious background and turbulent nature, faced the curse of the rulers and suffered a lot with men and money. It is said that Mewatis usually raided the Sultanate territory beyond the gates of Delhi. As the Ulugh Khan was the governor of Hansi and Rewari (part of the Mewat region), he also suffered a lot from the Mewati turbulences.[16]

Balban invaded the Mewat country second time on 29th January 1260 as the Meos of Mewat were in revolt and the latter had carried off a large number of Balban's camels. In retaliation Balban attacked the Mewat region with a huge force of ten thousand horsemen in armour, and a large army of brave and warlike soldiers. For twenty days the work of slaughter and pillage continued, and the ferocity of the soldiery was stimulated by the reward of one silver tanga for every head and two for every living prisoner. On March 9 the army returned to the capital with the chieftain who had stolen the camels, other leading men of the tribe to the number of 250, 142 horses, and 2,100,000 silver tangas. Two days later the prisoners were publicly massacred. Some were trampled to death by elephants, others were cut to pieces, and more than a hundred were flayed alive by the scavengers of the city.[17]

Balban after ascending the throne of Delhi as Sultan around 1266, once again attacked Mewat towards the end of the first year of his reign. It is stated that in this campaign one hundred thousand of royal army were slain by the Miwatis and most probably the same number of the Mewatis were also put to the sword by the royal forces of Sultan Balban. The final attack of Balban was so disastrous that no turbulence was heard about two hundred years following that grave episode. Consequently, the capital Delhi was delivered from the attacks of Miwatis.[18]

After their repression, it took about two centuries for the Mewatis to rise again to a significant position. During the rule of Tughlaqs, the Mewatis played most important role in the central politics of Delhi, particularly under their first most important ruler Bahadur Nahar Khan, the reputed founder of the Khanzadas. He was the king maker during the rule of the late Tughlaqs, Sayyed dynasty and at the time of Timur's invasion on Delhi. The other important period of the Mewatis was the time when the Battle of Kanwaha was fought. In this battle, Hasan Khan Mewati bravely fought against Babar and met to death. The death of Hasan Khan Mewati finally ended the 200 years' dynastic rule founded by Raja Bahadur Nahar Khan. Since then there has never been an exclusive and independent ruler of Mewat, which at British time was partitioned between Alwar, Bharatpur and Gurgaon.

The first glorious period in Mewat was the rule of Raja Bahadur Nahar Khan under whom the Mewatis arrayed and established a unique social setup. However, according to the Meo scholars, the Mewatis fought different battles against the invaders like Mahmud of Ghazni and Muhammad Ghauri. In 1002, Sayyed Salar Masud Ghazi attacked on Mewat region and left a far-reaching effect on the local religion due to his benevolent attitude. In 1017, Abu Baqar Shah Qandhari, a General of Mahmud Ghazni, attacked upon Bayana (Vijaymandgarh),[19] a part of the Mewat region. At the time of Mahmud's attack on Mathura in 1018, the Mewati fighters fought against him. Syed Ibrahim Barahazari, a General of Mahmud Ghazni, attacked on Rewari and directly faced the Mewati forces. Muhammad Ghauri also attacked Bayana in 1195 and conquered the Fort Tahangarh, which was earlier known as Vijaymandgarh. Mohammad Ghauri deputed Bahauddin Tughril as governor of Bayana.[20]

Raja Bahadur Nahar Khan (1360-1400), earlier name was Kunwar Samar Pal, was the son of Lakhan Pal, the local chief or zamindar of Sarehtha near Tijara. Samar Pal came to Delhi and joined the military service under Firoz Shah Tughlaq. Through his bravery and honesty, he gained the name, Bahadur Nahar, and the title, "Khana-i-Zad". The term Khana-i-Zad afterwards changed as Khanzada. He also acquired the area of Mewat as his Jagir and began to rule with his capital at Kotila. Bahadur Nahar was in great influence of Sultan Firoz Shah Tughlaq due to his saintliness and benevolence. In the company of Sultan, he came to know the true sense of Islam, and he fully decided to embrace Islam. He finally met with Sufi Saint Hazrat Nasir-ud-Din Mahmud Roshan Chiragh-i-Dehli, a disciple of Chishti Shaikh

Hazrat Nizam-ud-Din Auliya, along with the other *deshmukhs* of his kingdom and accepted Islam.[21]

A Meo scholar Mohammad Swaleh Khan states that in order to strengthen his Mewati kingdom, Bahadur Nahar Khan made certain divisions in the society. These divisions were known as *Got* and *Pal*. Mohammad Swaleh Khan states that at the time of later Tughlaqs there was complete anarchy in the court of Delhi, and most of the *Amirs* declared themselves as independent. At that time, Mewat was under the rule of very influential ruler Bahadur Nahar Khan, who divided his area into twelve divisions known as *Pals*. The chiefs of twelve divisions were known as *Deshmukhs*. Perhaps they all accepted Islam on the call of Bahadur Nahar Khan. These twelve divisions or *Pals* were further divided into fifty two *Gotras*. Those members who accepted Islam were called as Meos and those who did not accept Islam became famous as Meenas.[22]

Bahadur Nahar Khan was one of the most prominent figures in Delhi history for about a dozen years just before and after the invasion of Timur. He was the kingmaker to the Delhi Sultans. He was fully involved in every single activity related to central politics of Delhi. For some time, after the death of Ghayasuddin Tughlaq II, he even occupied and ruled the area of Firozabad. Bahadur Nahar Khan was enjoying a high reputation at that time, and it is proven by the fact that from Delhi, Timur sent him two envoys Sayyed Shamsuddin and Alauddin to his court. His envoys presented to Timur two white parrots sent by Bahadur Nahar. These two parrots must have been 75-80 years old survived from the time of Sultan Mohammad Tughlaq. Timur himself praises the gift of Bahadur Nahar in his Memoire by saying, "The sight of these parrots and the sound of their voices gave me great satisfaction, so I gave directions that they should be brought before me in their cages every day that I might listen to their talk."[23]

Bahadur Nahar Khan was killed by his father-in-law Jhamu Singh Chauhan in 1400 and was succeeded by his son Bahadur Khan.[24] However, Raja Jalal Khan (1422-1442) was the next most important and influential ruler of Mewat after his predecessor Bahadur Nahar Khan. At the time of his succession Jalal Khan, earlier known as Jallu, was the Jagirdar of Dhadoli. The people of

Mewat enthroned Jalal Khan, with his capital at Indore, as the ruler of Mewat. Jalal Khan proved himself one of the most powerful rulers of Mewat by his ability and quality. He faced several attacks of the Delhi rulers, particularly Sultan Mubarak Shah. At every invasion, Jalal Khan was assisted by his brother Qadar Khan (Qaddu), the Jagirdar of Jhimrawat.[25]

The bone of contention between the Delhi rulers and Jalal Khan was the revenue or annual tribute, and proclamation of Jalal Khan as an independent ruler. In this connection, Qadar Khan or Qaddu was mercilessly murdered at Delhi on the order of Sultan Mubarak Shah. Raja Jalal Khan was also having enmity with the Rajput ruler of Amber. It is said that he attacked the Kachhwaha Raja of Amber Fort and carried away one of its gates to his capital Indore. He was died in 1442, before the accession of Bahlol Lodi, and succeeded by his son Ahmad Khan with his capital at Alwar. There are some copper coins found with inscription of *Fateh-ud-Duniya-wa-Deen* Jalal Shah, dated in the Hijri years 841, 842, 843 (AD 1437, 1438, 1439).[26]

The last great warrior and patriotic Mewati ruler of Mewat was Hasan Khan Mewati (c1517-1527), who successfully ruled the Mewat region from his capital Alwar. He was the son of equally important ruler Alawal Khan. It is said that around 1517 due to his old age, Alawal Khan appointed his son Hasan Khan as the ruler of Mewat. The date of his accession is not sure, and it is also not clear that his coronation took place or not, but it is the fact that Hasan Khan was ruling the area of Mewat from the time of Ibrahim Khan Lodi as his father Alawal Khan was too old in age. Being the brother-in-law of the ruling monarch Ibrahim Lodi, Hasan Khan had full power and position at the Imperial Court of Delhi. Hasan Khan's formal coronation after his father's death could not have taken place as his father was found dead in his camp in the battlefield of Kanwaha and thereafter Hasan Khan also killed in the same battlefield in fighting against Babar.[27]

The hard times knocked the door of Hasan Khan Mewati when Babar advanced toward Panipat with the strong military of 12,000 against 100000 forces of his enemy Ibrahim Lodi. The two forces met at Panipat in April 1526. In this fateful battle of Panipat, Hasan

Khan along with his father Alawal Khan, favored the imperial army and send a force under his son Nahar Khan in the battlefield. Babar became victorious and Ibrahim was slain during the battle. Nahar Khan the son of Hasan Khan was also kept in Mughal captivity.[28]

In order to get the favour of Hasan Khan, Babar set free to Nahar Khan, the son of Hasan Khan, who was his prisoner from the time of Battle of Panipat. According to Babar, "....Nahar Khan, Hassan Khan's son. I again received him into favour, and bestowed on him a *Pargana* of several lakhs for his support........"[29]

Rushbrook has quoted from Babar that after the battle of Panipat, the Indian rulers became independent of Delhi and started a campaign against Babar. Kasim Sambhali set himself up in Sambhal, Nizam Khan in Bayana, Hasan Khan Mewati in Mewat, Mohammad Zaitun in Dhaulpur, Tatar Khan Sarang-Khani in Gwalior, Husain Khan Lohani in Rabiri, Kutub Khan in Etawa, Alam Khan in Kalpi. Among all the above-mentioned people, Babar considered Hasan Khan most dangerous one. Babar himself called Raja Hassan Khan Mewati as an infidel, the prime mover, and agitator in all these confusions and insurrections.[30]

Elliot & Dowson has cited Ahmad Yadgar's quotation, of his *Tarikh-i-Salatin-i-Afghana,* that Hasan Khan was a man of royal descent from several generations, and his family had possessed regal power from the time of Firoz Shah Tughlaq. Rana Sanga, who was at that time a most powerful chief tried to make an alliance with Hasan Khan against Babar. He sent a message to Hasan Khan saying, "The Mughals have entered Hindustan, have slain Sultan Ibrahim, and taken possession of the country. It is evident that they will, likewise, send an army against both of us, if you will side with me, we will be allies, and not suffer them to take possession."[31]

Rana Sanga showed himself to Hasan Khan as the well wisher of Hindustan but in a real sense, he was a big opportunist and one of the traitors of India whose infidelity was exposed by Babar in his memoire. Babar says in his memoire about Rana Sanga, "Although Rana Sanga, the pagan, when I was in Kabul, had sent me an ambassador with professions of attachment, and had arranged with me, that, if I would march from that quarter into the vicinity of Delhi, he would march from the other side upon Agra; yet, when I defeated Ibrahim, and took Delhi and Agra, the pagan, during all my operations, did not make a single movement."[32]

In this battle which was fought at Kanwaha in 1527, Babar again became victorious by leaving behind thousands of dead. Raja Hasan Khan Mewati and other associates were among the slain. Babar says in his memoire about the slain people, "Many were slain, and fell in the battle, and some giving up their lives for lost, turned to the desert of ruin, and became the food of crows and kites and hillocks were formed of the slain, and towers raised of their heads. Hassan Khan Mewati was enrolled in the band of the dead by a matchlock shot"[33]

Nahar Khan carried away his father Hasan Khan Mewati's dead body to Tijara and buried him in the complex of the mosque built by Hasan Khan in his lifetime. Nahar Khan constructed a dome over the grave. Nahar Khan also established his rule over the area of Tijara. A local poet has very beautifully written about Hasan Khan in the following couplets:[34]

"Dhaulo Anda Titar Ko, Aur Daulo Hi Chaubaro Re,

Kood Pado Langda Ko Poto, Nau Sau Gai Sanbhalo Re,

Lakho To Mero Lakh Taka Ko, Dahi Doodh So Palo Re,

Doodh Dahi Ko Bhooko Na Hai, Pani Ko Lapsayo Re,

Agam Dekho Pichham Dekho, Kahin Na Paani Payo Re,

Lal Das[35] *Ki Kothi Chal Rahi, Jaaye Jar Jhukayo Re"*

(His (Hasan Khan's) Palace was white in colour and looked like a white egg of Partridge. Hasan Khan, the grandson of lame (Zakaria Khan) jumped into the war (against Babar), was the owner of nine hundred cows (a proverb for the richest man). His annual income was one lakh tanka from his kingdom, and he was grown up eating with curd and milk. However, he was thirsty for water (divine thirst) not of the curd and milk. He looked forward and backward (all around) but could not find the water (divine blessings).

Eventually, he drunk the divine water (blessed of benevolence) from a Sufi Saint Lal Das, who was very famous at that time.)

Babar after controlling his power over the Delhi and suburbs marched towards Mewat to subdue the Nahar Khan but seeing no other means of safety Nahar Khan submitted to the authority of Babar. Babar divided the Mewat region into three parts and assigned one of its portions having the revenue of few lakhs of revenue to Nahar Khan for his living. The other two portions were assigned to his son Humayun and his general Chin Timur Sultan.[36]

Raja Hasan Khan Mewati was a brave and loyal subordinate of Ibrahim Lodi. His fight with the Babar in Panipat was not because of any political motives but sided with Lodis to prove his loyalty to his suzerain. Another reason for his support was that Hasan Khan was the real cousin of Ibrahim Lodi. However, unfortunately, he was defeated along with his master. He passed the restless day and night on the repeated call of his inner sense for the revenge as the defeat has blotted on his political career. He found it a fair chance to take the revenge when Rana Sanga appealed to him to join against the Babar. He had not only given his military support to Rana but also played a leading role to manage the confederacy against the invader. However, perhaps due to the treachery he was unable to achieve the goal. He was not the power hungry but a master of his own will.

After elimination of Mewati rule in Mewat by Babar, the Mewatis never regained their power and prosperity. The region was controlled by the Delhi chiefs like Mirza Humayun, Mirza Hindal, Khwas Khan, Haji Khan, etc. and ruled the region for many years. Some of the Mewati jagirdars also emerged in the heydays of Mughal rule, but they were completely subjugated. At the time of Akbar, a local Mewati chieftain Raja Todarmal of Deeg (Bharatpur) tried to hold up the half revenue but he was pardoned by the Emperor. A jagirdar of Patan (Alwar) also refused to pay personal homage on the call of Emperor Akbar. Another instance of defiance was the capture of royal camels laden with royal treasury, which was moving from Agra to Delhi. It was captured by Rai Bhan Pahat and Masand Khan Godhala. Emperor Akbar subjugated these insubordinate chieftains. He also sent Peer

Mohammad Sherwani to Mewat to suppress the kinsmen of Hemu and other rebellious Afghans.[37]

As Akbar was very liberal in all contexts, he tried to pacify the Mewatis by giving them employment. Cunnigham has quoted the words of Abul Fazal that the natives of Mewat were known as Mewrah and they were famous as runners. He further says that one thousand of them were employed by Akbar as post-carriers, and were called Dak Mewrahs.[38]

After Akbar, the Mewatis were subdued during the rule of Shahjahan. For their subjugation the Emperor Shahjahan assigned the Kaman and Pahari pargana of Mewat region to Raja Kesari Singh, the son of Raja Jai Singh. The Palwal, another region of Mewat was assigned as jagir to Dara Shikoh. Dara Shikoh was liberal to the local population and helped in assigning a jagir to a local loyalist Mao named Firoz Mewati.[39]

Although Mughal Emperor Aurangzeb is being branded as a staunch Musalman by some second-rate scholars but he too subdued the Mewatis. The Emperor favoured Churaman Jat and Hathi Singh Badgujar of Badshahpur against a Mewati insurgent Sanwalia Meo of the village Sahnula.[40] Another Meo sardar Sanwant of Tijara also rebelled against Aurangzeb and plundered the imperial territories of Aurangzeb. He was defeated and killed at Alwar by the forces sent by Aurangzeb.[41]

Overall in the reign of Emperor Aurangzeb, the Mewatis were subdued vehemently and even today he is not known in good words in the Mewat region. A Mewati song is needed to be quoted here in this regard:

"Dilli Shahar Suhaono Kanchan Barse Neer,

Sabke Kanth Bator Ke Le Gayo Alamgir,

Suno Sakhi Saheliyan Mile Bandhao Dheer,

Sukhi Suhagan Hongi Ja Din Bigde Alamgir"

(Delhi is the pleasant city where gold rains along with water; the Emperor Alamgir has brought all the youths of Mewat for punishment; Listen, O friends and companions have patience and think that all the brides would remain happy when Alamgir's days would be bad.)

After Aurangzeb, the Mewat region was divided into the local principalities like Bharatpur, Alwar, Firozpur Jhirka and Hathin. Subsequently, in the first half of the nineteenth century Hathin and Firozpur Jhirka merged into the British district of Gurgaon. In 1857, when the revolt was started, the Meos who comprised the majority population of the Mewat region including Bharatpur and Alwar state fought against the British along with other co-inhabiting communities of Jats and Goojars.

A Meo scholar Hashim Amir Ali writes that in 1857, Meos rose against the British and carried out massacre of both army and civil personnel in the British cantonments. They looted government property and burnt down offices and godowns and considered themselves independent. Reprisals were inevitable and having been soon subdued, they were massacred with equal ferocity by the British.[42]

References

1. Haig, Sir Wolseley, *The Cambridge History of India, Volume III, Turks and Afghans*, Cambridge, 1928, p. 43.
2. George Thomas, an Irish mercenary, was the most successful general in India in the 1790s. He left his job from the British Navy in Madras in 1781 and led the Pindaris of north India by 1787, where he took service under Begum Samru of Sardhana. However, he shifted his allegiance to a Maratha chieftain Appa Khande Rao in 1793, and placed a battalion of Sepoys under him. George Thomas worked for Appa Khande Rao for four years from until 1797. During this period, Thomas was raising fresh troops, collecting revenue by force from the ever-refractory peasantry of Mewat, and supporting his unpaid soldiery by looting Gurgaon and other villages in the Jagir of Begum Samru. As Appa Khande Rao enlarged the contingent of George Thomas, he assigned him Tijara, Tapukta and Firozpur Jhirka as fiefs for the maintenance of his troops. Soon afterwards Jhajjar, Pataudi and the neighbouring villages were added to his jagir. Panipat, Sonipat and Karnal were also assigned for maintenance of his army. Apa died on June 25, 1797, and his nephew Vaman Rao succeeded to his governorship and continued to keep Thomas in his service up to the end of 1797. After termination of his service, George Thomas

became a private robber-captain for his living. Early in 1798, he occupied Hansi and made it the capital of his kingdom extending from Ghaggar river in the north to Rewari and Pataudi parganas in the south. He was finally defeated and captured by Scindhia's army and died on 22 August, 1802. (*Gurgaon District Gazetteer*, Chandigarh, 1983, pp. 56-57, see also Atkinson, Edwin Thomas, *Statistical Descriptive and Historical Account of the North Western Provinces of India*, Vol. II, Allahabad, 1875, p. 251).

3. Begam Samru was a beautiful lady of Kashmiri origin, earlier a dancing girl and later on the princess of Sardhana near Meerut. Her native name was Farzana and Joanna after embracing Christianity. She married to Walter Reinhardt Sombre in her fourteen years of age in 1867, who died in 1778. On the death of her husband Sombre, she succeeded to his principality of Sardana. On the introduction of British rule in 1803 in north India, she managed to retain her possessions as an independent ruler. She always led her troops to the attack in person and displaying, in the midst of carnage, the greatest intrepidity and presence of mind. Her Diwan was Rae Singh, who was the great-grandfather of Motilal Nehru. In 1788, when the Rohilla Chief Ghulam Qadir attacked Delhi, Emperor Shah Alam appealed to Marathas and Begum Samru for help. On her quick response and loyalty, she was bestowed the pargana of Badshahpur and Jharsa, near Delhi. She died immensely rich on the 27th January, 1836 at age of 88 years. See for details Beale, Thomas William, (Revised by Henery George Jeene), *An Oriental Biographical Dictionary*, London, 1894, pp. 373-374 and James Burgess, *The Chronology of Modern India, for Four Hundred Years from the Close of the Fifteenth Century, A.D. 1494-1894*, Edinburgh, 1913, p. 270, and *ELTWeekly*, Vol. 5, Issue-16, 13 May, 2013, from the Book Reviewed by Kranti Sharma of '*Begum Samru of Sardana*' by Micheil Larneuil.

4. Channing, F.C., *Land Revenue Settlement of Gurgaon District*, Lahore, 1882, p. 22, (hereafter quoted as Channing), see also Malleson, George Bruce, *Kaye's and Malleson's History of the Indian Mutiny of 1857-8*, Vol. IV, London, 1911, p. 76, (hereafter quoted as Key&Malleson), *Punjab Gazetteer, District Gurgaon, 1883-84*, Lahore, 1884, pp. 23-24, *Gurgaon District Gazetteer*, Chandigarh, 1983, pp. 58-59, and Yadav, K.C., *1857: The Role of Punjab Haryana and Himachal Pradesh*, New Delhi, 2013, pp. 124-125, (Hereafter cited as *The Role of Punjab Haryana and Himachal Pradesh*).

5. *Punjab Gazetteer, District Gurgaon, 1883-84*, Lahore, 1884, pp. 24-25.

6. *The Role of Punjab Haryana and Himachal Pradesh*, pp. 121, 124 & 126.

7. Powlett, W., *Gazetteer of Ulwur*, London, 1878, p. 38, see also Rose, H. A., *A Glossary of the Tribes and Castes of the Punjab and North-West Frontier Province*, Vol. III, New Delhi, 1977, pp. 79-80, (hereafter cited as *A Glossary*) , see also Ibbetson, Denzil, *Panjab Castes*, Lahore, 1916, p. 179, (hereafter cited as Ibbetson).
8. *A Glossary*, p. 82.
9. Powlett, W., *Gazetteer of Ulwur*, London, 1878, p. 2, (hereafter cited as Powlett).
10. Sayyed Salar Masood Ghazi (1025-1033), born in Ajmer, was the son of Satar Maali, the sister of Mahmud Ghaznavi, and Sahu bin Ataullah Ghazi, the governor of Ajmer. He fought many battles with Indian Rajas of Delhi, Kannauj, Kara, Manakpur, etc. He was also a reputed Sufi Saint. His tomb is in Bahraich (U.P), where both the Hindus and Muslims come to pay him respects. In Mewat area also he is loved and respected even today. The custom of saluting the flag of Sayyed Salar Masood Ghazi was prevalent in many villages of Mewat until 1960-70. In that custom, the *Mujawars* (servants of Ghazi) used to bring the flag and hoisted it in the village Chaupal. The children and women devotees perform *Nazar-o-Neyaz* (offerings), and youths performed military drill. On the third day of the ceremony, the *Mujawars* departed along with the flag. Another practice was the worship of the flag of Sayyed Salar Masood Ghazi. Nevertheless, due to the influence of the Maulvis and Tabligh movement these practices slowly and gradually came to an end. See for detail, Khan, Habibur Rahman, *Tazkira Sufia-i-Mewat*, Delhi 1985, pp. 67-68, (hereafter cited as *Tazkira Sufia-i-Mewat*) and 180, see also *The Panjab Past and Present*, Vol. XXXVIII, Patiala, April 2007.
11. Miran Sayyed Hussain Khang Sawar was the military officer in the army of Sultan Shahabuddin Mohammad Ghauri. He was appointed Governor of the fortress of Taragarh and said to have been slain in 1202 in a night attack. This attack was organized by Rathore and Chauhan Rajputs who jointly launched an attack when all the soldiers and army men were resting. All were killed and on getting information Hazrat Moinuddin Chishti performed their burial on Taragarh hill.
12. Powlett, p. 2.
13. *A Glossary*, p. 85.
14. Aitchison, Charles, *Rulers of India: Lord Lawrence*, Oxford, 1892, pp. 29-30.
15. *A Glossary*, p. 82.

16. Cunningham, Alexander, *Reports of the Tour in Eastern Rajputana in 1882-83*, Vol. XX, Calcutta, 1885, p. 13, (hereafter cited as Cunningham).
17. Siraj, Minhaj, *Tabaqat-i-Nasiri*, (Urdu Trans. Ghulam Rasul Mehar), Vol. II Lahore, 2004, pp. 99-100, see also Haig, Wolsley, *The Cambridge History of India, Volume-III, Turks and Afghans*, Cambridge, 1929, pp. 72-73, Cunningham, p. 13, and Elliot, H.M. and Dowson, John, *History of India, as told by its own Historians, The Mohammadan Period*, Vol. II, London, 1869, p. 359, (hereafter cited as Elliot&Dowson).
18. Abdul Shakoor, Hakim, *Tarikh Meo Kshatri*, Shikrawa, 2010, p. 152, (hereafter cited as *Tarikh Meo Kshatri*), see also Ahmad, Aijaz, *Mewat: A Retrospective*, Ghaziabad, 2013, pp. 86-87, (hereafter cited as *Mewat: A Retrospective*).
19. A stone slab of Vijaymandgarh Fort bears the bears the couplet, "*Gyarah Sau Tihattar Phag, Teej Roovi Bar, Vijaymandgarh Toriya Abu Baqar Qandhar*" (On 3rd day of Falgun moth of 1173 Samvat, Abu Bakar Qandhari had broken the Fort of Vijaymandgarh.) Khan, Mohammad Ashraf, *Meo Qaum Aur Mewat*, Nuh, (ND), p.51, (hereafter cited as *Meo Qaum Aur Mewat*).
20. *Meo Qaum Aur Mewat*, pp. 50-52.
21. *Mewat: A Retrospective*, pp. 90-91.
22. Athar, Mohammad Swaleh Khan, *Tarikh Meo Mehar*, Firozpur Jhirka, 2009, pp. 458-466, (hereafter cited as *Tarikh Meo Mehar*), pp. 458-466, (Another Meo Scholar Hakim Abdus Shakoor states that this division was done by great Meo ruler of Mewat, Maharana Kaku Rana of Balot clan, in the thirteenth century in his stronghold, Garhdhamna, near Mehroli. It is said that at his time the Meos were in great distress due to the Balban's policy of suppression. Kaku Rana in order to organize the whole population of Mewat started division and sub-division of the area and its chiefs. The chiefs of the clans were organized and committed to fighting against the Balban's forces. See for details, *Tarikh Meo Kshatri*, p. 257).
23. Elliot&Dowson, Vol. III, London, 1871, p. 449, see also *Mewat: A Retrospective*, pp. 92-96.
24. *Tarikh Meo Mehar*, pp. 291-292.
25. *Mewat: A Retrospective*, p. 105.
26. Elliot&Dowson, Vol. IV, London, 1872, p. 75 see also Cunningham, pp. 18-19 and Haig, Wolseley, *The Cambridge History of India, Vol. III, Turks and Afghans*, Cambridge, 1928, p. 218, (hereafter cited as *The Cambridge History of India, Vol. III*).

27. *Mewat: A Retrospective*, p. 116.

28. Cunningham, p. 19.

29. Babar, Zaheeruddin Mohammad, *Tuzuk-i-Babari*, (Eng. Trans. John Leyden and William Erskine, *Memoirs of Zaheeruddin Mohammad Babar*), London, 1826, p. 369.

30. Williams, Rushbrook, *An Empire Builder of the 16th Century*, London, 1918, p. 140 (hereafter quoted as *An Empire Builder*), see also *Tuzuk-i-Babari*, pp. 335 & 361.

31. Elliot & Dowson, Vol. V, London, 1873, pp. 35-36 see also Sharma, S. R., *Mughal Empire in India, 1526-1761*, Part-I, Bombay, 1934, pp. 37-38.

32. *An Empire Builder*, p. 140 see also *Tuzuk-i-Babari*, pp. 335&361.

33. Lane-Poole, Stanley, *Babar*, Oxford, (ND), p. 177 see also *Tuzuk-i-Babari*, p. 360.

34. *Meo Qaum Aur Mewat*, pp. 100-101, (Hasan Khan Mewati was the son of Alawal Khan and the grandson of Zakaria Khan, a physically handicapped son of Raja Ahmad Khan. That's why Zakariya Khan was called *Langda* (Lame) by the poet in his couplets. It seems that after the death of Raja Ahmad Khan, his son Zakaria Khan was physically unfit to control the Mewat kingdom and eventually the throne passed to his son Alawal Khan. After Alawal Khan, his son Hasan Khan became the ruler of Mewat.)

35. Lal Das, a Meo Saint of Alwar, was born in 1540, much later to the time of Hasan Khan Mewati. Like all the other Meos, Lal Das was a Musalman by faith and followed the Hindu observances. Lal Das lived many years at Dhaoli Dhub, and used to wander over the hills behind Alwar, and began to work of miracles. One of his miracles was that an excited elephant stopped in full career and saluted him. The people usually quote another miracle that a Musalman Saint, Chishti Gadan, of Tijara, found him standing in the air in meditation. After some time, Lal Das went and lived at Bandoli, sixteen miles north-east of Alwar. He lived on the top of a hill, and went through great austerities in the hottest weather. Throughout his stay on the hills, he was safe from snake and tiger, and cured the sick. Once Lal Das appeared before a Muslim Faujdar of Bahadurpur in connection of a case; Faujdar expressed surprise at his being followed by both Hindus and Musalmans, and asked him what he was. Lal Das replied that the question was a foolish one, what he was in truth he knew not, but he got his garment, the flesh, in a Meo's house. The Faujdar cunningly offered him water from a poisonous well, but by the miracle, the whole water of the well became sweet. Afterwards, Lal

Das left Bandoli and resided at Todi, a village now in Gurgaon, on the Alwar border, where, being persecuted, he went away. At Naroli, the people refused him water, whereupon their wells dried up. At Rasgan, in Ramgarh, he was well received, and there he remained a while, repeating God's name, and teaching disciples the right path. Lal Das had a daughter Sarupa and a son Pahara. It was reported to Sahib Hukm, Mughal Governor of Tijara that Lal Das did not pray as a Musalman, nor performs ablutions, nor call on the prophet, but that he taught Hindus and Musalmans the same doctrine. The Hakim invited him and treated kindly, offered him meat, saying that it was the food of the Muslims. Lal Das replied, "Love God. God is one and separate from all. There is one path for Hindu and Turk, by which they come and go. Whoever kills another cuts his own throat, for the murdered is avenged by Gods casting the murderer into hell. Let me be shown how to escape before the judgment-seat, where God himself will do justice. The good keeps in mind the fear of that day." Lal Das then took the food into his hand, and the meat turned to fine rice. Lal Das died in Samvat 1705 (A.D.1648), at the age of 108, at Nagla, a Bharatpur village on the Alwar border, and was buried at Sherpur, in Ramgarh, Alwar, where there is now a fine shrine. See for details, Powlett, pp. 54-56, and *A Glossary*, pp. 102-103.

36. Firishta, Mohammad Qasim Hindu Shah, *Tarikh-i-Firishta*, (Eng. Trans., John Briggs, *History of the Rise of the Mohammadan Power in India, Till the Year 1612*, Vol. II), London, 1829, p. 59, see also *Journal of the Research Society of Pakistan*, (*History of Mewat: An Outline*, Shahabuddin Khan Meo) Vol. 48, No. 1, University of the Punjab, Lahore, 2011.
37. *Meo Qaum Aur Mewat*, pp. 107-111.
38. Cunningham, p. 22.
39. *Meo Qaum Aur Mewat*, pp. 115-116.
40. It is said that Sanwalia Meo had captured some elephants and camels of Churamal Jat. This incident was reported by a local bard in his words: "*Deeg Khalbali Mach Gai, Kagad Bacho Kumher, Oont Sanwalia Le Gayo, Kadi Na Dego Pher*," (There was an uproar in Deeg (capital of Churamal Jat), how Kumher (another stronghold of Churaman) would be saved. The camels had captured Sanwalia and he would never return.) *Meo Qaum Aur Mewat*, pp. 117-118.
41. *Ibid*, pp. 118.
42. Hashim, Amir Ali, *The Meos of Mewat: Old Neighbours of New Delhi*, New Delhi, 1970, p. 28, (hereafter quoted as *The Meos of Mewat*).

2

Nature and Causes of Mewati Rebellion

The beginning of the nineteenth century witnessed the emergence of British East India Company as the major political power in India. Consequently, not only was the power of the Mughal Empire broken, but also most of the independent principalities that had come into existence as a result of its disintegration were subjugated by the British. The mighty Marathas Empire, Mysore kingdom and many other Indian principalities were defeated by the British forces. Nevertheless, the crushing defeat of Sindhia of Gwalior at the battle of Laswari by Lord Lake in 1803 was the most significant and had far-reaching political consequence. The defeat of the Sindhia laid to the British protection of the Mughal Emperor and the British control to all over north and central India.

After establishing their rule over India, the British East India Company started its tyrannical rule over the Indian masses in order to fulfill their imperial interests. The British rule affected all the political, social, economic and religious spheres of lives of the Indian people. It created a misunderstanding between the ruler and the ruled. The British oppression and misunderstanding burst into a Rebellion in 1857 at the completion of hundred years British rule after the historic battle of Plassey.

The Rebellion of 1857 has been regarded as a most memorable episode in Indian history. It was in a sense one of the first formidable revolts that had broken out against foreign domination. After suppression of the Rebellion, a series of research works was started by the British as well as Indian intellectuals describing its nature and causes. The problem of how to read the Rebellion of

1857 has been a long-standing one in the historiography of India. The British historiography continuously claimed its mutinous character irrespective of the adverse remarks of Benjamin Disraeli and Karl Marx. The British historians wanted to justify their acts behind the iron curtain of the Whiteman's burden.

The British historiography in advocating the theory of mutiny was only an attempt to save their colonial interest. They used the history or historical figures as the instrumental to save their rule or identity in India. When the British were setting their feet in Indian sub-continent, they called the Mughal Emperor as the sole proprietor of India. They fully utilized the authority of the Emperor for their imperial cause. However, when the same Mughal Emperor Bahadur Shah Zafar tried re-establishing his power, the British authorities and even historians generally denoted him as the King of Delhi. They tried him for waging war against the ruler and deported him to a foreign land Rangoon.

Sir Syed Ahmad Khan was the first who described about the unrest of the people due to the unfavourable policies of the East India Company. Next most important propagator of popular theory was John William Kaye in 1867; while describing it as mutiny, Kaye settled that the event was an entire people's attempt to overthrow an alien domination. Kaye stated that hurting of religious sentiments, violation of caste rules and the greased cartridges led to the 'mutiny'. Malleson, too while advocating the theory of mutiny, very interestingly put the blame, not on Hindu superstition or Muslim fanaticism, but on the functionaries of the East India Company, who, in trying to preserve their own domination, extending over a hundred years, had completely failed in attaching even one section of the population to British rule.

From the early twentieth century or during the golden jubilee of the Rebellion, the new generation of radical nationalists began to challenge the decrees of colonial historiography and to write their own versions of the past. Vinayak Damodar Savarkar was one of those radical nationalists who advocated the theory of war of independence. Following the ideas of Savarkar, a new thought of nationalist historiography developed with a deep research on the gross-root level. Savarkar while advocating the theory of war of independence described the annexation of Awadh and the introduction of greased cartridges as accidental causes not as causative factors. There is, of course, a reason for this assumption. This thesis fully grown during Indian National Movement and was one of the sources of inspiration for the nationalists of the first half of the twentieth century.

After the completion of hundred years after the Rebellion in 1957, a new mode of research started in the Indian historiography. In the re-examination of the same question of nature of the Rebellion, the newly independent government of Indian National Congress took a keen interest. Surendranath Sen wrote an official history that concluded, carefully and with admirable restraint, that it was a war of independence that assumed a national scope. Subsequently, the Marxist historians also began to write the history of the Rebellion keeping in view the problems and participation of the common people. S.B. Chaudhuri, Eric Stokes, Rudgrangshu Mukherjee, Gautam Bhadra and Tapti Roy gave much stress to the peasants and common people's participation in the Rebellion by raising the subaltern theory.

During the 150th year celebrations of the Rebellion, a new study gained momentum while thorough discussion of different perspectives of the Rebellion of 1857. Apart from the stereotype rake in about the old theory of war of independence, a new thesis of religious nature was given much importance overall. William Dalrymple was the main propagator of this theory. He emphasized the role of the religious class of the Muslim society by highlighting the ideology of the Wahabis and Faraizis. He pronounced that the Rebellion of 1857 was a sort of fundamentalist religious war, a *Jihad.* Irfan Habib also while emphasizing the Marxist views stressed the role of Wahabis and Faraizis. William Dalrymple's religious factor may be considered advancement of great conspiracy theory with slight modifications. It is evident that the writers like Major General Hearsay, Alfred Lyall, and James Outram wrote about Muslim conspiracy by giving the examples of passing of chapattis and the spreading of a different kind of rumour. However, at the beginning of historiography of the Rebellion, the theory of Muslim conspiracy did not get wide approval. Even the pro-British Sir Syed Ahmed Khan did not consider the revolt as premeditated.

Notwithstanding, at most of the cases, the Indian historians are unanimous in asserting that the Rebellion of 1857 was a popular uprising against the British. However, the role of different communities in the revolt is a matter of debate by historians and intellectuals. In this work, it has been properly emphasized the role of the common Mewati people, especially the peasants and farmers, calling it a popular Rebellion by intelligently evading the controversy. More emphasis has been given to the people of gross root level, who fought against the British due to their personal and collective grievances.

Regarding the popular or common people theory, the intellectuals feel that a Rebellion on such a large scale could not have been planned and carried out with the help of only few groups of people. It needed the active participation of all the people to make it a success. Since the Indian society comprises a large number of lower and backward castes, a Rebellion on such an immense scale could not have been planned and executed without their cooperation. This debate might be fueled by the Mewati history scholars who have started demanding a share in the development pie of the country that had earlier been divided among the elite upper classes by asserting their role in the nation-building process and in the Rebellion of 1857.

The British East India Company began to rule the country after their victory in the battle of Buxar, but most of the regions of north India came under British rule much later in 1803. The British rule of about half a century from 1803 to 1857 produced a great deal of discontent and disaffection among almost every section of the northern India, including Haryana and more especially Mewat. However, unfortunately, the role of Mewatis as a whole has a little mention in the accounts of the Rebellion of 1857.

For the popular uprising, the Mewat region was the most suitable example, where the common people and peasants were the leader as well as the fighter in the absence of the ruling family. It happened for the first time in Indian history when almost all the rural as well as urban population of Mewat raised their banner of revolt against the British tyranny and tried their level best to uproot the foreign yoke from their homeland. The Mewati enthusiasm regarding the Rebellion could be gazed that even after the re-conquest of Delhi by the British, the Rebellion continued in Mewat for two months more. After getting the opportunity of the Sepoys revolt, all the Mewatis jumped into Rebellion irrespective of their caste and religion.

The long lasting war waged by the Meo community against the British definitely bears a lot of causes, which deeply affected the lives of the Mewatis from last several decades. Charles Raikes writes that the late disturbances were caused, firstly, by a general mutiny of the Native Army. Secondly, by the violence and rapacity of the Goojar, Mewati, and other clans, disposed in the best times to predatory habits; furthermore by the cruelty of the lower town-mobs and cantonment rabble. Lastly, by the attempts of certain quasi-royal pensioners and landholders to revive their lost local ascendency.[1]

Not only the Raikes, but a lot of historians have stressed the participation of the Mewatis into the Rebellion. As the Mewat region is culturally and geographically different to those of others, some of the most important causes related to Mewat have been discussed under the following headings. These causes would through much light on the real facts behind the participation of the Meos in the Rebellion.

Heavy Taxation and Miserable Position of Peasantry

Mewat is a hilly region, and most of its soil is alkaline and barren. Even its underground water is salty. Most of the agriculture crops in Mewat area are rain fed. The crops yielded are not sufficient for the livelihood of the population of Mewat. The Mewatis are bound to do more labour for fewer benefits. Perhaps this is one of the reasons that the Mewatis are most hard working, brave and courageous. The alkaline and barren lands of Mewat yielded very low crops of both Rabi and Kharif. Some of its areas were useless as there were full of water accumulated for the whole year.

Some British officers had also explained the miserable position of Mewati peasantry by quoting the position of several lakes in Mewat. About the Khalilpur Jhil, Mr. Maconachine, the Deputy Commissioner, Gurgaon, writes in 1898, "During the ordinary season the whole of this is flooded.......Its area may be reckoned at about 1500 acres." About the Chandeni Jhil, he says, "Here is another permanent swamp....... The permanent basin is perhaps somewhat smaller, say about 1000 acres." The Sangel-Ujina Jhil spreads over a larger area than it covered at Khalilpur or Chandeni. The Kotila Jhil is the largest in the district covering three miles long and two and half miles broad.[2]

In the medieval times, the Meos found it difficult to pay the land revenue, in any circumstances, which was imposed by the Delhi Government. So the differences and skirmishes started from the Delhi Sultanate continued until the end of the Mughal suzerainty. After the downfall of the Mughal Empire, the Mewat area came under the influence of the Jaipur kingdom. However, the two principalities, Alwar and Bharatpur, emerged out of the eastern territory of Jaipur. Accordingly, the western area of Mewat was divided into Alwar and Bharatpur. Some of its area also came under the Marathas and the European officers like Begum Samru and George Thomas, who obtained the grants over there. After battle of Laswari in 1803, Daulat Rao Sindhia, the Maharaja of Gwalior, was ousted by the British from the Mewat region. Consequently, a vast tract of land of Mewat fell into the hands of the British.[3]

Following the defeat of the Marathas under Sindhia, most of the areas of north-west came directly under the rule of the British Government. However, the Mewat region under the principalities of Bharatpur and Alwar remained the same. Out of the conquered territories, Sohna, Nuh and Tauru were taken under the direct administration of the British Government, and the administration established in Delhi territory was implemented in these areas. In 1806, Firozpur Jhirka and Punhana were given to the British ally Ahmad Baksh Khan as Jagir, until 1836; Hathin was assigned to Faizullah Beg, the brother of Ahmad Baksh Khan; Hodal was given to Murtaza Khan, and Palwal was assigned to Mohammad Ali

Khan Afridi. Some of the European officers like Sombre and George Thomas were also given Jagirs. Pataudi, an adjoining area of Mewat was assigned to Faiz Talab Khan.[4]

The Mewat region was summarily settled in 1809, and heavy taxation was imposed. The new British government was more concerned with the collection of revenues in time, which were fixed at high rates. Growing burden of taxation, eviction from land led to the impoverishment of a large section of the peasantry. The revenue collectors were least concerned about the paying capacity of the cultivators and forcefully collected the taxes. In meeting the increasing demand of taxes, the peasants were compelled to sell their lands, or they were caught in the trap of moneylenders. Justice could not be expected from the local administration because it was under the influence of the rich. Thus, under the British rule, the nexus of the official, the landlord and the money lender combined together to exploit the peasantry.

In 1809, Seton assisted by Charles Metcalfe made the first effort to establish regular administration in Mewat region. At first, settlements were made for short periods, but by 1820, conditions became stable enough to make settlements from three to twenty years. The land policy pertaining to the settlements ruined the peasantry of Mewat. They were not implemented with the consent of the people. On the other hand, when the settlements were made, the headmen were imprisoned until they agreed to the terms offered and having accepted them, and furnished security for payment. The poor farmers could not pay the revenue which their village headmen had agreed to pay under compulsion. They had to visit jails several times in this connection. The mode of collection of land tax was extortionate as the assessment was oppressive. The collections were made in February and September, long before the harvest.[5]

The harsh and unsympathetic policy of heavy revenue greatly demoralized the people and shattered the peasant's economy. Not only the peasantry, but the jagirdars were also suffered a lot due to the British policy. It moreover must not be forgotten that much before the time of the Rebellion almost all the Jagirs of Mewat region assigned after 1803 were confiscated and settled according to the British revenue policy. The heavy taxation and miserable position of the Mewatis forced them to take active part in the uprising and uproot the British paramountcy.

Sir Syed Ahmad Khan opines about the system of land revenue settlement by the British Government that, "The assessment imposed by the English Government have been fixed without any regard to their various contingencies. Land lying fallow pays in the same proportion as other land. Such lands as are for a time left uncultivated in order that they may aquire strength are not considered free from assessment.... The cultivators were obliged to borrow money in order to pay the revenue. The interests on these loans ran up." Sir Syed quotes the statement of Thomason, a Settlement Officer that the settlements under the regulation 9 of 1833 were light on good villages, but pressed heavy on poorer ones.[6]

However, the taxation was burdensome as the agricultural production in Mewat area was very low in comparison to the other adjoining areas. F. C. Channing, the Land Settlement Officer of Gurgaon district (later the collector of Gurgaon district), gives the details that wheat occupied only 5 per cent of the crop area and cotton, which is grown chiefly in the Firozpur tahsil, 8 per cent. There was hardly any sugar cane, very little indigo or vegetables, and no maize. Oil or seedy which in late years had been a very paying crop, were grown to a very small extent. The autumn crop, chiefly consisting of millets and pulse, which were generally retained for home consumption, occupied in this district double the area of the more marketable spring crops. Among the millets, bajra, except in the east, generally prevailed over jowar, which requires a better soil. Even on well lands barley, and not wheat, was the common crop. Wheat had the preference only on naturally irrigated (dahri) lands.[7]

In Mewat region, the British Government fixed the revenue beyond the paying capacity of the peasantry. Most of the areas of Mewat, such as Nuh, Sohna, Palwal, Tauru, Rewari, Firozpur, etc. affected badly and the conditions of Mewati peasantry became miserable. The peasants were bound to sell their cattle and stock in order to pay the revenue. Channing himself describes that the Summary Settlements in Gurgaon, like those of most parts of the old Delhi territory, were not favorable examples of fiscal arrangements. The assessments were generally based on the excessive demands of the former Native Rulers and Jagirdars. In Rewari, it was said that the villages were settled by Mr. W. Fraser with the highest bidders. The same officer's assessments in Bahora completely broke down; the parganas of Nuh and Sohna greatly deteriorated; Tauru was equally unfortunate. Repeated reductions became necessary, but were often followed by further enhancements and renewed failures. The policy of moderation in revenue matters was but slowly learnt. Palwal was very heavily assessed in 1820, and in Firozpur as late as 1836 the Nawab's high demand was maintained.[8]

The British Government realized the folly much later when the severe famine clutched the area of Mewat. During the famine, in 1837 a Regular Settlement of the Gurgaon district was commenced under Regulation IX of 1833, and in that and the following year almost the whole of the district came under settlement. In Tauru, considerable relief was given; but the assessments of Mr. Lawrence in Palwal and of Mr. M. Gubbins in Firozpur were still decidedly high. Unfortunately, the introduction of the new assessment was accompanied by a severe famine which continued its starvation and suffering until 1841. This was the hard time for the Meos because, on the one hand, they were suffering from the heavy taxation of the British Government and a severe famine at the same time on the other. By this Regular Settlement, the land revenues were reduced only in some areas of Mewat.[9]

However, these reductions of revenue rates in Mewat were still burdensome. British Government further decided to revise the rates of the land revenue. In 1841, Mr. M. Gubbins revised his own assessment of Firozpur, and Punhana made three years before, reducing it by about 20 per cent, for the term of settlement, and remitting all outstanding balances. About the same time Mr. Barnes revised the assessment of parganas Palwal and Tauru made by Mr. Lawrence in 1837 and 1838, granting here also reductions of about 20 per cent. Mr. Barnes also assessed the Nuh tahsil at similar rates. The Rewari and Gurgaon tahsils had not suffered so much from the bad seasons as had the south-east of the district, and Mr. Lawrence's original assessments of those tahsils were allowed to stand.[10]

The rate of land revenue in Mewat was different in accordance with the type of land, fertility, and means of irrigation. The rate of revenue on the land irrigated by well was from Rs. 3.80 to Rs. 4.00 per acre. However, where there was no means of irrigation except rainy water, the rate of revenue was Rs. 2.80 per acre for *Narmot* (good loam) lands.[11]

F.C. Channing remarks about the heavy taxation policy of the British Government, "1842, as also in previous years, it would appear as if successive calamities were caused by high assessments and cured by their reduction. I believe this inference to be incorrect. The assessments of 1842 and previous years were higher than any we now make, prices were lower, and our collection proceedings were rigid; but what broke the agriculturists down was a succession of bad years (famine years), and what restored their prosperity, equally in those days and on the last and most recent occasion, was the reoccurrence of good years (end of the famine years). I earnestly hope that this will be remembered when trouble next comes."[12]

These reduced rates of revenue by Regular Settlement were also much high which comprehensively beyond the paying capacity of the Mewati farmers. In order to pay these revenues they usually fell in the clutches of the *Mahajans* and other moneylenders. The British torture regarding revenue collection was surplus on the Meos. The conditions of the Mewati peasantry were very miserable. Due to their misery and suffering, some of them were bound to theft or even beg. K. C. Yadav quotes an incident that one Mewati was caught for stealing one and half *Seer* paddy (unprocessed rice) and produced in the court of Mr. Metcalfe. Metcalfe sentenced him life imprisonment for that petty crime.[13]

Government did not care the Meos' sufferings, and no relief operations were noted during the whole period of famine in Mewat. More ridiculously government blamed the Mewati population for their suffering from the natural curse famine.

According to F.C. Channing, "The Meos are an unsatisfactory class of peasantry. They are reckless in prosperity and helpless when in trouble, but their behaviour during recent times of distress has not confirmed the opinion that they readily relapse into predatory habits. The standard of living in the case of this class is certainly low."[14]

In his *Settlement Report* in 1882-83, Channing showed his satisfaction by criticizing the pre-Rebellion land revenue settlements of Mewat area in the Gurgaon districts. He says, "It is undeniable that the condition of the agriculturist in many respect enormously improved as compared with the state of affairs which prevailed before 1860. Produce sells now at a much higher value; there are greatly improved qualities of export, and it is therefore easier to sell, and it is probable that even the inferior grains and pulses can be and are sold in the market to a very much larger extent than was the case formerly. Moreover fluctuations of prices are now less severe and sudden than was the case 40 years ago."[15]

No serious attempts were made to improve the conditions of the people and their related land. This added more filth in the ongoing miseries in Mewat. This disgusting situation was also in many parts of India. Angels, the friend of Karl Marx writes in a letter to him that British Government in India has completely avoided the agriculture that's why it is damaging and destroying.[16]

All the peasants of Mewat, including the Meos, Jats and Ahirs heavily taxed by the British Government had no substitute but to mortgage and ultimately sell their lands to the moneylenders. In Mewat, even the high-class land owners were reduced into the position of tenants. They were in great distress and perhaps waiting for the opportunities to overthrow the tyrant British rule. The Mutiny at Meerut, and the Sepoys move towards Delhi, provided them the long-awaited opportunity to end the British rule from their homeland.

Imperial Gazetteer of India also reports about the same situation of the Mewat region. Although, the data provided by the Gazetteer is of the much later period of 1879 but more or less the situation was the same during the Rebellion of 1857. The Gazetteer says,

"During the past fifteen months about five per cent, of the cultivated area of the two Meo tahsils of Nuh and Firozpur has been mortgaged, and now 17 per cent, of the total cultivated area is so burdened that there is little hope of its ever being redeemed. The Meo landowners are rapidly becoming practically reduced to the position of tenants. Their condition loudly calls for special consideration, though it is difficult to see what can be done for them. A large amount of revenue due from them has been suspended, but they have had to borrow for food, and the evil has only been reduced, not removed."[17]

After the termination of the Rebellion, Mewat region was very liberally settled. Channing reports that in the year of droughty 1860-61, special leniency was shown in the collection of the revenue, and liberal relief was given by Government, by which means serious distress was averted.[18] Most probably the leniency by the British Government was not because of the drought but due to the fear of defection by the local population who played most important role in the Rebellion of 1857.

In the Bharatpur princely state, the Meo population was inhabited the tehsils of Nagar, Gopalgarh, Kaman and Deeg. Nagar and Gopalgarh were most sensitive due to the periodic rebellions of the Meos as they were suffering the heavy taxation policy of the state. In 1844, about ten thousand agriculturist Meos surrounded the Diwan and his group of Bharatpur state, who were rescued only after the intervention of the Darbar Regiment. In 1853, when the Naib Diwan came to collect revenue at Saimla in Nagar, he was shot at, and two of his party including a Goojar Risaldar, were killed. The Diwan brought a strong force of Cavalry and Artillery to chastise the rebellious Meos but they had meanwhile fled to the neighbouring state Alwar.[19]

Subsequently to the Nagar and Gopalgarh incident, the Meos' unrest was again bursted at Sikri and Bharatpur in 1854 and 1855. The British Officers Lawrence and O'Dwyer, in their reports severely blamed the Diwan, the Princely State and the native land revenue and administration. In view of the popular resentment, the demand was reduced by 19.8% in the summary settlement of 1855-56 to 1857-88. That's why the Rebellion in Bharatpur State could not gain much momentum. After the termination of the Rebellion, the Bharatpur State once again raised the revenue by 12.5 % in the three-year settlement of 1859-62.[20]

The Mewati area in Alwar State was troublesome, but the Maharaja had not imposed heavy taxation policy during the Rebellion. However, after the suppression of the Rebellion in 1858, the revenue was raised 5% by the Settlement Officer Captain Impey for three years. In 1861, the revenue was again raised by 20% by the same officer for further ten years.[21]

The land revenue policy of the British Government caused much damage when the natural disasters also followed in the same years. *Imperial Gazetteer of India* reports that due to the regular famines in the years of 1833 and 1837, many villages of Mewat region lost their entire population through death and emigration.[22] As a result of the Regular Settlement of 1837-38 in Mewat and subsequently famine in 1837-39 in the entire area of Mewat, left no choice for the Mewatis except loot and plunder.[23] The Mewati people made the British Government and its tyrant policies responsible for all their distress and disaster. They find it fair opportunity to overthrow the British power during the rebellion of 1857.

The unrest of the peasantry could be felt that the time when the revolutionaries attacked Gurgaon, they completely burnt the land revenue records of the tahsils and district headquarter. They did the same wherever they could find especially in the Government offices. They wanted to remove the records of the debts, land transfer and land and revenue-related court cases. Not only the Government records, but they burnt the records of the mahajans and other moneylenders. After the termination of the war, a new agrarian policy was introduced to guarantee the security of the tenure and to fix the rent for lands. This policy freed cultivators from tedious settlements and excessive demands of the state. The Bengal Rent Act of 1859 served as a model for this enlightened approach to an age old but a vexatious problem.

Chivalry and Martial Background of the Meo Community

The Rebellion of 1857, which broke out from Meerut and a day after in Delhi, firstly, attracted the Meos of Mewat. They were one of the communities in the suburb of Delhi who joined the Rebellion on the same day on its outbreak. They could not control their nerves from the active participation in the Rebellion, which provided them a chance, after many centuries, to prove their chivalry and patriotism. Their historical background goaded them to do or die for their motherland.

Historically, the Meos belonged to the martial race, which was always engaged in the warfare. It is being proved that their origin was from the belligerent Med community belonging to the Greek and Iranian Empire, well known at that time as Media. At the time of Alexander's invasion in India, most of the Meds of his army showed their courage to conquer the Indian territory of Sindh and consequently, continued to enter the Sindh territory following the Alexander's invasion. It is well known that, Alexander left an army under his Governor, Seleucus Nicator, to guard the Indian territory of Sindh, and he himself returned to Babylonia. Subsequently, the Meds, who were major part of Macedonian army also settled over the region occupied by the Greeks, and became well-known inhabitants, particularly in the coastal and hilly areas of Sindh.[24]

The area to which the Meds inhabited in Sindh was not very fertile so the livelihood of the inhabitants was a little difficult. The martial history of this tribe forced them to engage themselves into the sea piracy. While doing that job, they came in contact with the Arabian traders of that time. They fought many battles with the Arab traders on the issue of piracy. Consequently, the Arabs under Mohammad bin Qasim conquered the Sind territory. Hard pressed by Arab conquest, the Meds were drove away to hither and thither and finally took their shelter into the hilly areas of Arawali ranges, covering modern states of Haryana and Rajasthan, which were safe for their livelihood. Subsequently, they embraced Islam and called themselves as Meos in order to distinguish themselves from their Hindu brethren now known as Meenas.[25]

After their settlement in the suburbs of Arawali, they did not forget their main occupation of warfare and agriculture. The alkaline soil and barren land of Mewat made the Meos' life very tough, and consequently, it made them brave and warring in comparison to other communities of India. Due to their courage and bravery, they engaged themselves in loot and plunder at the time of the famine and other natural disasters. That's why most of the British scholars explained the Meos of India as robber and plunderer.

The Meds after settling themselves in the area of Mewat, divided themselves into two groups. One group formed the ruling class and other group of the subjects, just like the Chaukidari and Zamindari of the Meenas. Most of the peoples of both the groups started accepting Islam throughout time. After accepting Islam, they changed their nomenclature. Ruling class became known as Khanzada, at the time of Bahadur Nahar Khan, and the subjects were known as the Meos.[26]

The first known example of chivalry of the Meos after their settlement in the region of Mewat was their fight in 1256, 1260 and 1266 against Balban, the Prime Minister and later on the despotic ruler of the Delhi Sultanate. In 1256, the Meos fought bravely but could not resist long due to the heavy imperial forces. However, they were waiting a chance to revenge their defeat. In 1260 when Ulugh Khan was in the way to Rewari, the Meos carried off a large number of Balban's camels from his army. It was the signal of their open rebellion against Balban. About 12,000 Mewati ladies, gents, and children were put to death. After twenty days slaughter, Balban returned to the capital with 250 chieftains of the Meo tribe, who had stolen the camels and other 250 leading men of the tribe, 142 horses, and 2,100,000 silver *tankas*. Two days later the prisoners along with their leader Malkha were publicly massacred with great cruelty near Hauz Rani in front of the Badaun Gate. Some were thrown under the feet of elephants; others were cut in halves with knives.[27]

Even after repression of Balban, the Meos continued their terror for the Delhi Government. According to the Ziauddin Barani in his *Tarikh-i-Firoz Shahi*, the daring of the Mewatis in the neighborhood of Delhi was carried to such an extent that the westerly gates of the city were shut at afternoon prayer. Meos plundered the travelers on the roads, entered the city by night, and robbed the inhabitants in their houses, and even by day robbed and stripped water-carriers and women drawing water from the large reservoirs *Sar-Hauz* just within the city walls, so that it became necessary to shut the gates on the western side of the city immediately after the hour of afternoon prayer. No one dared to go out of the city in that direction after that hour, whether he traveled as a pilgrim or with the display of a sovereign. These daring acts of the Mewatis caused a great ferment in Delhi. Barani further says that the Sultan felt the repression of the Mewatis and for a whole year, he was occupied in overthrowing them and in scouring the jungles.[28]

When Balban ascended the throne of Delhi in 1266, he again attacked on Mewat. The Meos fought with full of their strength. One lakh of the royal army was slain by the Mewatis, and the most probability the same numbers of Mewati were also put to the sword.[29]

At the time of Firoz Tughlaq, the Meos under Bahadur Nahar Khan became successful in forming their government in Mewat. It was the height of their chivalry and bravery that the Meos under Khanzada rulers became the king maker during the rule of the late Tughlaqs and early Sayyeds of the Delhi Sultanate. Although, they also faced the wrath of the Delhi imperial army time to time with the loss of their men and money. They fought many battles, against Delhi rulers, under Jalal Khan, Qadar Khan, Aqlim Khan, Ahmad Khan, Alawal Khan, etc. During the Babar's invasion on India, the resistance of Raja Hasan Khan Mewati in the battles of Panipat and Kanwaha is well known. In the battle of Kanwaha, the Meos lost their king and cherished leader Hasan Khan Mewati.

Alaxander Cunningham mentions about the Meos' resistance against the rulers of Delhi as follows:[30]

> "As Hindus the Meos often successfully resisted the arms of the Muhammadan kings of Delhi until the time of Feroz Tughlak, when they became converts to Muhammadanism. But in spite of their change of religion the Moslem Meos were just as turbulent as their Hindu ancestors — and they remained virtually independent from the time of Timur's invasion until the conquest of Northern India by Babar."

Emperor Akbar was cautious enough about the bravery of the Meos and utilized their energy in nation building. He employed the Meos in large scale. Abul Fazal in *Aine Akbari* writes the name Mewrah, and says that they were natives of Mewat. He praises the Meos by saying them as famous runners and one thousand of them were employed by Akbar as post-carriers, who were called *Dak-Mewrahs*. He quotes as "Mewatis are natives of Mewat, and are famous as runners. They bring from great distances with zeal anything that may be required. They are excellent spies, and will perform the most intricate duties. There are likewise one thousand of them, ready to carry out orders."[31]

At the time of Rebellion of 1857, the Meos, whose history witnesses the chivalry, bravery and patriotism for their land, worked a lot in their participation in the war against the British. They find the British oppressors equal to the Arab and Delhi rulers and reminded their glorious past while fighting against the British rule.

Meos' Unrest over Annexation of Firozpur Jhirka

The Meo community was naturally very loyal to their motherland Mewat and its rulers. A little bit humiliation was never tolerable to the Meos, on any conditions. In this connection, the humiliation, dethronement and execution of Nawab Shamsuddin Khan of Firozpur Jhirka and its annexation to the British territory was foremost. This infamous and humiliating episode added more fuel on the burning episode of heavy taxation policy of the British Government in Mewat.

The principality of Firozpur Jhirka was awarded to Ahmad Baksh Khan, on his role played in helping Lord Lake, during Second Anglo-Maratha War in 1803. Firopur Jhirka principality, including the other parganas of Punhana, Bichhor and Sakras awarded by the British Government, was bringing in the revenue of almost Rs.80,000. It was in addition to the Loharu principality, granted by Raja Bakhtawar Singh of Alwar to Ahmad Baksh Khan, at the same time.[32]

Although Ahmad Baksh Khan was not a Meo Nawab but his marriage with a Meoni of Ghata village, named Maddi, and nomination of her son as his heir, acquired enough sympathy from the Meo community or his subject. Nawab Ahmad Baksh Khan had two sons from the Meoni wife Maddi Begum named Shamsuddin Khan, born in 1809 and Ibrahim Khan, born later on and died in his childhood. From another wife, Begum Jaan, there were also two sons named Ameenuddin Ahmad Khan, the Nawab of Loharu and Ziauddin Ahmad Khan.[33]

Before his death, Nawab Ahmad Baksh Khan had divided his principality into his sons; Firozpur Jhirka to his firstborn son Nawab Shamsuddin Khan and Loharu to Nawab Ameenuddin Khan. The eldest son of the family Nawab Shamsuddin Khan (1827-1835) was succeeded after his father's death. However, his reign did not last long, and he was executed at Delhi for compassing the murder of Sir William Fraser,[34] the Resident to Delhi in 1835. Subsequently, the *Pargana* of Firozpur was taken away by the British, and the state of Loharu was given to his brothers Aminuddin and Ziauddin Khan.[35]

The enmity between William Fraser and Nawab Shamsuddin Khan bears many stories. William Fraser's pleasure loving nature and political interference became the sole cause of his murder. Faulkner states that Shamsuddin wished to deprive his younger brother Ameenuddin of his proper share of the estate, which William Fraser opposed. Mohammad Ashraf in his book '*Meo Qaum aur Mewat*' also repeats the same story and says that Fraser was the friend of Ahmad Baksh Khan and wanted to implement his last wishes. Fraser not only supported Nawab Ameenuddin Khan but instigated him to appeal in the court of Governor General for justice. The court gave an order for the division of the principality according to the wishes of Nawab Ahmad Baksh Khan. Nawab Shamsuddin Khan then employed his servants to murder William Fraser.[36]

Channing also gives more or less the same details that an order was passed by the British Government that Nawab Shamsuddin Khan should administer Loharu as well as Firozpur and Punhana, his brothers being provided for by pensions. Mr. W. Fraser, the Commissioner of Delhi, objected to this decision, and procured a delay in its being given effect. According to Nawab Sarwarul Mulk

Bahadur, a relative of the same family, Mr. Fraser had an eye on the sister of Nawab Shamsuddin Khan. General Hervey recorded that the provocation was that Mr. Fraser had enquired about the Nawab's sister by name.[37]

According to the novel of Shamsur Rahman Faruqui entitled, "*Kai Chand The Sare Aasman,*" quoted in the *Dawn* magazine, that the mother of Mirza Dagh Dehlavi or wife of Nawab Shamsuddin Khan, Wazir Khanam was the most beautiful lady of his time. However, living in Delhi as a widow, she with her charms attracted the attention of Mr. Fraser and Nawab Shamsuddin Khan at the same time. Nawab succeeded in winning her, which led to the hostility between the two men ending in the murder of William Fraser and the consequent hanging of Nawab Shamsuddin Khan and confiscation of his principality.[38]

Another reason comes in limelight in recent researches that Mirza Ghalib, one of the scions of Nawab Shamsuddin Khan from the side of Begum Jaan, wanted to enhance the reduced pension. In this connection Mirza Ghalib started backbiting Mr. Fraser against Nawab Shamsuddin Khan. Mirza Ghalib also made spiteful remarks about the low origin of Nawab Shamsuddin Khan. It is said that in the influence of the opponents of Nawab Shamsuddin Khan, Fraser denied to even meet him at his residence in Delhi. These humiliations and ill-remarks enhanced the enmity between the two and subsequently murder of William Fraser.[39]

Whatever was the exact reason of open hostility between the two, but it was sure that the reputation of the Nawab was damaged and the dignity of the household was shattered. The illegal intervention of Mr. Fraser in political affairs of Firozpur Jhirka added more filth to their relations. The Meos as a whole were also indirectly felt humiliated over the attitude and undue intervention of William Fraser.

Nawab Shamsuddin Khan deputed Karim Khan, a famous Meo sharp shooter of Rangala village of Mewat, for the murder of William Fraser. Karim Khan was popularly known as "*Bhar Maru*" (sharp-shooter), due to his sharp shooting, courageous and murderous characteristics. Karim Khan easily agreed to end the game of William Fraser, and accordingly went Delhi along with his servant Annia Meo, a famous runner, at the end of 1834. Karim Khan stayed in a building of Mughal Beg at Daryaganj and began to watch Mr. Fraser at his residence in Bara Hindu Rao. In between, Nawab Shamsuddin Khan made correspondence with Karim Khan in code words, which proved that Nawab wanted to purchase a dog through Karim Khan.[40]

Karim Khan Meo, after a long wait of many months, finally got the opportunity on 22nd March 1835, and at 11 pm of the same night, he shot dead Mr. Fraser near his residence. His servant Annia Meo ran away from the spot and reached Firozpur Jhirka covering ninety miles in twenty four hours. Karim Khan also rode away by his famous black horse. Charles Metcalf's nephew Tom Metcalf, who later on succeeded as Resident of Delhi reached on the spot and enquired from his servants and became known that the murderer was on a black horse. Tom Metcalf quickly followed the killer but failed to trace him in dark night.[41]

On hearing the news, John Lawrence also reached Delhi from Panipat. After a detailed enquiry, they reached on the conclusion that Nawab Shamsuddin Khan was behind the murder of Mr. Fraser. They arrested Annia, the servant of Karim Khan Meo, made him the government witness on the condition of sparing his life. On the witness of Annia, both the Nawab and Karim Khan arrested and executed on Thursday morning, 3rd October, 1835, close outside the north of Kashmiri Gate, leading to the cantonments.[42]

Nawab prepared himself for the execution in a rich and beautiful dress of light green, the sacred colour of Muslims. After his death, his principality was confiscated and attached to district Gurgaon. It is said that after the execution of Nawab, his face automatically changed to west side. Notwithstanding, the implication of Section 144 by the British Government, about 8000 people participated in the burial ceremony of both Nawab Shamsuddin Khan and Karim Khan Meo. Maulana Shah Mohammad Ishaq, the maternal grandson of Maulana Shah Abdul Aziz Dehlavi offered the burial prayer.[43]

By the execution of both the Mewatis, and confiscation of the Firozpur Jhirka State, there spread the resentment and noncooperation to the government in Mewat. Many leaders even revolted against the British Government. Maulana Abdullah Khan Mewati of Firozpur rose in an open revolt in which hundreds of Mewatis arrested and killed, including Maulana Abdullah Khan Mewati. Although, the British Government brutally crushed the Mewatis before their rising, but they could not be controlled at the time of the Rebellion of 1857. Many scholars believe that the execution of Nawab Shamsuddin Khan was one of the reasons of Mewati Rebellion of 1857.[44]

Despite the jagir was confiscated in 1835, but the family continued to play an important part in the public affairs throughout the period of British rule and even after. Several members from the family have been among the finest poets and literary figures of the Urdu language. Among them, Dagh Dehlvi, the son of Nawab Shamsuddin Khan, and Mirza Ghalib and Sir Syed Ahmad Khan, both connected by marriage to the family.[45]

Interference in the Village Communities

After assuming the central authority in Indian subcontinent, the British Government directed their attention towards the peasants and their agrarian conditions. The time-honoured institutions like the village communities and panchayats were abolished by the British. In fact, these institutions were the centers of all the social and economic life of the villagers. The village communities and the panchayats were built up according to the requirements of the people and under these institutions they felt themselves secure and happier. Their destruction brought social instability, and people felt insecure and unhappy. Adding more distress to the village communities, the British Government had broken the backbone of the farmers by imposing heavy revenues and cesses.

There was a strong reaction in the local society against the British intervention in their age-old customs and traditions. As for the Mewat region, the whole area was rural and the cities like Gurgaon, Rewari, Kanaud, etc. were just like villages. All the villages were self-sufficient and were regulated by the village constitution forming a community. The decision of the panchayats, the ruling body of the village community, was obeyed unanimously with religious bounds. Though living in different realms of their respective religions and castes, they generally adhered the common village deities, Pirs, Sadhu saints and common customs and traditions, forming a composite culture. This common identity and composite culture goaded the villagers to take a united stand whenever the need arose.[46]

The past rulers like Afghans, Mughals, Marathas and Sikhs, who ruled over this region always realized the practical utility of this arrangement, and except the collection of revenue, never tried to disturb it. The British also did not find it easy to administer the area without the existing system. Nevertheless, in order to improve the lot of the rural masses, the British implemented their own system of governance. The process of their so-called improvements somewhat directly or indirectly disturbed the social set-up of the Mewatis.

K.C. Yadav writes that the British public officials, both revenue and the police interfered in the internal affairs of the villages. Their courts took up the work of dispensing justice, throwing the panchayats into oblivion. Yadav gives the example of Metcalfe that he punished offenders without weighing their guilt or fault. Metcalfe gave to one Roshan Khan, a policeman, life imprisonment accompanied by hard labour for having been accused of stealing 7 lbs. of thread. Yadav further says that even death penalties were awarded without printed regulations.[47]

The people did not find the British system to their taste and always regarded the British as no better than usurper and plunderer. The British system administration greatly affected the martial races of that tract such as Meos, Goojars, Ahirs, Jats and Ranghars, who lost no chance in resisting the British whenever and wherever they could find. The British system of administration and its interference with the long existing village communities greatly provoked the villagers of Mewat to rise against the British during the Rebellion of 1857.

These village communities were having no obligation to the Government or any other authority except for the payment of taxes. These communities independently managed most of their local affairs. D.C. Verma & Sukhbir Singh has quoted Metcalfe, which has shared his experiences that, "The village communities are little republics, having nearly everything they want within themselves and almost independent of any foreign relations. They seem to last where nothing else lasts. Dynasty after dynasty tumbles down; revolution succeeded to revolution; Hindu, Pathan, Mughal Mahratta, Sikh, English are masters in turn, but the village communities remain the same."[48]

The observation of another British officer Gubbins needs to be quoted here, although it was observed for the Awadh peasantry, but it has been explained exactly as of the Metcalfe for peasantry of Haryana and Mewat. The quote is as follows:[49]

> ".... Of these the most marked and universal feature was that of the village communities. The brotherhood which resided in each village was the only real proprietor of the soil, and among its members, the ancestral fields are divided. Each village was a separate little republic and having its accountant, public servants, the priest, the carpenter, the smith, the washer man, and the watchman, who were generally paid by dues claimable from the grain produce of each shareholder. The payment of a land tax was one of the oldest institutions of the country. It was levied from the several shareholders, by a rate upon the land, the shares, the ploughs, or the grain produce, and was paid to the Government officer through the head man of the village. As the numbers of these communities increased, their land no longer afforded them a sufficient maintenance, and numbers leave their villages to seek service, returning on the leave of absence to visit their families; and retiring when pensioned to live and die in their ancestral home. Such were the features which distinguish the class from which the Sepoys were drawn. They were originally proprietors of the soil, and they valued this right of property in the land above all earthly treasure."

Some scholars believe that the socio-economic measures adopted by the British administration were for the betterment of the peasantry, but Mewat was not reconciled to that system. D.C.

Verma & Sukhbir Singh quotes Percival Spear in which he attributes the failure to two causes. Firstly, the over assessment of land which was bitterly resented as it brought into operation oppressive methods. Secondly, the tampering with the age-old institutions such as the panchayats.[50]

Most of the areas of Mewat region were inhabited by the peasantry or agro based people. They were living the simple rural life established by their ancient forefathers. As many scholars described, their village community system was a small republic governed by the panchayats. The British interference into their system deeply hearted their feelings and they were alarmed of the destruction of their age-old social setup. All these changes dealt a serious blow to the rural society, particularly the cultivators and tribes of Mewat region. For the peasant, the new changes in agrarian economy and social structure meant more intensive and systematic exploitation. During the Rebellion of 1857, these Mewatis rose vehemently against the British in order to save their social set-up, honour and dignity to which they cherished from many centuries.

After disturbing the entire social setup, the British Government introduced a unique type judiciary which was unknown to the Indian masses. The newly judicial setup was much disgusting, repressive, arbitrary and expensive. There was no proper check on the judges, and a provision for appeal was not made in the legal system. It was neither liked by the people of the country nor appreciated by the efficient and reasonable administrators. It is said that bribery and corruption among the judges were prevalent.

Religious Factor

After the annexation of the Indian territories, the British Government, apart from most of its barbaric policies, adopted the unholy secret design of promoting the conversion to Christianity. The Government-missionary nexus gave further credence to the rumour about the use of cow and pig fat for the cartridges of Enfield Rifles. These blasphemous episodes of the British policies increased the people's growing disaffection with the Government. The Ulema or the Muslim theologians quickly responded over the issue and mobilized the people, particularly Muslim masses to rise against the Government during the Rebellion of 1857.

The Ulema, right from the British occupation of Delhi, were bitterly against the British rule in India. The first example of such resentment was the fatwa of Shah Abdul Aziz (1746-1824) the illustrious son of Shah Waliullah Dehlawi (1703-62). He issued the famous fatwa in 1803 declaring that India had ceased to be a *Dar-ul-Harb* or "Country of the Enemy". This fatwa from politico-religion point of view was a landmark in the history of India in general and for the Muslims of India in particular. It amounted to a call to religious conscientious Muslims to mobilize them in the absence of a powerful Muslim ruler, under whose popular leadership they would rise in defence of foreign power.[51]

Following the call of their cherished leader, every section of the Muslim community responded positively. During the Rebellion, the Muslim Ulema showed their resentment following the plea of the religion. They adopted the Wahabi ideology and fought against the British; although, they were arrayed initially against the tyrannical rule of Ranjit Singh of Punjab. They thought that the introduction of English medium of instruction in the schools, changing of Court language, propagation of Christianity, were the instruments of converting the Indian masses into Christianity as well as the direct attacks on their religion. In the schools run by the Christian Missionary or the British Government, the boys heard much about the Christian religion, of which the parents disapproved, but they were unable to withdraw their boys in the desire of Government jobs. Any measure of development started by the British was considered as a prelude to the conversion into Christianity.

These Muslim Ulema with a purported or avowed religious agenda were commonly termed *Ghazis* or *Jihadis* and *Mujahideen* in British sources. This terminology implied that they were holy warriors, fighting for Islam and their country. The modern historians prove this fact of religious perspective of the Rebellion of 1857 based on very authentic contemporary documents. This religious perspective was fully coloured undoubtedly with Wahabi ideology. Like many of the researchers about the dominancy of the religious factor, a modern historian Dalrymple's research also emphasizes the religious factor based on Urdu documents in the National Archives. The words *Deen* and *Dharma* (the Muslim and Hindu words for religion) appear constantly in revolutionary proclamations, and were used as war the cry by the combatants. These facts show the extent to which religious feelings goaded the revolutionaries; it goes well beyond the question of greased cartridges.

Although, the Muslim intellectuals such as Sir Syed Ahmad Khan, Mirza Ghalib, Maulvi Zakaullah, etc. who had seen the horrific scenes of the insurrection, thoroughly denounced the call of *Jihad* by the Ulema. According to them, the Muslim religious fervour against the British during the Rebellion of 1857 was surely supported by the followers of other communities of India. Undoubtedly, the intellectuals' plea was based on saving the Muslims from the heavy hands of the British. Certainly, at most of the places the people belonging to both the religions were fought shoulder to shoulder against the British. The Ayodhya episode in such a reference was the fine example. Maulana Amir Ali, a well-known Maulvi and the chief priest of Hanuman Garhi, Baba Ramcharan Dass of Ayodhya took up arms and fought gallantly against the British. They both hanged together in Ayodhya.[52]

The other revolutionaries, without any doubt, at most of the places not only supported the *Mujahideen* whole heartedly but jointly carried the struggle for a long time. The contemporary British chronicler Thomas Lowe also testifies the same opinion by writing about this thesis in 1860. Thomas Lowe writes, "The infanticide Rajput, the bigoted Brahmin, the fanatic Musalmans, and the luxury-loving fat-paunched ambitious Mahrattah, for they all joined together in the cause; cow killer, cow worshiper, the pig hater and pig eater the crier of 'Allah is God and Mahomet his Prophet,' and the mumbler of the mysteries of Bram!"[53] Thomas Lowe concluded that they all joined together against the British during the Rebellion of 1857.

However, it surely could not be denied that the Wahabi and Faraizi fighters and other likeminded freelance *Mujahideen's* involvement were in greater extent. The sacrifices of lives and property of the Ulema clearly shows their intention of love for their religion and nation. The Ulema were not at all the Sepoys, but a freelance fighter and they maintained their identity as a separate class. These Ulema not only participated themselves in the Rebellion but aroused the sentiments of the other Muslims to fight against the British. The people rushed to fight against the British on the call of the Ulema. Regarding such an influx, some of the intellectuals believe that the preaching of such Ulema did indeed have an effect on those soldiers, who later joined the *Mujahideen* at the outbreak of the Rebellion. Some of them also argue that the *Mujahideen*, who took part in what they conceived as a *Jihad*, did so in the belief that the Rebellion of 1857 was an extension of the egalitarian and reformist Shah Waliullahi Movement.

However, the factor of religion was having little importance, especially for the people of Mewat but it could not be completely ignored. The greased cartridge episode was the burning example of the religious interference by the British. It hearted both Hindus and Muslims as the cartridges were greased with the cow and swine fats. However, the peasantry in Mewat had no direct concern with this matter, but it also could not be ignored that many peasant family members were in the military service of the government and were deeply hearted due to this act. It not only infuriated the related families but all the villagers as use of the greased cartridges had polluted the religion of the brotherhood or the village communities.

Undoubtedly, the people of Mewat were not educated but due to the religious policies of the British Government, some of the Maulvis played instrumental in arousing their religious feelings against the Christianity or the British. Right from the occupation of Mewat territory, the British custom and traditions indirectly affected the people, and they felt that the British Government was bent on interfering their religion and age-old established customs. Doing away the Arabic, Persian and Sanskrit and imposing English on its place confirmed the local intelligentsia that they would be deprived of knowledge of the principles of their own faith.[54]

Right from the beginning of the British occupation of Mewat, the Ulema class of that region was bitterly against the British. The religious interference and uncordial behavior of the British Government further added fuel in the existing hostility. Just after the annexation of the Mewat region, Maulvi Evaz of Notki village along with other Maulvis and Meo people attacked upon the British army in 1806 and harmed them severely. Fearing the defection of the Mewati people, the British Commissioner, Mr. Seton advised his officers for cordial behave with the people of Mewat.[55]

Most probably the religious interference was the chief cause of the Wahabi revolution much before the Rebellion of 1857, which affected a lot in the Mewat region. The Maulvi class of the Mewati society was in constant touch with the other Maulvi *Mujahideen* of Frontier who were constantly fighting against the British. They were not only in touch with the *Mujahideen* but also fought shoulder to shoulder against the British. Revolutionary emissaries from the Frontier found the Mewat region a fertile field for their activity. As mentioned in *Tarikh-e-Meo Kshatriya*, a Mewati named Haji Abdullah Khan of the village Kankarkhera of Tijara Tehsil in Mewat went to the Frontier along with his followers to fight in the battle of Balakot. After their defeat, he returned to his country and began to organize his people for the new mission, or war against the British. Haji Abdullah Khan was closely supported by another Mewati named Miyanji Karimullah Gohanvi.[56]

After the battle of Balakot, Maulana Mahboob Ali Dehlavi and Maulana Sayyed Hyder Ali Tonki, the close associates of Maulana Sayyed Ahmad of Rai Bareli, toured the whole area of Mewat and mobilized the Mewatis to fight against the British to save their religion and nation. They became successful in creating the great followers in Mewat, who were ready to sacrifice their lives and property for the sake of their religion and nation.[57]

When the Rebellion started in Delhi, the revolutionaries from frontier areas rushed towards Delhi to fight for the nation. Most of them were having close connection from the region of Mewat. They motivated the youths of Mewat to fight against the British by the name of religion and nation. They became successful in recruiting the freelance Mewati *Mujahideen*, which later joined the other revolutionaries of Delhi. This fact is being proved by the letters written to the Commander-in-Chief General Bakht Khan by the Mewati *Mujahideen* (*Fidawiane Jameeye Mewat*) and their leader Alif Khan. The letter written on 13th August 1857 is as follows:[58]

> "Aali Jaah! As we, the hundreds of *Mujahideen* from the district Mewat, promptly rushed to sacrifice our lives on your request after leaving our children and other family members on the mercy of God. We have been doing so for several months. Other revolutionary fighters are getting the proper salary and we the *Mujahideen* are without diet, living on the blood of our heart, and being martyred in the same condition of thirst and hunger. Our sacrifices are well-known among the other revolutionaries. We had sold one of our horses and got one female horse and 45 rupees for our daily subsistence. Nevertheless, we are sorry to say that you have taken over the rupees and female horse and also made serious allegations of mismanaging the Government property. Our team leader Alif Khan had many times submitted his request before you but you have not heeded his appeal. We have no concern for mixing the lead. The lead defaulters had run away and somehow we the innocents were arrested in the way, and you have still not enquired about the matter. This is improper according to the constitution and justice. On doomsday, we have to show our face before God, who has given us the present life. That's why we are here to seek justice otherwise we the hundreds of *Mujahideen* would have gone to our homes after informing you formally. If you would not give us justice, we surely would be given on the Day of Judgement. Now we are requesting to your honour. Whatever we deemed fit we said."

After the suppression of the Rebellion at Delhi, the same *Mujahideen* came to Mewat and fought against the British at different fronts. Among these *Mujahideen*, Maulvi Noor Ali, Maulvi Mohammad Mureed, Maulvi Abul Hasan Afghani, Huzoor of

Kheti, Dr. Nazar Mohammad of Badshahpur, etc. were in the fore. At the time, when the British completely suppressed the Rebellion in Mewat, some of these *Mujahideen* permanently settled in this region and began the tabligh work in Mewat.[59]

Maulana Abdul Shakoor quotes the version of Dr. Nazar Mohammad Badshahpuri that in July 1857, four persons came to his house at Badshahpur. One of them known as Maulvi Mohammad Mureed was injured with a bullet. The bullet was poisoning his leg. Dr. Nazar provided him medical aid and arranged for their stay in a dome which was two furlongs away from his house.[60]

As the four aforesaid revolutionaries were hiding in the dome for long time, they became known to the people of Badshahpur. It was the time when the Rebellion in Mewat was suppressed, and the British forces were combing and hanging the revolutionaries. Dr. Nazar advised them to change their destination. They all moved towards Mewat. Maulvi Mohammad Mureed settled at Firozpur Jhirka. One of them Maulvi Noor Ali had chosen his destination at Rewari. The third one lived at Kheti village in Alwar State and was more popular with the name of Huzoor. The fourth, Maulvi Abul Hasan settled himself at the village Bhoonri in Mewat.[61]

The religious unity of both Hindus and Muslims was a great threat to the British. The British were extremely worried and horrified with this kind of unity of the people of two religions. After suppression of the Rebellion, they tried to break the unity in a most horrendous and sickening manner. A story of Hansi is one of such examples of breaking the unity. At Hansi, Hukumchand Jain and Muneer Beg were leading the revolutionaries of the Rebellion. They led many successful military campaigns in the area but were defeated and captured. After hanging them on the same tree at Hansi on January 19, 1858, Hukumchand Jain was buried and Muneer Beg was cremated against the custom of their respective religions. It was done with the obvious purpose of making fun of the unity of these two revolutionaries belonging to different religions and show hatred towards their comradeship.[62]

Interference in the Cottage Industries

After the annexation of India, the British started its most unpopular policy, the de-industrialisation of India. Due to the Industrial Revolution in England, there was a heavy demand of the raw materials from India and market for their finished products. The de-industrialisation policy of the British Government closely affected the petty industries of Mewat region. The import of Europeans clothes and objects to India rendered traditional artisan communities like weavers, carpenters, iron smiths, shoe smiths and so on, jobless and without any alternative sources of income except begging. Thus, most of them actively joined in the Rebellion against the British as a protest against this social and economic injustice. During the Rebellion, they find a fair opportunity to avenge the oppressor by murder, loot and plunder.

Artisans and handicraft's men were largely affected by the British Government policy of promoting the British manufactured goods and neglect of indigenous industry in Mewat region. There were a large number of cottage industries in the Mewat region, including the tahsil of Rewari. *Imperial Gazetteer of India* reports that the Rewari town was ranking as one of the chief trading emporiums in the Punjab. Its merchants transact a large part of the commerce between the States of Rajputana and the Northern Provinces of British India. Salt from the Sambhar Lake, together with iron, forms the principal import; while sugar, grain, and English piece-goods compose the staple items of the return trade. Hardware of mixed metal is the chief manufacturing industry.[63]

The Mewat region was the centre of important manufacture of hardware and famous handicrafts. Nuh, Firozpur Jhirka, Palwal, Hodal, and Hasanpur were the chief minor marts for country produce. Fine class shoes were made at Sohna. Beautiful glass bangles were manufactured at Sohna, Basai Meo in Firozpur and Rangala in Nuh; iron vessels were made at Darapur and Tankri in Rewari, and there were the usual manufactures of coarse cotton cloth and rough blankets. These industries were shattered due to the import of the British goods. Manufacture of salt another important industry in Mewat, that too suffered by unjust policies of the British Government. The salts were prepared by the evaporation of brine raised from wells; this is carried on in the clusters of villages near Nuh.[64]

In Firozpur Jhirka, there was the cotton industry in which many types of clothes were prepared for the people. Even the cotton was sent in large quantities from Alwar State for petty manufacturing of cloths in Firozpur Jhirka and other surrounding areas. Powlett mentions that the manufacture of iron was in former times a great industry in the Alwar State, as is testified by the large hillocks of slag, which are to be found in all directions; but it has fallen off largely of the late years, the value of the native iron having been extremely lessened by the large quantities imported from Europe.[65]

Unrest of Meo Sepoys Serving under British and Native States

In 1857, the British East India Company controlled a vast area protected by a huge military force, composed of three distinct armies centered around the presidencies of Madras, Bombay, and Bengal. By 1857 the Bengal army was considered as the showpiece of the Indian army due to its hugeness and the most active role in the conquest of north India. The British Government recruited native volunteers in large numbers because of the vast British territory in north India, large resources of manpower that various Indian populations offered, and as the native soldiers were less expensive, better disciplined, and healthier than their European counterparts.

Following the people of different areas, the Mewati youths were employed in the Bengal army, Contingents of the principalities paid by the native governments as well as the local army of the native governments. They proved themselves a better fighter for their employer. The introduction of the new Enfield Rifles and rumor of the cartridges greased in swine and cow fats, surely would have affected the Mewati Sepoys like the other Sepoys serving under the British Government. It is said that the rural panchayats issued the decree that the Sepoys using the greased cartridges would be treated as outcastes and expelled from all communion. Instances of such a decree were firstly noticed at

Ambala. It was more probable that the Mewati panchayats would have also issued such decrees.

The Meos, historically as the martial community, were largely employed by the British Government directly under Bengal army, their contingents of the princely states such as Gwalior and Kota Contingent, as well as the native governments of Alwar, Bharatpur, Gwalior, Dhaulpur, Rewari, Ballabhgarh, Jhajjar, etc. Even the Meos under the princely states were employed by the British Government for different contingents.

The Alwar State, which was including hundreds of Meo villages, naturally forming a major part of its army from the Meos and other martial communities. Out of 6795 Artillery, Cavalry and Infantry forces of the Alwar State, 1860 Muslims were from Alwar State and 292 were foreign Muslims (Pathans-630, Shaikhs-630, Sayyeds-320, Mughals-140, Khanzadas-360, Meos-12, others-40); 2342 from Alwar Rajputs and 546 from foreign Rajputs; 1580 from other Alwar Hindus, 172 from other foreign Hindus and three Eurasians.[66]

As for the military service under British from the Alwar State, it was also proportionately enough. Powlett gives the description of the Meos and other people serving under British military service from Alwar State. According to Powlett, the British Cavalry and Infantry were consisted Brahmins, 9+35=44; Hindu Thakurs, 9+26=35; Jats, 2+31=33; Goojars, 0+40=40; Ahirs, 12+34=46; Shaikhs, 8+2=10; Sayyeds, 30+3=33; Pathans, 5+3=8; Khanzadas, 28+17=45; Qazis, 8+2=10; Meos, 11+34=45; Muslim Thakurs, 110+4=114; Saqqas, 6+14=20; thirteen othe castes, 15+15=30.[67]

In the State of Dhaulpur Mewati inhabitants were in abundance. In the military forces of Dhaulpur Rana, there was a Mewati contingent consisting of 100 to 1200 Cavalry.[68] Surely they would have played a very remarkable role during the Rebellion of 1857.

Apart from the military services in the princely states, the Meos were directly recruited in different regiments of the British Government. The exact numerical strength of the Mewati Sepoys is not known from the records, but some of the Mewati Sepoys, who were hanged after a short trial by William Ford, the Gurgaon

Deputy Commissioner, is shown in the Appendix-V. The Mewatis were largely recruited in the British army in the 10th Regiment of Irregular Cavalry, Punjab Cavalry, 2nd Regiment of Gwalior Contingent, 4th Regiment of Gwalior Contingent, 2nd Troop, 5th Regiment of Gwalior Contingent, 3rd Regiment of Gwalior Contingent, 3rd Regiment of Punjab Cavalry, 2nd Regiment of Punjab Cavalry, 15th Punjab Regiment, 4th Irregular Cavalry, 15th Irregular Cavalry, 2nd Irregular Cavalry, Kota Contingent, Gwalior Contingent, 3rd Regiment of Gwalior Contingent, and Haryana Light Infantry.[69]

The Sepoys had their own reasons for resentment. The Sepoys were unhappy for low pay and racial discrimination in matters of promotion, pension and terms of service. However, the immediate cause of their mutiny was to the introduction of the Enfield Rifles which were loaded with the cartridges greased by swine and cow fats. They were in the suspicion that they would be forced to renounce their cultural ethos of centuries' old society was also an important cause of their insurrection. As far as Mewat region is concerned, most of the soldiers who were basically hailing from the peasant families were also unhappy with the new land revenue settlements introduced by the British Government.

Regarding the participation of the Mewati Sepoys in the Rebellion of 1857, they fought many battles in Mewat against the British. These battles which were fought in Mewat region were the battles of Raiseena (Alipur), Ghasera, Mahu, Rupraka, etc. In these battles, the Meo peasants and farmers were equally assisted by the Mewati Sepoys with their arms and ammunitions. After their defeat at Ghasera, the Meos completely evacuated the village and when the British force made house to house search they find the Sepoys' uniform and other belongings in most of the houses. For the British force each village, where they fought, was a regiment in itself. The Meo Sepoys not only fought in Mewat but showed their bravery at the battle of Nasibpur (Narnaul) and other various fronts. The Meo chaudharies also sent an army of Sepoys and civilian to fight in Delhi, on the call of General Bakht Khan and Mughal Emperor Bahadur Shah Zafar. It is needless to say that mere civilian could never be so courageous to fight against the most advanced and well equipped British army.

References

1. Raikes, Charles, *Notes on the Revolt in the North-Western Provinces of India*, London, 1858, pp. 123-124.
2. *Mewat: A Retrospective*, p. 13, see also Shams, Shamsuddin, *Meos of India*, New Delhi, 1983, pp. 41-43, (here after quoted as *Meos of India*).
3. Channing, (Letter of the Officiating Secretary, Govt. of India, Revenue and Agriculture Deptt. to Secretary, Government of Punjab), p. 4.
4. Meo, Siddiq Ahmad, *Sangram 1857: Mewatiyon Ka Yogdan*, Nuh, 2006, pp. 21 & 31, (here after quoted as *Sangram 1857*).
5. *Haryana State Gazetteer*, Volume I, Chandigarh, 2001, pp. 276-277, see also Verma, D.C. & Sukhbir Singh, *Haryana*, New Delhi, 2009, p. 33, (here after quoted as *Haryana*).
6. Khan, Syed Ahmad, *Asbab-e-Baghawat-e-Hind*, Patna, 1999, pp. 29-30.
7. Channing, (Letter of the Officiating Secretary, Govt. of India, Revenue and Agriculture Deptt. to Secretary, Punjab Government), p. 5.
8. *Ibid.*
9. *Ibid*, (Letter of the Senior Secretary, Punjab Financial Commissioner to the Junior Secretary, Punjab Government), pp. 5-6.
10. *Ibid*, (Letter of the Senior Secretary, Punjab Financial Commissioner to the Junior Secretary, Punjab Government), p. 6.
11. *Ibid*, (Letter of the Officiating Secretary, Govt. of India, Revenue and Agriculture Deptt. to Secretary, Government of Punjab), p. 6.
12. *Ibid*, (Letter of the Senior Secretary, Punjab Financial Commissioner to the Junior Secretary, Punjab Government), p. 23.
13. Zakir, Kashmiri Lal, *Tahrik-e-Azadi Aur Mewat*, Panchkula, 2008, p. 17, (here after quoted as *Tahrik-e-Azadi Aur Mewat*).
14. Channing, (Letter of the Officiating Secretary, Govt. of India, Revenue and Agriculture Deptt. to Secretary, Government of Punjab), p. 3.
15. *Ibid*, (Letter of the Senior Secretary, Punjab Financial Commissioner to the Junior Secretary, Punjab Government), p. 23.
16. Karl Marx and Angels, *Collected Works*, Part-39, Moscow, 1986, p. 339.
17. Hunter, William Wilson, *Imperial Gazetteer of India*, Vol. V, London 1885, p. 219, (hereafter cited as *Imperial Gazetteer of India*).
18. Channing, (Letter of the Officiating Secretary, Govt. of India, Revenue and Agriculture Deptt. to Secretary, Government of Punjab), p. 7.
19. Mayaram, Shail, *Against History Against State: Counterperspectives from the Margins*, New Delhi, 2004, pp. 188-189, (hereafter cited as *Against History Against State*).

20. *Ibid.*
21. *Ibid*, p. 209.
22. *Imperial Gazetteer of India*, Vol. V, London 1885, p. 221.
23. *Against History Against State*, p. 192.
24. *Mewat: A Retrospective*, p. 22.
25. *Ibid*, p. 23, (Ibbetson writes that the Mina, a caste which is in the Punjab at least invariably criminal. In Gurgaon, the Meena cultivates land, but this does not prevent his being a professional thief. They are boldest criminal classes in the Punjab. Their enterprises are on a large-scale and, they are always prepared to use violence if necessary. They travel great distress in gangs of from 10 to 20 men, practicing robbery and dacoity even as far as the Deccan. See for details, *A Glossary*, pp. 102-103).
26. *Ibid*, p. 39.
27. Siraj, Minhaj, *Tabaqat-i-Nasiri*, (Urdu Trans. Ghulam Rasul Mehar), Vol. II, Lahore, 2004, pp. 99-100, see also Cunningham, pp. 13, 29-30, *The Cambridge History of India, Vol. III*, p. 73, Elliot&Dowson, Vol. II, London, 1867, pp. 359&381, *The Meos of Mewat*, p. 20, *Tarikh Meo Kshatri*, pp. 151-152, and *Tarikh Meo Mehar*, p. 239.
28. Barani, Ziauddin, *Tarikh-i-Firoz Shahi*, (Urdu Trans. Sayed Muinul Haque), Lahore, 2004, p.104, see also Elliot&Dowson, Vol. III, London, 1867, p. 104, Firishta, Mohammad Qasim Hindu Shah, *Tarikh-i-Firishta*, (Eng. Trans., John Briggs), *History of the Rise of the Mohammadan Power in India, Till the Year 1612*, Vol. I, London, 1829, p.255 (Hereafter cited as Briggs Firishta).
29. *Tarikh Meo Kshatri*, p. 152 see also *Mewat: A Retrospective*, p. 69.
30. Cunningham, p. iv.
31. Abul Fazal, *Ain-i-Akbari*, (Eng. Trans., H. Blochmann), Vol. I, Calcutta, 1873, p. 252.
32. Frowde, Henry, *Imperial Gazetteer of India*, Vol. XVI, London, 1908, p. 169, see also Alexander Smith, Faulkner, *An Historical Sketch of the Naruka State of Ulwar in Rajputana*, Calcutta, 1895, pp. 26-27, (hereafter cited as *An Historical Sketch*) and *Meo Qaum Aur Mewat*, p. 128.
33. Horace, W. Carpentier, *Imperial Gazetteer of India*, Provincial Series, Vol. II, Calcutta, 1908, p. 364, see also Thornton, Edward, *A Gazetteer of the Territories under the Government of the East India Company*, Vol. II, London, 1854, p. 372.
34. William Fraser, a Scotman, self imaged themselves as the Mughal noble. He was a scholar of Persian, composed poetry in that language,

befriended as the Urdu Poet Mirza Ghalib and loved to discuss ancient Sanskrit texts. He was a brilliant scholar, metaphysician, and philosopher. He followed Indian customs, wore Indian clothing and a Rajput style beard, refused to eat pork and beef, and was virtually a half Hindustani. He frequently chatted and joked with his servants in their own language. Fraser had a harem and many wives; the senior most was a Jat lady. In Mewat he built a fort and called it the "Fraser Garh", in which he maintained one thousand Sepoys of his own raising and disciplining. There he lived like a Nawab, being as absolute in his domain as Bonapart of France. See for details, *Against History Against State: Counterperspectives from the Margins*, pp. 190-191.

35. *Meo Qaum Aur Mewat*, pp. 129-130.
36. *An Historical Sketch*, p. 27, see also *Meo Qaum Aur Mewat*, p. 130.
37. Channing, p. 22, see also Nawab Server-ul-Mulk Bahadur, *My Life, Being the Autobiography*, Eng. Trans. Nawab Jiwan Yar Jung Bahadur, London, (ND), pp. 61-62, and Cunningham, Vol. XX, p. 22.
38. *The Dawn*, Magazine, July 30, 2006, quoted from the novel of Shamsur Rahman Faruqui '*Kai Chand The Sar-i-Asman*'.
39. Ahmad, Iqbal, *Nawab Shamsuddin Khan Aur Karim Khan Meo*, Lahore, 2010, pp. 17-20, (hereafter cited as *Nawab Shamsuddin Khan*).
40. *Meo Qaum Aur Mewat*, pp. 131-132, see also *Nawab Shamsuddin Khan*, pp. 20-21.
41. *Nawab Shamsuddin Khan*, pp. 26-27, see also *Meo Qaum Aur Mewat*, pp. 134-135.
42. *Ibid*, pp. 28-39.
43. *Meo Qaum Aur Mewat*, p. 134, see also *Nawab Shamsuddin Khan*, p. 29.
44. *Nawab Shamsuddin Khan*, p. 30.
45. Nawab Server-ul-Mulk Bahadur, *My Life, Being the Autobiography*, Eng. Trans. Nawab Jiwan Yar Jung Bahadur, London, (ND), p. 59.
46. *The Role of Punjab Haryana and Himachal Pradesh*, pp. 123-124.
47. *Ibid*, p. 131.
48. *Haryana*, p. 36.
49. Gubbins, Martin Richard, *An Account of the Mutinies of Oudh and of the siege of the Lucknow Residency; With some Observation on the Condition of the Province of Oudh and of the Causes of the Mutiny of the Bengal Army*, London, 1858, pp. 66-67.
50. *Haryana*, p. 40.

51. *World Policy Journal, (The Hidden Roots of Wahhabism in British India-* Charles Allen), Vol. 22, No. 2, Massachusetts, USA, Summer 2005, p. 88, (W.W. Hunter, summaries this fatwa in his own words, "when infidel get hold of Muhammadan country and it become impossible for the Muslim of the country, and of the people of neighboring district to drive them away or to retain reasonable hope of ever doing so, and the power of infidels increasing to such an extent that they can abolish or retain the ordinance of Islam according to their pleasure and no one is strong enough to cease on the revenue of the country without the permission of infidels. And the Muslim inhabitant does no longer live so secure as before. Such a country is politically a country of the enemy (*Darul Harb*)." Hunter, William Wilson, *The Indian Musalmans*, London, 1876, p. 142).
52. Shamsul Islam, *Hindus and Muslims in the First War of Independence of 1857 & Emergence of Two-Nation Theory*, Paper presented in a conference at Trivandrum, Kerala, on May 19, 2007.
53. Lowe, Thomas, *Central India During the Rebellion of 1857 and 1858, London, 1860*, p. 324.
54. *Asbab-e-Baghawat-e-Hind*, pp. 16-17.
55. *Sangram 1857*, p. 31, (quoted from the File No. R-89, DC office, Gurgaon).
56. *Tarikh-e-Meo Kshatriya*, pp. 381-382.
57. *Ibid*, p. 381.
58. *Ibid*, p. 457.
59. *Ibid*, p. 382, see also *Meo Qaum Aur Mewat*, p. 199.
60. *Ibid*, p. 382.
61. *Ibid*, pp. 383-384.
62. Hunter, William Wilson, *Imperial Gazetteer of India*, Vol. V, London 1885, p. 221.
63. Channing, pp. 60-61, see also Hunter, William Wilson, *Imperial Gazetteer of India*, Vol. V, London 1885, p. 222.
64. Powlett, p. 78.
65. *Ibid*, p. 76.
66. *Ibid*, p. 107.
67. *Ibid*, p. 49.
68. Muir, Sir William, *Records of the Intelligence Department of the Government of the North-West Provinces of India during the Mutiny of 1857*, Vol. II, Edinburgh, 1902, p. 48, (hereafter cited as *Records of the Intelligence Department*).
69. *File No. R/189*, Deputy Commissioners Office, Gurgaon.

3

Beginning and Progress of Rebellion in Mewat

The Rebellion of 1857, which lasted for more than two years from the rising at Meerut in May, 10, 1857 to the fall of General Bakht Khan and Nana Sahib in June 1859 in the Terai border of Nepal, is the most written about an event in the world history. It was by far the largest, most widespread, and dangerous threat to British rule in India in the nineteenth century. In spite of the voluminous works about the Rebellion of 1857, but unfortunately, the rise of the peasantry of the Mewat region has not been seriously introduced to the readers. The names and involvements of the great personalities like Bahadur Shah Zafar, General Bakht Khan, Maulvi Ahmadullah Shah, Kunwar Singh, etc., in the Indian Rebellion of 1857, are well known to history; those of Rani Luxmi Bai, Tantia Tope, Begum Hazrat Mahal, are household words. However, the common people, Sepoys, working class and peasants, farmers were never emphasized except some Marxist writings.

The Rebellion started as the mutiny at Meerut by the Sepoys but it soon snowballed into the national war against the British due to the large-scale involvement of the people of every class, race and religion. It started with the mutiny of the Meerut Sepoys of the three Native regiments. Mewati people, especially the Meo peasantry, were among them, who jumped into the war and gave popular diversion to the Rebellion.

The Sepoys after their loot and plunder in the Meerut cantonment reached to the Delhi in the morning of 11th May. The Kashmiri Gate and Calcutta Gate were opened, and the Sepoys entered the city with shouting of *Deen! Deen!*-Religion! Religion!,

'*Badshah Zindabad*- Long live the Emperor, *Badshah ki Jai*- Victory to the Emperor'. The revolutionaries soon spread into the palace and the city and killed all white men and women they found. They also attacked the church, and every house occupied by Christian or Europeans. They not even left the Indians who were converted to Christianity. The revolutionaries, in the city, were greeted with lotus flowers and chapatis and were urged to clear Delhi from the British.

The 82 years old Mughal Emperor Bahadur Shah Zafar, initially showing some hesitation, agreed to give his countenance to the Rebellion. He was formally declared the Emperor of Hindustan. Bahadur Shah Zafar gave a stirring call to the countrymen to throw off the foreign yoke in 1857 and he himself became the symbol and focal point of hopes of the people of all over India. Subsequently, after the arrival of General Bakht Khan, the administration of the national government was carried on by a council consisting of both the military and civilian officers. The name of the Council was *Jalsa-e-Intizam-e-Fauji-wa-Mulki* but popularly it was known as Military Council.[1]

The Delhi episode greatly affected the nearby region of Mewat. The Meos, a brave and freedom-loving community, were living from many decades in the system of heavy taxation and exploitation by the British Government. Their dissatisfaction burst in 1857, when the Rebellion broke out from Meerut and Delhi. They had shown their resentment in 1838, much before the Rebellion of 1857. It was reported that during the famine years in Mewat in 1837-38, Mewati and Rajput zamindars of Shahjahanpur had led their men against the moneylenders of the towns. Following that episode, the Mewati military gentry resumed their depredations on the route between Delhi and Mathura.[2]

After the advent of the revolutionary Sepoys in Delhi, the fury reached to the rest of the northern India in the next few days. The neighbouring area of Mewat, closely attached to the Delhi and Gurgaon could not remain calm over that burning episode. They responded over the Rebellion as soon as it overpowered Delhi and subsequently Gurgaon. Since half a century, the Meos were feeling themselves enslaved on their own land and when they found the opportunity of the Rebellion, they jumped into it with men and money. The Mewati revolutionaries were mostly Meos and other sects of the Muslim community. They were fully coloured in national passion of ousting the British from their homeland.

In this Rebellion, the Mewatis threw themselves into the war with their ancient velour and bravery. It was really amazing that without any commonly accepted leader, the Meos ousted the British and formed their own government under the different chaudharies of the villages. They quelled the British force and freed themselves after a long slavery. In Mewat region, there were no native chiefs, nobles or lords, that's why, the command of the Rebellion in Mewat was taken by the chaudharies of the 52 *Gotras* and 12 *Pals* of the Meo community.

Among the chaudharies, Sharfuddin Mewati of Pinangwan was the commonly accepted leader during the Rebellion of 1857. Apart from him, many other local leaders rose to the occasion and did the wonderful job against the British. Saadat Khan headed the revolutionaries from Firozpur Jhirka area. Sadruddin of Pindhua took charge of the Nuh-Tigaon region; Firoz Shah Mewat organized the revolutionaries of Sohna, Tauru and Raiseena areas; Ali Hasan Khan was the hero of the Nuh and Ghasera areas. Maulana Mehrab Khan, although a religious leader, also worked a lot to mobilize the people of Mewat and successfully created a band of the revolutionaries by preaching *Jihad* against the British.[3]

In Mewat region, there was no military cantonment, base or controlling headquarters of the British Government. There was no British officer to guard the area. By the name of the British administration in Mewat, there were only few Police Stations attended by the Indian police personnel, and some Custom Chaukis attended by the Custom Officers and Clerks. The Custom Chaukis were on the Custom Line, which was going from Mathura to Lahore via Mewat.[4]

The Khanzada community of Nuh was loyal to the British government and aided them and fought against the Meos or Mewati revolutionaries. Very surprisingly, the Khanzadas of Mandikhera and other many other places were anti-British and fighting along with the Meos and other Mewatis of this region. Khanzadas of Nuh town were in the league with police personnel and gave tough resistance to the Meo revolutionaries in occupying the different areas of Mewat and particularly the Nuh town. Even then the police and the loyalists were unable to check the revolutionaries who were mostly belonging to the Meo population of Mewat.

After being freed from the British slavery, the Mewati revolutionaries controlled the towns and villages of the Mewat area through the chaudharies or village headman. The chaudharies, after controlling the administration under their jurisdiction, accepted subordination of the Mughal Emperor Bahadur Shah Zafar and paid homage by sending the revenue collected by them.

Immediately after assuming the charge of revolutionary government of Hindustan, Emperor issued orders to the rajas and local chiefs to cooperate the Emperor with men and money. He issued orders to the Rajahs of Jaipur, Jodhpur, and Bikaner personally to attend, or to send soldiers to rally around the King. Mirza Aminuddin Khan (Brother of Nawab Shamsuddin Khan) was ordered to proceed to Firozpur, to arrange for a Mohammadan administration, and to raise a force of Mewatis. Mirza asked for orders to allow him free egress and ingress to and from the city, and the orders were accordingly issued.[5]

Emperor was sure that his order would be honestly obeyed in Mewat region. Ultimately, an order was dispatched from the Emperor to the chaudharis and nambardars of Mewat in which it was instructed to follow Sayyed Musharraf Ali, the newly appointed tahsildar of Mewat region. Sayyed Musharraf Ali tahsildar was also instructed to do his job with honesty, responsibility and loyalty.[6]

After the fall of Delhi, the British suppressed the Meos and other Mewatis with full force and restored the British Government in Mewat area after a three-month continuous siege. The Meos paid a heavy price of their patriotism by facing the barbaric British wrath after suppression of the Rebellion. The details of the events, both the Mewati rising and British efforts to continue their rule in Mewat region, has been widely discussed under the following headings.

William Ford, Deputy Commissioner of Gurgaon

When the Rebellion of 1857 started from Meerut and gave a national shape in Delhi, the neighbouring area of Gurgaon was under Deputy Commissioner William Ford. The Mewat region, where the Meo population was in majority, was also under the jurisdiction of the Gurgaon district. The Meos and Goojars of the neighbouring areas assisted the troopers, when about 300 troopers of 3rd Light Cavalry attacked the Gurgaon on 11th May, immediately after looting and plundering the city and enthroning the Bahadur Shah Zafar as the Emperor of Hindustan. They were assisted by the local farmers, artisans and the other people of that area. Even the local feudal nobles like Ahmad Mirza and Nawab Dula Jan tried to lead the revolutionaries, but the rebellious Sepoys took control of the attack in their own hands. The revolutionaries were repulsed by the William Ford, the Deputy Commissioner of Gurgaon.[7]

In the morning of 12th May, William Ford, at first, with the assistance of a body of Pataudi Horses who were in attendance on him, drove off some troopers of the 3rd Light Cavalry at Bijwasan village, 12 km from Gurgaon. He furthermore seized their 10 men and 20 horses. William Ford also suppressed an outbreak in the jail.[8]

However, hundreds of peasants from the neighbouring villages and artisans and poor people from the towns of Gurgaon swelled the Sepoy's ranks in no time. Subsequently, in the next attack at Gurgaon, the seat of the district administration, William Ford and his forces were defeated by the heavy revolutionary force. He was compelled to leave the station, which was thereupon plundered and burnt by the victorious revolutionaries. William Ford proceeded to Hodal *via* Sailan and Palwal, where he reached on 14th of May. At Gurgaon, the revolutionaries set fire to the houses, and plundered the treasury, bringing away about seven lakhs and 84,000 rupees along with arms and ammunition.[9]

The revolutionaries at Gurgaon seized and occupied a gun, four camels and many of the tents. They also killed 25 Englishmen, burnt all the revenue records of the district administration and records of the Mahajans. The withdrawal of the British from the station resulted a complete political vacuum thus caused the people to believe that the British rule had ceased to exist. The revolutionaries also attacked the jail and freed the prisoners and took the whole administration of the district in their own hand.[10]

The worst of all for the British, that the fire of Rebellion soon caught the neighbouring area of Mewat immediately after the Gurgaon victory by the revolutionaries. At the initial phase of the Rebellion in Mewat Ali Khan Mewati was most active. Shamsuddin Shamsh while highlighting historical importance of the nomenclature, Hasan Khan Mewati, says that in the Rebellion of 1857, Ali Hasan Khan Mewati was the main hero against the British. He further says that William Ford while fleeing towards Mathura and Hodal fought a battle with Mewati revolutionaries under Ali Hasan Khan Mewati at Ghasera. The battle was so fierce that British were completely routed, and William Ford saved his life by fleeing towards Mathura cantonment.[11]

While moving towards Hodal, William Ford was accompanied by four or five clerks and others. In addition, he picked up the Customs Officers from Bhondsi, Sailani and Palwal in his way. On the 15th May, he reached Mathura, whence he returned to Hodal on the 20th, accompanied by four or five Englishmen and one hundred Bharatpur Horse. At Hodal, he remained until 29th May, when he was compelled to leave due to the mutiny of some Bharatpur and Alwar troops, which had meantime joined him. On the day before the revolt at Hodal, he had proceeded to a large village of Soondh, a few miles distant, and had compelled the people to give up a gun which they had taken from Hodal.[12]

On the 29th of May, William Ford started for Palwal, accompanied by some thirty Europeans. Customs Officers, fugitives from Delhi and others also joined him. On the 30th May, the party proceeded from Palwal to the ferry over the Yamuna river at Chhaensa, intending to cross over to Bulandshahar. Hostile demonstrations on the Bulandshahar side of the river prevented this, and the party then proceeded to Mohna, where they were hospitably entertained by Risaldar Mir Hidayat Ali of 4th Bengal

Irregular Cavalry. Mir Hidayat Ali was subsequently rewarded by a grant of a village as Jagir. On the 8th June, Mr. Ford left Mohna for Sohna, where he reached on the 9th of June. At Sohna William Ford found a force of the Jaipur Contingent, under Captain Eden, which had come across the Tauru, after a fight with the Meos. This force afterwards marched to Palwal and Hodal, and on the 1st July, William Ford joined the British camp at Delhi, where he remained until the 13th October.[13]

For the whole month of May, the Mewat witnessed full of burning episodes such as setting free to the villages of Mewat from British tyranny; regular attack on the towns of Mewat where local police and some loyalists were giving tough fights; setting up the village administration by the panchayats and village headmen by owing allegiance to the Mughal Emperor Bahadur Shah Zafar.[14]

The towns like Tauru, Sohna, Firozpur Jhirka, Punhana and Pinangwan were easily overpowered by the revolutionaries. However, Nuh town proved a little tough for the revolutionaries. The loyalist Khanzadas and local police gave a tough fight to the revolutionaries, but subsequently, they occupied the Nuh town and controlled the administration. The Surot Jat of Hodal, Pathans of Seoli and Meos attacked the towns of Hodal and Hathin. The loyalist Rawat Jats of Hodal and Rajputs of Hathin gave the tough fight to the revolutionaries, and ultimately, the loyalists were routed. A British force came with their rescue, but it too was defeated badly. Eventually, the town Hodal was left by the revolutionaries due to the heavy enforcement of the British.[15]

The fire of revolt also reached the neighbouring area of Hodal, Kosi and Mathura, where the Meo population was in abundance. Mr. Thornhill, the Collector of Mathura, received intelligence from the magistrate of Gurgaon that the revolutionaries were also approaching the Mathura city. For the precautionary measure, the English non-combatants and women in the Mathura district were evacuated to Agra. On hearing the possibility of the disturbances, a British army reached Kosi on May 25, where detachment of 300 Bharatpur infantry and two guns (under Raghunath's command) were retained. Mathura was at stake as the Sepoys rebelled on 29th of May. Due to the Rebellion at Mathura, the Government treasure was dispatched to Agra on the same day. The Sepoys stormed over the treasury and raised the cry that it would be taken to Delhi. They shot dead Mr. Burlton, who was commanding the detachment. A number of fighters then rushed into the office firing at the Europeans who ran towards the city where they procured horses and escaped. Thornhill also started for Hodal where Nixon was camping.[16]

William Ford stayed at the Ridge at Delhi until the re-conquest of Delhi and suppression of the revolutionaries. In between, the Mewat region was left independent under Mughal Emperor Bahadur Shah Zafar administered by village panchayats and the respective chaudharies. William Ford again arrived at Gurgaon on 13th October 1857, took charge of the administration and began to settle the turbulence in Mewat. In his guidelines many officers such as Assistant Collector Mr. Clifford, Brigadier General Showers, Captain Drummond, and Captain Ramsey, etc. attacked the Mewat region to quell the Rebellion.

Captain Nixon and Mark Thornhill

The areas of Hodal, Kosi, Mathura and Chhata, which were also included in Mewat region at that time, were disturbed during the revolt of 1857. The Mewati revolutionaries along with other co-insurgents and Sepoys occupied these areas and expelled the British suzerainty after looting and plundering the British treasury. In order to settle the disturbances of the region, Captain Nixon, the political agent of Bharatpur State, accompanied by Chaudhari Ratan Singh, chief of the five Sardars, and Gobardhan Singh, the Faujdar, came with a small force to Kosi and there stayed for a time in readiness to check the approach of the Mewatis of Mewat and the other revolutionaries from Delhi.[17]

Meanwhile another British officer Mr. Mark Thornhill, the Magistrate of Mathura, arrived at Chhata, with a small boby of Bharatpur Horse. Chhata is a small town on the high-road some eight miles short of Kosi. This village was the centre of disaffection and the revolutionaries possessed a fortified *sarai*, a stronghold capable of long resistance against the British. Subsequently, Mark Thornhill went to Kosi, the another revolutionary stronghold.[18]

The first outbreak, however, was at Mathura itself, where Mr. Mark Thornhill was the Magistrate. The sum of money then in the district treasury amounted to rather more than five and half lakhs, and arrangements were made for its dispatch to Agra, with the exception of one lakh kept in reserve for local requirements. The escort consisted of a company of soldiers from the cantonments, supported by another company, which had come over from Agra for the purpose. In the way, very close to the Mathura city, the revolutionaries attacked on the party and killed Lieutenant Burlton, commandant of the escort. Besides Lieutenant Burlton, one of the treasury officials also was killed. The revolutionaries then seized the treasure and went off in a body to the Magistrate's Court-house, which they set on fire and destroyed all the records. They broke open the jail and carried all the prisoners with them as far as the city, and then took the road to Delhi.[19]

This was the time when the Bharatpur and Alwar forces were at Hodal with Harvey the Commissioner, Captain Nixon of the Bharatpur Residency, and other European Officers. Mark Thornhill, the Magistrate of Mathura, was at Kosi, some eight miles on this side Hodal, with a small body of Bharatpur horse. When the revolutionaries appeared with the treasure at Kosi, the Alwar troops were fraternised with them and that the Bharatpur Horse were not acted against them. Ultimately Mark Thornhill made off to the force at Hodal on the 31st May 1857. At Kosi the revolutionaries burnt down the Customs bungalow and pillaged the police-station, and plundered the tahsil. But some Rs. 150 was all they could find in the treasury. While Mark Thornhill was departing to Hodal, the revolutionaries came up in the midway and the whole British force was a mass of confusion. Mark Thornhill fled back towards Mathura.[20]

Progress of the Rebellion

The Rebellion of 1857 completely undertook the whole area of Mewat into its clutches in a very short time. Gurgaon again became the seat of the administration but this time the collector was Maulana Abdul Haq Khairabadi, the revered son of Allama Fazle Haq Khairabadi. He was being appointed by Mughal Emperor

Bahadur Shah Zafar sometimes in May after the outbreak of the Rebellion. He controlled the area and collected the revenue with the help of the Mewati chaudharies and other revolutionaries.[21]

On 20th May 1857, the Meo leaders and chaudhries of Punhana, Pinangwa, Hathin, Nagina, Nuh, Ferozpur Jhirka, Rupraka, Kaman, Dig, Bharatpur, Dhausa and Alwar held a Meo Mahapanchayat and declared Bahadur Shah Zafar as their leader in this war of independence. By the last week of May almost all the rural Mewat came under the rule of the Emperor Balhadulshah Zafar. The chaudharies began to conduct the management of their villages and localities in accordance with the instructions of the Emperor. However, the fight between the Meo revolutionaries and the British still continued.[22]

As soon as the Rebellion started, the Meos were up at once and plundered Tauru, Sohna, Firozpur Jhirka, Punhana, Pinangwan and Nuh. Sharfuddin Mewati, the most experienced revolutionary, was considered the commonly accepted leader of the Rebellion in Mewat began targeting the towns of Mewat region where some police personnel and loyalist Rajputs and Khanzadas were the main obstacle. Saadat Khan was much active in and around the Firozpur Jhirka, Doha, Rauli, etc. The revolutionaries of Mahu, Tigaon, Pinangwan areas were boosted by Sadruddin. Chaudhary Firoz Shah Mewati also quickly responded and organized the revolutionaries around Sohna, Tauru, Raiseena, etc. Ali Hasan Khan Mewati organized the revolutionaries of Nuh and surrounding villages. Here the fight was a little tough due to the Khanzadas assistance to the British.[23]

Even the Ulema class was most active in mobilizing the common people to wage war against the British. Maulana Mehrab Khan Mewati toured the village after village to encourage the Mewatis to fight against the British for the sake of their religion and nation. Maulana also distributed the talisman to the Mewati fighters and assured their victory.[24]

Every Meo was bent upon to fight and die against the tyrant British. There were a lot of enthusiasm and emotions pertaining to the Rebellion of 1857. Mirza Ghalib, in his diary '*Dastamboo*', has openly described the rebellious enthusiasm in Mewat, "In the areas of Sohna and Nuh, the Mewatis have run amuck as if crazy mrn had thrown off their shackles and rampaged. Under the devil's guidance, the rebel Tula Ram, who was fighting in Rewari, joined forces with the Mewatis and this group has been fighting the British savagely in the plains and on the mountains. The warfare is so bitter that it seems as if the entire land of India is engulfed in whirling storms and flaming fires."[25]

The revolutionaries of Mewat very easily occupied the rural areas of the Mewat region, but the urban Mewat still owed its allegiance to the British through their native officials and wealthy persons. The gatherings of Mewatis attacked such towns. In this campaign of the Meo revolutionaries their leader was Sadruddin Meo, a farmer of Pindhua village. He targeted basically urban educated Khanzadas, Mahajans and government officials. The Meo revolutionaries did not meet any serious opposition from Tauru, Sohna, Ferozpur Jhirka, Punhana and Pinangwa and overpowered these towns and controlled the administration.[26]

About Sohna, *Punjab District Gazetteer* says that the Meos, after attacking Sohna started loot and plunder like they did at other places.[27] According to *Tarikh-e-Meo Kshatriya*, Sohna had become the center of freedom fighters that comprised of the Meos and Goojars.[28]

Nuh town proved very tough for Ali Hasan Khan Mewati and his fellow men because the local police and the Khanzadas, loyal to the British, gave a stiff battle to the Meo revolutionaries. However, due to his numerical strength, Ali Hasan Khan became victorious and Khanzadas suffered heavy casualties. A large number of them were treacherously put to death after their surrender. The Khanzadas along with other loyalists and British troops were completely routed by the Meo revolutionaries. The victory of the Meo revolutionaries at Nuh town resulted the complete withdrawal of the British administration from Mewat.[29]

After the victory over Nuh, the Mewati revolutionaries intended to chastise the loyalist of Rawat Jats of Hodal and the Rajputs of Hathin. These loyalists were attacked by a large gathering of Surot Jats of Hodal, Pathans of Seoli and the Meos. The fight continued for several months, and the loyalists suffered heavy losses. The Rawats informed the British authorities and sought their help. A small British force was dispatched, accordingly, from Delhi to Hodal to help their supporters. The loyalists and the British troops fought well but they were completely routed by the Mewati revolutionaries.[30]

The inhabitants of Mewat became happy to become independent and they celebrated by singing heroic songs. An excerpt of a song sung by Mewati girls has been quoted as follows:[31]

Kid Jaigo Firangi Ya Biraj Me Su,

Chiriya Chirangla Sab Marwaya,

Mora Maru Bar Me Su,

Kid Jaigo Firangi Ya Biraj Me Su,

(Oh Foreigners! Where you will go from this land of Brij? You have killed innocent birds and even peacocks from the Banyan tree. Oh Foreigners! Where you will go from this land of Brij?)

After many hundred years, the Meos were happy to hold their homeland in their own hands; independent from the foreign yoke. They were full of national and religious passion. They not only killed the British and their employees but also killed their co-inhabitants, the Khanzadas, the Rajputs and other loyalist population of the Mewat region. In this period of revolution, Firoz Baksh reported to the Tahsildar of Firozpur Jhirka on 8th of August that a revolutionary named Majlis Khan along with his revolutionary band had killed five persons and arrested 29 persons belonging to the loyalists of the British. It was also reported that Majlis Khan had gone to Rewari for some hidden purpose and returned to his abode.[32]

The revolutionaries of Mewat organized themselves against the British in different fronts and controlled the administration in Mewat region. Emperor Bahadur Shah Zafar through General Bakht Khan, the Commander-in-Chief sent a *Farman* to the Zamindars of Mewat to dispatch the fighters or the revolutionaries to fight against the British at Delhi. The request was obeyed and accordingly on 25th of June 1857; about 400 revolutionaries were sent at Delhi in support of General Bakht Khan.[33]

The Mewati army was fighting against the British under the command of their leader Alif Khan at Delhi. However, unfortunately, no due attention was given to these revolutionaries due to the anarchy and mismanagement prevalent in revolutionary forces at Delhi. This fact is being proven by the letters written to the Commander-in-Chief by the Mewati *Mujahideen* and their leader Alif Khan.[34]

Alif Khan repeatedly wrote to Commander-in-Chief, to raise the subsistence allowances for his fighters. However, no action was taken by the administration. Finally, a letter was sent to Commander-in-Chief General Bakht Khan, from the revolutionaries of Mewat on 13th August 1857. In their letter, they said that on his call, they promptly came to Delhi after leaving their children and other family members on the mercy of God, and continuously fighting with the enemy from many months, without getting the proper subsistence allowance. They complained that the other fighters were regularly getting the salary, but they were being martyred at the position of hunger and thirst. They also wrote that their sacrifices were well-known among the revolutionaries. They futhermore complained that on the false report of the Goojars, their meager monthly amount was also discontinued. They threatened that if they were denied from justice, they along with hundreds of Mewati revolutionaries would return to their homes. However, unfortunately, no action was taken on their request, and the Meos bravely fought and martyred while fighting with the British.[35]

The Meos under their process of fight, loot and plunder, intended to loot the British treasury at Palwal, containing Rs. 50,000. However, the Mewati revolutionary controlled themselves when they heard that the Emperor already had ordered to Bhond Zamindar of Faridabad to capture the same treasury. The Zamindar also asked for one hundred horsemen and fifty men in arms to do the same. Although the assignment was not met to its end.[36]

At Palwal, the revolutionary activities were also gaining ground. Nawab Ameer Khan, the Zamindar of Palwal, and his son Usman Khan alias Dhoola were leading the revolutionaries at Palwal. However, as Palwal was on highway, it was frequently checked by the commanders of the British army. Nawab Ameer Khan and his son Usman Khan were not only active in their native place but also participated in many battles at Delhi against the British.[37] Mirza Ghafur Ali and Harkush Rai the small tradesmen of Palwal also lead the revolutionaries against the British.[38]

As large part of the area of Mewat still falling under slavery, was under Alwar State. Its Raja named Maharaja Vinay Singh, who was a staunch supporter of the British Government, decided to settle the turbulence prevailing in the areas of Mewat, adjoining to his state. In spite of his illness, Maharaja prepared a fort at Naugaon and encamped with his forces in July 1857. At the end of July or beginning of August 1857, Maharaja Vinay Singh sent his noble Deewan Nawab Ameen Khan alias Munshi Ammu Jaan (Ammu Jaan, and his two brothers were able Musalman gentlemen of Delhi, whom the king took into his service and made Diwans about 1838) as Tahsildar of Firozpur Jhirka. However, the Meos proved him as bone of the throat. He was many times attacked by the Meo revolutionaries. Subsequently, in order to save his life Ammu Jaan fled for Alwar.[39]

About the appointment of Ammu Jaan as Tahsildar of Firozpur Jhirka, the *Dehli Urdu Akhbar* reports, "The Raja of Alwar has managed the revenue collection of Firozpur, but this has been done on the instructions of the British."[40]

Maharaja Vinay Singh of Alwar, in spite of his severe paralysis illness from past many years, supported the British during the Rebellion. He sent a military contingent of four hundred cavalry, eight hundred infantry and four guns under Raja Bahadur Chimman Singh to Agra in support of the British. Nevertheless, they were attacked at Achhnera village, on the road between Bharatpur and Agra, by the revolutionary Sepoys of Neemuch and Naseerabad Battalion. Deserted by their leader Raja Bahadur Chimman Singh and the Mohammadan portion of the force, including the artillery, the Rajputs suffered a severe defeat, leaving on the field fifty-five men, among whom were ten Sardars of note. The leader of the defeated force Raja Bahadur Chimman Singh was said to have been connected by marriage with some of the rebellious Sepoys. The old king was on the point of death when tidings of the disaster reached Alwar; but his reason had fled, and he was spared the sorrowful news. The last order he is said to have given in writing, as having lost the use of his tongue, was that a lakh of rupees should be sent down from the fort and sent out to his small force.[41]

It is also said that when the remaining force was passing through villages of Doha and Raoli, they were again attacked by the Meo revolutionaries of those villages. The whole force was killed, and the rests were dispersed. Naugaon fort was destroyed and Maharaja met a heavy loss. It was a big shock for the ailing Maharaja and at the age of fifty, Maharaja Vinay Singh left the world forever.[42]

Major W.F. Eden

The loss of Delhi was a crushing blow to British prestige, and it took nearly two months for them to regroup and reclaim the imperial city. They reached Delhi on 7th of June with heavy enforcement under Henry Barnard and fought the battle of Badli ki Sarai, on the 8th June. The British became successful in driving the revolutionaries within the walls of Delhi. The gain of the British under Henry Bernard, in the battle of Badli ki Sarai, was the occupation of the Ridge, the finest base of operations against the Delhi revolutionaries.[43]

Undoubtedly, the Ridge was the safest place for the British to fight against the revolutionaries, but Mewati Rebellion was a bone of the throat for the British. In this position, the British were sandwiched between the revolutionaries of Delhi and Mewat. They were feeling insecure in these circumstances. The Mewati revolutionaries were also proved as barrier for the military assistance sent to the British from Rajputana States. The Mewati revolutionaries proved themselves a real patriot by disturbing the Major Eden's military aid to British forces at Delhi.

At the beginning of June 1857, Major W. F. Eden, Political Agent of Jaipur with a big Jaipur force comprising of 6000 men and seven guns marched to Delhi through Rewari and Gurgaon and Palwal. Eden was going Delhi to aid the British force fighting against the Delhi revolutionaries. Eden, however, soon found that his job would not be accomplished unless Mewat was settled. It is also said that in his way to Delhi Eden was disturbed by the Mewati revolutionaries. Major Eden ultimately decided to settle Mewat turbulence before going to Delhi. He started his work from Sohna. Mewati revolutionaries gave stiff opposition between Tauru and Sohna. Hundreds of the hard nut Meos, fully equipped with arms, fought valiantly at every step and suffered heavy losses. Eden's forces burnt and destroyed a number of villages, but the gallant Meos were never subdued. In these battles, the Meo leaders Saadat Khan and Mehrab Khan killed many army men of Major Eden. Had he not been in possession of the artillery guns, his force would have experienced heavy losses. Major Eden's artillery opened fire in different quarters, burnt villages and killed a number of the Meo revolutionaries.[44]

About the advance in Mewat by Major W. F. Eden, Political Agent of Jaipur, the *Dehli Urdu Akhbar* reports, "The Agent of Jaipur, along with the military force of Jaipur and two guns is roaming in Mewat".[45]

Major W. F. Eden stayed at Sohna for three days. William Ford, the Gurgaon Deputy Commissioner came from Mohna and joined Major Eden at Sohna along with his small army of 30 European officers. They jointly moved towards Palwal and fought with the revolutionaries of Palwal and Hodal for a long time. In the meantime, some of the Jaipur force under Major Eden fraternized with the revolutionaries and a discontent and spirit of revolt grown in his force. The prime mover of the discontent in the Eden's force was an ex-Minister of Jaipur named Shiv Nath Singh. On 20th July 1857, Shiv Nath Singh also made an attempt to murder Major Eden. Keeping in view of the growing spirit of discontent in his force, Major Eden was compelled to return to Jaipur in August 1857, leaving Mewat in its own condition.[46]

The *Dehli Urdu Akhbar* reports about the incidence of Mewat that, "*Chhota Sahab* (Deputy Commissioner) of Gurgaon along with his forces (in alliance of Major Eden) are there in Mewat. They are burning the villages but there is no restoration of order in their favour." The newspaper, while praising the loyalty and patriotism of the Mewatis, again says, "In Mewat, particularly Mewatis, have restored the order (in favour of the revolutionary Government under Emperor Bahadur Shah Zafar)".[47]

Malleson writes that after the troops from Bharatpur and Alwar had joined the rebels, Jaipur Political Agent, Major Eden, along with the Jaipur troops marched to Rewari and Gurgaon, and subsequently to Palwal, thirty miles to the south-east of Gurgaon. The Jaipur troops rescued several Europeans, and escorted them safely to Agra. They also restored order in the plundering villagers of Mewat, but when that had been accomplished, Major Eden receiving a hint from their officers whom it would not be prudent to try them further, wisely ordered them back to Jaipur.[48]

Faridabad District Gazetteer says that from Sohna, Eden moved towards Palwal and remained between that place and Hodal for some time. Interestingly, at this stage there was rebellion in a powerful group led by Thakur Shiv Nath Singh. Sickness, discontent and growing spirit of revolt among his troops obliged him to return to Jaipur in August, 1857.[49]

References

1. *Frontline*, Vol. 24, Issue 12, June 16-29, 2007.
2. *Against History Against State*, pp. 189-190.
3. *The Role of Punjab Haryana and Himachal Pradesh*, p. 146.
4. The Custom Chaukis were on the Custom Line, which was going from Mathura, Kosi, Mondkari, Seoli, Manpur, Hathin, Mandkola Khera, Indri, Sohna, Raiseena via Gurgaon, Jhajjar, Hisar, Firozpur, reaching at Lahore. See for details, *Tahrik-e-Azadi Aur Mewat*, p. 19.
5. Metcalfe, Charles Theophilus, *Two Native Narratives of the Mutiny in Delhi*, (Eng. Trans. of *Roznamcha Mainudin Hasan Khan* and *Munshi Jeewan Lal*), London, 1898, p. 90, (hereafter quoted as *Two Native Narratives*).
6. Qasmi, Ataur Rahman, *1857 Aur Haryana*, New Delhi, 2011, pp. 69-70, (hereafter quoted as *1857 Aur Haryana*).

7. *Arzdast, Mujahideene Mewat*, NAI, New Delhi. See also *Punjab Gazetteer, Gurgaon District, 1883-84*, Lahore, 1884, p. 25, Kaye&Malleson, Vol. V, London, 1896, p. 56, *Haryana District Gazetteers, Faridabad*, Chandigarh, 1993, p. 51, *Gurgaon District Gazetteer*, Chandigarh, 1983, p. 60, and Mead, Henry, *The Sepoy Revolt: Its Causes and its Consequences*, London, 1858, pp. 101-2, (hereafter quoted as *The Sepoy Revolt*).
8. *Punjab Gazetteer, Gurgaon District, 1883-84*, Lahore, 1884, p. 25, see also Kaye&Malleson, Vol. V, London, 1896, p. 56, *Haryana District Gazetteers, Faridabad*, Chandigarh, 1993, p. 51, *Gurgaon District Gazetteer*, Chandigarh, 1983, p. 60, and *The Sepoy Revolt*, pp. 101-2.
9. *The Sepoy Revolt*, pp. 101-2, see also *Punjab Gazetteer, Gurgaon District, 1883-84*, Lahore, 1884, p. 25, Yadava, S.D.S., *Followers of Krishna: Yadavas of India*, New Delhi, 2006, p. 78, (hereafter quoted as *Followers of Krishna*) and *Haryana District Gazetteers, Faridabad*, Chandigarh, 1993, p. 51.
10. *Akhbar-uz-Zafar*, 19 July, 1857, see also *Gurgaon District Gazetteer*, Chandigarh, 1983, p. 60.
11. *Meos of India*, pp. 31-32.
12. *Punjab Gazetteer, Gurgaon District, 1883-84*, Lahore, 1884, p. 25, see also *Followers of Krishna*, p. 78.
13. *Punjab Gazetteer, Gurgaon District, 1883-84*, Lahore, 1884, p. 25 see also, *Haryana District Gazetteers, Faridabad*, Chandigarh, 1993, p. 51, and *Haryana State Gazetteer*, Volume I, Chandigarh, 2001, p. 288.
14. *Gurgaon District Gazetteer*, Chandigarh, 1983, p. 60, see also *Meo Qaum Aur Mewat*, p. 138.
15. *Meo Qaum Aur Mewat*, p. 138, see also *Gurgaon District Gazetteer*, Chandigarh, 1983, pp. 60-61.
16. *Haryana District Gazetteers, Faridabad*, Chandigarh, 1993, pp. 51-52, and *Haryana State Gazetteer*, Volume I, Chandigarh, 2001, p. 288.
17. Growse, F. S., *Mathura: A District Memoire; With Numerous Illustrations*, Third Edition, North-Western Province And Oudh Government Press, 1883, p. 46, (hereafter quoted as *Mathura: A District Memoire*).
18. *Ibid*, p. 46.
19. *Ibid*, p. 47.
20. *Records of the Intelligence Department*, Vol. I, Edinburgh, 1902, pp. 34-35, see also *Mathura: A District Memoire*, p. 47.
21. Noorani, Khushtar, *Allama Fazle Haq Khairabadi: Chand Unwanat*, Idara-e-Fikre Islami, Delhi, 2011, p. 24.
22. *Meos of India*, pp. 30-32.

23. *Tahrik-e-Azadi Aur Mewat*, p. 18.
24. *Ibid.*
25. Mirza Asadullah Khan Ghalib, *Dastamboo*, (Urdu Trans. Khwaja Ahmad Faruqi), New Delhi, 2000, pp. 55-56.
26. Budh Prakash, *Glimpses of Haryana*, 1969, p.85.
27. *Punjab District Gazetteer*, Vol, IV-A, Lahore, 1911, p. 24.
28. *Tarikh-e-Meo Kshatriya*, p. 460.
29. *Punjab Gazetteer, Gurgaon District, 1883-84,* Lahore, 1884, p. 26, see also Yadav, K.C., *Revolt of 1857 in Haryana*, New Delhi, 1977, p. 58.
30. *Haryana State Gazetteer*, Volume I, Chandigarh, 2001, p. 287.
31. *Tarikh-e-Meo Kshatriya*, p. 455.
32. *1857 Aur Haryana*, p. 70.
33. *Akhbar-uz-Zafar*, Delhi, 13th September, 1857, see also *1857 Aur Haryana*, p. 140, and *Meo Qaum Aur Mewat*, p. 139.
34. *Tarikh-e-Meo Kshatriya*, p. 457.
35. *Ibid.*
36. *1857 Aur Haryana*, p. 67.
37. *Ibid*, pp. 126-130, After termination of the Rebellion, Nawab Ameer Khan and his son Usman Khan settled at Alwar but arrested, brought to Delhi and hanged. His family members went to Jawra and settled there.
38. *Haryana District Gazetteers, Faridabad*, Chandigarh, 1993, p. 53.
39. *Akhbar-uz-Zafar*, Delhi, 19th July, 1857, see also *Tarikh-e-Meo Kshatriya*, p. 475.
40. *Dehli Urdu Akhbar*, Delhi, 5th July, 1857.
41. Powlett, p. 23.
42. *Dehli Urdu Akhbar*, Delhi, 5th July, 1857, see also *Tarikh-e-Meo Kshatriya*, pp. 472 & 475, 432-433.
43. Vibart, H.M., *Richard Baird Smith: The Leader of the Delhi Heroes in 1857*, Westminster, 1897, p. 12, see also Malleson, George Bruce, *The Indian Mutiny of 1857*, New York, 1891, pp. 125-126, and Handcock, Arthur Gore, *The Siege of Delhi in 1857: A Short Account*, Allahabad, 1897, pp. 11-12.
44. *Gurgaon District Gazetteer*, Chandigarh, 1983, p. 61, see also Yadav, K.C., *Haryana, Itihas Avam Sanskriti*, part-2, New Delhi, 1992, p. 105, *Tahrik-e-Azadi Aur Mewat*, p. 79, Kaye&Malleson, Vol. VI, London, 1914, p. 159, and *Haryana State Gazetteer*, Volume I, Chandigarh, 2001, p. 287.

45. *Dehli Urdu Akhbar*, Delhi, 5th July, 1857.

46. Husain, Iqbal, *1857 Ke Swatantra Sangram Me Mewatiyon Ka Balidan*,(Unpublished) AMU Aligarh, p. 40, see also *Haryana State Gazetteer*, Volume I, Chandigarh, 2001, p. 288, *Gurgaon District Gazetteer*, Chandigarh, 1983, p. 62, and *Meo Qaum Aur Mewat*, p. 139

47. *Dehli Urdu Akhbar*, Delhi, 5th July, 1857.

48. Kaye&Malleson, Vol. VI, London, 1914, p. 159.

49. *Haryana District Gazetteers, Faridabad*, Chandigarh, 1993, p. 52, see also *Punjab District Gazetteer*, Vol. IV-A, Lahore, 1911, p.24, see also *Gurgaon District Gazetteer*, Chandigarh, 1983, p. 62.

4
Mewati Rebellion Beyond Mewat

The Mewati turbulence is well known during the reign of the Sultans and Emperors of Delhi. The rulers tried to subsidize the Mewatis more frequently by force, but sometimes the Mewatis by matrimonial methods and giving them employment in different departments of administration. Especially, Humayun and Akbar were more liberal with the Mewatis. During their times, the Mewatis settled in north-west and central regions of India. Emperor Humayun was the first Mughal ruler, who started matrimonial relations with the Mewati (Khnazada) chief Jamal Khan, nephew of the famous ruler Hasan Khan Mewati. Jamal Khan married his elder daughter Takht Gosain to Humayun and younger one Raj Gosain to Bairam Khan. The famous Jewel of Akbars' Court Abdur Rahim Khan-i-Khana was the son of Raj Gosain. In lieu of these relations, Jamal Khan was given the Jagir of some parts of Mewat area.[1]

It is well known that after fall of Bairam Khan, Emperor Akbar married Raj Gosain, the mother of three year-old child Bairam Khan. This marriage surely would have invited the sympathy of the Mewatis in favour of Emperor Akbar. It is also said that a Mewati from Bisru village had married his daughter to Akbar. However, as Mirasi sung the story that the Bisru daughter was taken aback by Dada Bahad of village Kot. He was finally settled with the Akbar's ex-wife at Papra village of Mewat.

The process of Mewati subsidization was continued until the time of Emperor Aurangzeb. Most of the Mewatis employed in the military and postal departments. Many of them were engaged in the age-old agricultural occupation. In the centuries of their royal services, the Mewatis settled in different areas of Mughal suzerainty. However, they could not forget their martial past and freedom-loving characteristics.

The Rebellion of 1857 gave them another chance to prove their martial chivalry against the British. They fought for this country not only in Mewat but also in various parts of the country. Charles Raikes writes that the predatory class, the Goojars, the Mewatis, felt instinctively that their day had come. Their natural enemy, the Magistrate, had perished at the hands of the mutineers, or was flying before them, protected only by the people over whom he lately presided.[2]

Following is the state-wise details of the Mewati Rebellion in all over north and central India, where the Meos, better known as Mewatis played a remarkable role in the rebellion of 1857. Whether they were the Sepoys or peasants or farmers or workers, they jumped into the fire of Rebellion to free their country from the tyrant British Government.

Madhya Pradesh

Madhya Pradesh, earlier known as Central Provinces, has a lot of Mewati villages in the regions of Satwas, Indore, Dhar, Mandsaur, Jaora, etc. These Mewatis were most active against the British during the Rebellion of 1857 and in many cases assumed the leadership. Mewatis, the real patriot of India never bowed before the British and subsequently suffered the heavy losses.

Satwas: In Madhya Pradesh or the Central Provinces, Satwas was one of the Mewati settlements beyond the Mewat region, where Meos were most active in the Rebellion of 1857. On 17th October, 1857, the Mewatis along with the Kukus community set up the standard of Islam and menaced the Nimawar Panch Mahal. Colonel Durand directed Major Orr to proceed with the Hyderabad Contingent Field Force through Nimawar to attack and disperse the rebels wherever he might find them, and to ascend into Malwa by Unchod, Piplia, and Raghugarh. Major Orr found the insurgents at Piplia on the 27th October, attacked and took the fort, and captured some forty-five prisoners, thus quelling the Mewati rising at Satwas.[3]

Jaora: Next to the Satwas, the neighbourhood of Jaora was emerged as another centre of Rebellion in Madhya Pradesh. At Jaora, the Mewatis were risen with their arms against the British and the loyalist Nawab of Jaora. Nawab of Jaora requested the Malwa Contingent at Mehidpur, to quell the Rebellion of the Mewatis. Mewatis were also active in Mallagarh and the north, south and east of Jaora. The petty States such as Dhar and Dewas were embarrassed rather than strengthened by the Mewatis.[4]

Mandsaur & Dhar: Mandsaur, a large and important town on a tributary of the Chambal river, about hundred and twenty miles from Indore, was the chief centre of the revolutionaries in Central Provinces. In the month of July, this place was occupied by some of Sindhia's revolted troops. Here the Mewati revolutionaries were very much active. The Mewati levies along with the other counterparts like Afghan and Makrani levies reinforced the revolted troops of Sindhia's army and assembled at Mandsaur. In August, the insurrection at Mandsaur threatened not only all western Malwa, but Neemuch as well.[5]

Firoz Shah, a prince connected with the Imperial House of Delhi arrived here to lead the revolutionaries. The green flag was raised by the Shahzada and Mewatis in Mandsaur. He preached a crusade (*Jihad*) against the British. The Shahzada's appearance before Mandsaur was the signal for a general rise of the Muslim population of the town and district containing some ten thousand Mewatis, and of the defection of the Makrani and Vilayti mercenary troops of the Subah. The chief Gwalior authorities of Mandsaur, the Komasdan (Civil Governor) and Kotwal (Chief of Police), in endeavouring to suppress the revolt, were wounded and taken prisoners; a third officer of the Subah was killed.[6]

Proclamations were issued to all the neighbouring princes and chiefs, claiming their allegiance and calling upon them to present themselves. Thus, the Raja of Partapgarh, Nawab of Jaora, chiefs of Ratlam, Seeta Mhow, and others received such proclamations.[7]

The revolutionaries also made a general assault on the Barah (government house). The treasury plundered, records burnt, and the Shahzada being brought in triumph was seated on the throne and proclaimed king under a royal salute. At Mandsaur, a person known as Mirzajee, was appointed Pardhan (Chief Minister).[8]

In September 1857, this rebel force, estimated at 15,000 men with 16 or 18 guns, had rallied around the standard of Shahzada, and this estimate was subsequently found to have been below the actual number. This huge force of the revolutionaries under the command of Prince Firoz Shah ravaged many areas in the Central Provinces. They plundered Bhopawar and Sirdarpur, and then marched on Dhar, which they occupied on the 31st August 1857.[9]

The British force under Durand along with Major Robertson, consisting of a troop of the 14th Dragoons, three companies, 25th Bombay Infantry, two guns, and some Hyderabad Contingent Cavalry, arrived before Dhar on 22nd of October. Major Robertson was assisted by Brigadier Stuart, Major Gall, Captain Orr and Captain Mayne. Another column under Major Keane also joined in the way. A tough battle was fought between the British and the revolutionaries. The revolutionaries evacuated the Dhar fort and fled towards Mandsaur.[10]

The same huge British force under Durand also attacked on Mandsaur in the last days of October. Malleson says that the revolutionaries were defeated and Shahzada and his two thousand Afghans, Mewatis and Makranis evacuated Mandsaur and retreated on Nangarh. After pursuit, they further fled through the country, avoiding towns and villages, and endeavouring to seek refuge in the jungles. One party of them, more daring decisive, than their fellows, suddenly appeared at Partapgarh. The loyal chief of that state, summoning his Thakurs, attacked them, killed eighty of them, and drove the rest into flight.[11]

Indore: At Indore, the people were also revolted against the British. Many of the revolutionaries were the Mewatis. Even the Poorbea Mewatis, who were in the service of the Maharaja, supported the revolutionary people of the city and rushed towards Delhi. Sir William Muir says that the Indore force would go to Agra — and then to Delhi. He quotes their statement, "The British Government will not let us go; therefore we are prepared to die."[12]

Gwalior: During the Rebellion of 1857, Maharaja Jayajirao Sindhia remained loyal to British, but his army, viz. 3000 Infantry, 3000 Cavalry and 2000 some kind of policemen revolted against the British. The other force led by the British known as the Gwalior Contingent also rebelled against British and fought boldly against the British army. The Gwalior Contingent created in 1844, was consisting the regiments of 1154 Cavalry, 74 Golundaz (Gunners), 26 Guns of Nine Pounder and Twenty Four Pounder Howitzer, and a regiment of Infantry of 6412 men in 1857. At the time of Rebellion there were four native regiments of the Gwalior Contingent were stationed at Gwalior, the rest being stationed at Neemuch, Seepree, Agra, Sultanpur, Burhanpur, and Jabalpur stations. These troops belonged to the Company, and were officered by them, but were paid by the Maharajah of Gwalior.[13]

A Sizeable number of the Sepoys and officers of the Gwalior Contingent were Muslims including the Meos. In the Cavalry regiments, the Muslims were in much larger strength. In the Macphersons report of 10th February 1858, it is said that 800 of Sindhia's Mohammadan Horse from British provinces were among the rebel Sepoys, who proceeded from Gwalior to Agra in September 1857. The Wahabi ideology was prevalent in the Contingent. In the influence of the Maulvis, the Muslim Sepoys fought along with the *Ghazis* against the British army.[14]

As most of the Mewati scholars claim that in Gwalior Contingent and other forces of the Sindhias army, the Meos were in good numbers and most probably it were the Meos or Mewati Muslims who played most active and leading role in the Rebellion of 1857. Exemplary to their patriotic and martial background, they tried to uproot the British supremacy even at the cost of annoying to their ruler Jayajirao Sindhia.

Uttar Pradesh

Almost all Uttar Pradesh or United Provinces was burning in the flame of the Rebellion of 1857. Apart from the other different communities, the Meos were very much active against the British. From the reports of the Intelligence Department, it becomes clear that the Meos, on the instruction of the local chiefs, fully involved against the British during the Rebellion of 1857. **Mainpuri:** Intelligence from Mainpuri reported that Nawab Raees of Farrukhabad had marched troops (two Sepoy Regiments, one Regiment of Cavalry, and 1000 or 1500 Pathans and Meos of Shamshabad) towards Kanpur. They were also assisted by the Raja of Mainpuri, who had advanced money to the Cavalry, and prepared supplies.[15]

Aligarh: Before the British attack under Lord Lake at Aligarh in September 1803, the Fort was under the Marathas. The Marathas under Pedron and Baji Rao were defeated although they were having a huge army consisting of a batallion of 800 under the charge of Saadat Ali, 1000 Bhadourea Rajputs, 500 Mewatis and 200 Golundaz. British captured the Aligarh fort but could not crush the dalliance and stubbornness of the people. In 1857, there was one last attempt to throw the British yoke and at the district-level Narayan, Rasul Khan and Mir Khan organized the revolt. However, the attempts were failed.

Aligarh was the strongest centre of the Mewati Rebellion in Uttar Pradesh, where hundreds of Mewati rose against the British and in cooperation of the rebellious Sepoys attacked the British officers. There was a British spy named Ghanshyam Chaubey reported every moment of the Rebellion from Aligarh to the Intelligence Department. According to a report, the Mewatis and Goojars were very active in the Rebellion at Aligarh and practically ruling the whole district. Panna Lal of Sasni was another British agent who helped the British at Aligarh.[16]

Ilahi Baksh was the most important Meo leader of Aligarh Rebellion. He quickly responded the 20th June's *Fatwa* of *Jihad* by Maulvi Abdul Jaleel of Chhatari. He goaded the Mewati community of all over the district to wage war against the British. The whole district was at razing. The houses, court and post office were burnt and looted by the revolutionaries with the assistance of British employee Rasul Khan and Meer Khan. They attacked and tried to kill the British officers such as Nichterlein, Connor, Clein, etc. eventually fled towards Sasni but targeted by the Mewati revolutionaries. In these skirmishes, the son of Nichterlein was killed. The revolutionaries finally evacuated the district from the tyrant British and set up their own administration.[17]

As the Mewatis were the staunch follower of Walidad Khan, the Nawab of Malagarh and relative to the Emperor Bahadur Shah Zafar, he took charge of Aligarh following the order of Emperor. Subsequently, the revolutionary panchayat (local administration), elected Ghaus Mohammad, son of Noor Khan of Sikandra Rau, as the ruler of Aligarh. He came at Aligarh on the invitation of Walidad Khan. Ilahi Baksh, a disaffected Mewati, was made Kotwal of Aligarh and later on Husain Khan Mewati was appointed as Kotwal at his place.[18]

The Aligarh revolutionaries also sent their forces along with Sepoys to Delhi in the assistance of the Emperor Bahadur Shah Zafar. *Dehli Urdu Akhbar* reports that four companies of Koel appeared before the king after disgracing the English, killing every Englishman they came across and allowed the people to loot the treasury. Consequently, the public began looting thoroughly and everyone grabbed what he would catch hold of.[19]

Unfortunately, the Mewati resistance at Aligarh could not last long due to the planned attack of the British forces. The revolutionaries were bound to flee towards Farrukhabad after their defeat at Aligarh. Atkinson writes that Aligarh was plundered during the Rebellion by the Mewatis of the neighbouring villages, by the passing rebel troops, by Nasimullah during his eleven days' rule, and by the British troops.[20]

Pilibhit: Pilibhit was also burnt in the Rebellion of 1857. A very important revolutionary of Paharganj, Pilibhit known as Ali Khan Mewati was active in the Rebellion not only at his native place but different stations of United Provinces. His brother Shahzad Khan was also very active against the British. Both the brothers fought very bravely against the Europeans in different fronts. On 20th of October 1857, Nawab Bahadur Khan sent a force of revolutionaries under Ali Khan Mewati at Nainital to expel the British Government. Ali Khan Mewati fought bravely but defeated due to some native traitors. Ali Khan Mewati also attacked the Raja of Puwain (Pilibhit), along with the revolutionaries and the local zamindars. Raja Puwain was a traitor and had treacherously killed Maulana Ahmadullah Shah in an earlier action.[21]

Farrukhabad: Farrukhabad was another important centre of the Rebellion, where Mewatis were most active. The Mewatis of Shamshabad were fighting against the British under Nawab Tafazzul Husain Khan. The Aligarh Mewati revolutionaries also joined Nawab of Farrukhabad in this sacred war.[22]

Hathras: At the town of Hathras, the Mewatis were very much active and in conjunction of the Mewatis of Koel, they not only engaged in the active rebellion at their respective areas but in the first week of September 1857, they also headed towards Delhi to fight against the British.[23]

Shikohabad: At Shikohabad, the Mewatis were also very much aggressive in the Rebellion. They rose against the British and threatened to burn the Shikohabad town, which was under the Raja of Mainpuri.[24]

Fatehpur Sikri: Fatehpur Sikri was another place, where Mewatis were in open revolt during the Rebellion of 1857. The rebel Mewati soldiers on the hills colluded with the Tilangas. They were having matchlocks and carbines, and some 10 or 12 flint guns. Some of the revolutionary force left for Bayana on the instance of the Mewatis but about 20 Mewatis of Gwalior force remained at Fatehpur Sikri. The Mewatis and other Musalmans with their native arms also arrived at Fatehpur Sikri from other places and concealed at Tahsildaari. The local Mewatis kept these people and gave them food.[25]

Etawa: At Etawa, the Mewatis were also very much active. The Mewatis along with other revolutionaries under Aladad Khan Mewati, Taj Khan Mewati, Ganga Singh Bhadosia and Kunwar Zor Singh were practically ruling the area. They attacked on jail and freed the prisoners. They also attacked police officers and British officials and burnt their bungalow. But somehow they spared the railway officers Parker and Hume. When the Gwalior Contingent mutinied on 16th June, All the Europeans of Etawa fled to another station leaving the city on the mercy of the revolutionaries. On their victory over Etawa, the revolutionaries turned towards Mainpuri.[26]

On 29th December, 1857, Brigadier Walpole's Column reached Etawa. The Intelligence Department reports that the revolutionary force, consisting of seven guns, 1500 matchlock men, and 350 horses, hastily abandoned Etawa under their leaders, Aladad Khan Mewati, and Ganga Singh Bhadosia. However, some of them, with Taj Khan Mewati, a subordinate leader, were surrounded by Kunwar Zor Sing's people in the Tahsil, where they were killed by a part of the Column on the morning of the same day. They had two telegraph guns, and resisted to the last.[27]

Mathura, Hodal and Kosi: Mathura, Hodal and Kosi were other important centres of the United Provinces attached to the region of Mewat. The areas of Mathura, Hodal, Kosi and Chhata were also a part of the Mewat region at that time. Here the Mewati revolutionaries bravely fought against the British during the Rebellion of 1857. Mark Thornhill, the Collector of Mathura heard that the Sepoys at Mathura rebelled on 29th of May, and subsequently fled for Hodal and Kosi. Captain Nixon, the political agent of Bharatpur State, accompanied by Chaudhari Ratan Singh, chief of the five Sardars, and Gobardhan Singh, the Faujdar, already came with a small force to Kosi and there stayed for a time in readiness to check the approach of the Mewatis and other revolutionaries of the area.[28]

The Mewati revolutionaries of Mathura and Hodal along with other co-insurgents and Sepoys occupied these areas and expelled the British suzerainty after looting and plundering the British treasury. They looted the treasury and when the revolutionaries appeared with the treasure at Kosi, the Alwar troops were fraternised with them and that the Bharatpur Horse were not acted against them. Ultimately, Mark Thornhill made off to the force at Hodal on the 31st May 1857. At Kosi, the revolutionaries burnt down the Customs bungalow and pillaged the police-station, and plundered the tahsil. While Mark Thornhill was departing to Hodal, the revolutionaries came up in the midway and the whole British force was a mass of confusion. Mark Thornhill fled back towards Muthura.[29]

Allahabad: Allahabad was the next place, where Mewatis played an important role in the Rebellion of 1857. It is reported that the

Mewatis held a panchayat at the house of Saif Khan Mewati in a village Samadabad on 5th June 1857. Excepting Saif Khan, every one promised to fight against the British and decided to rebel the same day. In Allahabad the Mewatis were the real contrivers of the Rebellion of the sepoys and the Risala. The ties of geographical vicinity represented by the Mewatis of all villages near Allahabad- Samadabad, Rasulpur, Mauza Beli, Baghara, Shadiabad, Jonhol, Shevri, Fatehpur Bichhua, Katra, Karnail Ganj, Mahadpuri, Bakhtiara, Bakhtvari, Rasulpur (village), Minhajpur, Dara Ganj, Chhitpura, Kasya, Sarai Mir, Roohi, Shaikhpur and others- again helped them here to rise as a community against the British.[30]

Maulvi Liaqat Ali[31] led the revolutionaries against the British. Both the civilian and Sepoy revolutionaries appointed him as the Governor of Allahabad Subah under the Mughal Emperor Bahadur Shah Zafar on 6th June 1857. He had many followers; many people were his devotees. At his call, the Gwyn Platoon along with a Risala and a large number of Mewatis jumped into the war against the British. All the British and Sikh soldiers were imprisoned in the fort. The revolutionaries burnt British officers' bungalows and looted the treasury.[32]

Maulvi Liaqat Ali made his headquarter at Khusru Bagh, hoisted green flag, looted the treasury worth 30 lakh of rupees and freed around three thousand victims from the jail. Maulvi along with the revolutionaries waged continuous war against the British until his fall on 16th of June 1857. During the retribution, thousands of the revolutionaries, including innocents were shot dead, most of the villages were burnt and buildings razed on the ground.[33]

Muzaffarnagar: The Mewatis of Muzaffarnagar were also in the fore and fought, shoulder to shoulder against the British, along with the Jats and other communities of the area. Iqtidar Alam Khan says that in the Muzaffarnagar district, the rival *khaps* of the Jat peasantry came together for defying the English authority under the leadership of a Mewati Muslim. The Jat peasantry of the same Muzaffarnagar district had also aligned itself with 'the petty Muslim gentry elements' then fighting last ditch battles against the advancing English troops.[34]

Kanpur: At the time when the Rebellion arose in Kanpur, the Mewatis were actively allied with the rebellious Sepoys. With the assistance of Raja Bhao and Qalandar Girgosain, the Mewati revolutionaries controlled the administration of the Mewati dominated villages like Bhoganpura, Sikandra, and Akbarpur. Definitely, they might have faced the tyrant British Generals like Havelock, Neill, and G. W. Sherer and met the heavy losses of men and property.[35]

Rajasthan

A large part of the Mewat region was in Rajastha or Rajputana under the State of Alwar and Bharatpur, where a lot of Mewati resides in their villages. During the Rebellion of 1857, they were also actively involved following their brethren in Mewat and other parts of north India. However, their efforts didn't become successful due to the loyalty of their respective rajas.

Alwar: The city of Alwar, which is situated near the centre of the State, is in Mewat, of which it is now the largest and most important town. More than half the territory of the State, too, was in Mewat region. In the Mewat region of Alwar State, the Mewati revolutionaries took active part in the Rebellion of 1857. Mohammad Ashraf Khan writes that the Mewatis of Alwar State in Rajputana looted and burnt the granaries of the Alwar Government, but they could not become successful in capturing towns and villages of that region. The loyalist Raja of Alwar was severely crushed the movement where there was any doubt he could find.[36]

Maharaja Vinay Singh of Alwar encamped himself along with his forces in Naugaon and tried his level best to crush the revolutionary Mewatis. He also sent a military force to Agra to help the British army, but his force was completely routed by the rebellious Sepoys of Neemuch and Nasirabad Battalions at Achhnera and subsequently Mewati revolutionaries of village Doha and Raoli. During the Rebellion, the Alwar principality was the shelter place for the British fugitives.[37]

In Alwar principality, the Meos showed their resentment by burning and looting the state property, but due to retribution of the government, the insurrection could not attain success. Ibbetson writes that in 1857, the Meos assembled burnt state riches, carried off cattles, but did not succeed in plundering any town or village in Alwar. In British territory, they plundered Firozpur and other villages and, when a British force came to restore order many were hanged.[38]

Bharatpur: In the Bharatpur princely state, the Meo population was inhabited in the tahsils of Nagar, Gopalgarh, Kaman and Deeg. Nagar and Gopalgarh were most sensitive due to the periodic rebellions of the Meos as they were suffering the heavy taxation policy of the state. The Meo unrest was clearly seen in 1844, 1853, 1854 and 1855 but in view of these popular resentments, the revenue demand was reduced by 19.8% in the summary settlement of 1855-56 to 1857-88. That's why the Rebellion in Bharatpur state could not gain much progress in 1857.[39]

During the Rebellion of 1857, Bharatpur faithfully rendered good service to the British Government and the young Maharaja Jaswant Singh sent a large body of troops of all arms to quell the Rebellion in neighbouring area of his State under the Political Agent Captain J.P. Nixon. Jwala Sahai says that one of the regiments Bharatpur state was preserved in the Mathura district throughout the troublous period. Three hundred Sawars were served for a long time under the Lieutenant Governor at Agra. The revolutionaries which entered the state or passed on its border were attacked and such of them arrested were made over to the British authorities. A strong body of Bharatpur troops under Bakhshi Ganga Ram fought with Captain Nixon against the revolutionary Sepoys led by Tantia Tope at Deosa in Jaipur and put them to flight.[40]

Dhaulpur: Apart from the Mewat regions of Alwar and Bharatpur in Rajputana, there were many instances of Mewati Rebellion in the province. Dhaulpur in Rajasthan was also the centre of Rebellion, where the Mewatis were active like other parts of the country. About 20-25 Mewatis plunderers of Sont ki Mundee, to whom the British Government called as horse stealing Mewatis attached to the rebellious force Ghulam Mohammad of Dhaulpur. They marched towards Delhi in order to join the revolutionaries of Delhi in the first week of September 1857. They also got much strength when they were being followed by the Mewatis of Koel and Hathras.[41]

Although the Dhaulpur was completely under the revolutionaries, the Rana of Dhaulpur never resisted them and encamped himself in his Purani Chaoni, 2 coss off the Dhaulpur city. He was accompanied with two Paltans. One Risala of Mewatis consisting of 1000 to 1200 Cavalry and one Risala of Vilayatis consisting 3750 to 4000 men.[42]

Haryana

Haryana was not in the existence in 1857, but as part of Punjab province and took active part in the Rebellion of 1857. Most of the area of Mewat, densely populated by the martial Meos, was the part of Haryana province. Undoubtedly, the Mewati revolutionaries took active part in the Rebellion not only in Mewat but other adjoining areas of Haryana.

Hisar: Among the rebellious centres of the Mewati revolutionaries during 1857, other than the Mewat area was Hisar. Five British companies which were stationed at Hisar mutinied in June 1857. The Mewatis of that district quickly responded over the incident and joined them in bulk, numbering about 300. Nawab Samad Khan led the whole movement against the British. The revolutionaries killed the district collector and looted the treasury. They moved to Delhi along with the treasury, following the examples of the other revolutionaries of the north India. The Emperor Bahadur Shah Zafar managed their stay near Delhi jail and ordered to fulfill their living requirements.[43]

Mahendragarh: Mahendragarh, better known at that time as Kanaud, was also the centre of the Rebellion, where Mewatis were active in the Rebellion of 1857. Mahendragarh was under the Nawab of Jhajjar in 1803 and continued up to 1857. About 17th or 18th of October, Brigadier-General Showers attacked Mahendragarh, where they met the revolutionaries of Jhajjar and Delhi along with the Mewatis and other likeminded people, and a fierce battle took place. The revolutionaries' loss was 40 men, 50 cavalry horses and a few nine-pounder guns. The leader of the revolutionaries was General Abdus Samad Khan, the father-in-law of Nawab Abdur Rehman Khan of Jhajjar. He gave the inspiring lead to the people who rose up vehemently against the British. Eventually, the British force under Showers became successful in occupying the fort along with a treasury worth nine lakhs and a heavy ammunition.[44]

For further subjugation, Gerrard was sent with a huge army. He stayed at Gurgaon in the night of 10th November, and then proceeded to Narnaul via Mahendragarh and Rewari. Gerrard reoccupied Rewari on the 13th, and here he was joined by two squadrons of the Carabineers. At Mahendragarh, where he reached two days later, he was met by a detachment of the Hariana Field Force of the three arms, including, in addition to the police and native levies, the 23rd Panjab Infantry under Captain Stafford. Thence he pushed on over a very sandy plain difficult to traverse to Narnaul, where it was understood, the enemy had mustered in considerable force.[45]

Narnaul: Narnaul was the next most important centre of Rebellion in Haryana, which was also gifted to Nawab of Jhajjar in 1803, who remained its ruler for about half a century, up to 1857, the year of the Rebellion. At Narnaul, the Mewatis along with other revolutionaries were very much active during the Rebellion of 1857. After Showers departure to Delhi, the revolutionaries moved into the northern Rajasthan, where they met a rebel force, the Jodhpur Legion from Rajasthan and formed a junction with it. Then they marched to Rewari and reoccupied it. Nevertheless, strategically speaking, Rewari was not a good place to camp, so they abandoned it in the first week of November and occupied Narnaul.[46]

The British authorities at Delhi were alarmed by these developments. They sent a strong column under Colonel Gerrard, an officer of conspicuous merit. Colonel Gerrard of 1st Bengal Fusiliers left Delhi on 10th of November for Narnaul where the revolutionaries were led by General Samad Khan, father-in-law of Nawab Abdur Rahman Khan, and had seized the fort of Narnaul. Colonel Gerrard's force was consisting of about 2500 men of the 1st Fusiliers; two squadrons of the Carabineers; a troop of Bengal

Horse Artillery; a Eurasian Battery, commanded by Colonel Yan Cortland; the Sikh Guides' Corps, Cavalry, and Infantry; the Multani Horse; and some Sikh Infantry Regiments, forming the Brigade.[47]

The revolutionaries were arrayed at Narnaul under Rao Tula Ram and Samad Khan. A fierce battle took place at Narnaul on 16th of November 1857, but as the British got a helping force from Jaipur, the revolutionaries lost the ground and took refuge at a nearby village Nasibpur. The British forces followed the revolutionaries, and another battle began between the revolutionaries and the British. Rao Tula Ram's first charge was irresistible, and the British forces scattered before them. Rao Tula Ram's ally Prince Mohammad Azim,[48] the hero of Hisar Rebellion, also fought well but never heard after this battle. The Patiala Infantry and the Multani Horse on the British left were completely disheartened. The whole of the right flank fled. However, at this juncture, the Guides and the Carabineers came to their rescue and saved the situation.[49]

The Guides, led by Kennedy, and the Carabineers by Wardlaw fought splendidly against the revolutionaries. At this crisis Gerrard, riding in front, conspicuous on his white Arab charger, was mortally wounded by a musket-ball. The Fusiliers charged and drove the revolutionaries into flight, and completed their expulsion from the fort of Narnaul. Caulfield was succeeded to the command and a few days later by Seaton. However, under orders from headquarters, the British force went back to Delhi. The British took nine Indian guns and many other standard arms from the revolutionaries.[50]

This battle of Nasibpur set another example battle of Kanwaha and battle of Buxar, in which the combined front of Indian rulers fought against the foreigner. This time also, the Indian nobles, including freedom fighters and Sepoys of Jodhpur Legion were defeated. On the Indian side, the number of dead in the battle was supposed to have gone beyond many hundreds. Rao Kishan Gopal, Ram Lal, General Samad Khan's son and many other top-ranking officers were killed in the action. Rao Tula Ram fled from the field and joined Tantia Tope in Rajasthan and afterwards fled towards

Kabul. The total loss of the British force as stated were 70 killed and 45 wounded. They lost their commanders Colonel Gerrard and Captain Wallace, while Lieuts. Graise, Kennedy, Peaise and Hamphreys were wounded in action.[51]

Jhajjar: Just half a century before, a vast territory, consisting of Jhajjar, Badlee, Kanaud, Narnaul, and other districts, the whole producing revenue of above twelve lakhs of rupees, had been granted to Nawab Nijabat Ali Khan by the British Government, the only service required of him in return being to furnish a given number of Sawars to the civil authorities of the neighbourhood. However, during the Rebellion Jhajjar Sawars never helped the Magistrates of Gurgaon and Rohtak, but they joined the revolutionaries in loot and plunder.[52]

At the time of crisis in Delhi Sir Thomas Metcalfe, after having lain concealed for some days in Delhi, escaped to the fort of Kanaud, and entreated shelter and assistance, neither shelter nor help was there for him. The Nawab refused to see him, and driving him away without escort, guide, or arms, warned him to leave the territory immediately, having taken away, too, his own horse, on which he had escaped. The Nawab's involvement in the Rebellion can be understood by his presence at Delhi on 11th May 1857.[53]

Jhajjar was one of the strong centres of Rebellion where Mewatis along with rebellious Sepoys and other revolutionaries were active against the British. Abdul Rahman Khan, the Nawab of Jhajjar, was the leader of the Rebellion. He sent one hundred Sawars under his father-in-law Abdus Samad Khan to fight against the British in Delhi. Nawab also helped the Emperor by sending one lakh of rupees. Apart from his father-in-law Abdus Samad Khan, his grandfather Ibrahim Ali Khan was also constantly fighting shoulder to shoulder along with the revolutionaries of Delhi against the British. However, unfortunately, Delhi fell into the hands of the British and the Jhajjar revolutionaries again sheltered in their native place.[54]

After the suppression of the insurrection Brigadier General Showers with a strong column moved towards Jhajjar and reached Dadri, where the British forces killed twenty men of Jhajjar Nawab, to whom they had arrested from Gauria village. Showers arrested Abdur Rahman Khan, the Nawab of Jhajjar from Chhuchakbas, a hunting resort of Nawab Jhajjar, on 18th of October. On the next day at Jhajjar, the British forces killed Bakshish Husan, Colonel Paltan Husaini, Hawaldar Major Jawahar Singh, Ranjeet Singh Subedar, and Jaswant Singh Jamadar, who were gathered to handover the arms and ammunition. It followed a large-scale massacre of the innocents.[55]

Brigadier General Showers left for Delhi via Rewari, Farrukhnagar, Ballabhgarh, Tauru and Sohna at the end of that month. Nawab Abdul Rahman Khan was hanged in Delhi on 24th December, 1857, after a two-day short trial. His State was confiscated and on 4th January, 1861, his parganas of Kanaud (Mahendragarh) and Narnaul were awarded to Maharaja Narendra Singh of the Patiala state.[56]

Rewari: Rewari (including Narnaul) was the part of the Mewat region in the ancient times, and many of the Meos were settled along with the majority population of the Ahirs. During the time of Emperor Aurangzeb, this area worth twenty lakhs per annum was granted to the fore fathers of Rao Tula Ram. About half-century before the Rebellion, the forefathers of the Raos had helped the Marathas in 1803 in their fight against the British. Unfortunately, the British became victorious and confiscated their jagir and gave instead an *istamarari* grant of about 58 villages. This was a great blow to the Raos which shattered their position and made them unhappy with British Government. During the Rebellion of 1857, Rewari and Bahora were the centres of Rebellion where Mewati fighters, both Meos and Ahirs, were fighting against the British. Rao Tula was the rebellious leader of the revolutionaries. His cousin Gopal Dev also stood by him.[57]

On 17 May, 1857, the Raos went to the tahsil headquarters at Rewari with four to five hundred followers and deposed the tahsildar and thanedar. They appropriated the cash from the tahsil treasury, took all the government buildings in their possession and proclaimed, under the sanction of Emperor Bahadur Shah, their rule over the pargana of Rewari, Bahora and Shahjahanpur. For their headquarters, they chose Rampura, a small fortified village, one mile south-west of Rewari. Rao Tula Ram, the elder Rao became Raja and Gopal Dev his commander-in-chief.[58]

In the process of subjugation, a British force was dispatched from Delhi under Brigadier General Showers and Hodson of Hodson's Horse, just after the re-conquest of Delhi. The force comprised of 1500 men with a light field battery, 18 two-pounder guns and two small mortars, was advanced to attack and destroy Rao Tula Ram and his followers. The column had light skirmishes with some of the Rewari revolutionaries on 5th October at Pataudi. The column next advanced to Rampura but Rao Tula Ram fled before the arrival of Showers. Showers reached on Rewari on 6th of October and occupied the fort without any serious opposition.[59]

The column under Brigadier General Showers returned to Gurgaon via Rewari, Farrukhnagar and Ballabhgarh on 22nd of October. Here Showers settled the Meo revolutionaries at Tauru and Sohna and at the end of October, he finally unsuccessfully went back to Delhi.

On 13th of November 1857, the British authorities sent a strong column under Colonel Gerrard, who occupied the abandoned fort of Rampura. Rao Tula Ram was at that time at Narnaul, where the revolutionaries and Jodhpur Legion were ready to face the British. Colonel Gerrard, after a few days stay at Rewari went towards Narnaul on 16th of November via Mahendragarh.[60]

It must not be forgotten that the Meos were not in support of Rao Tula Ram, although they were fighting under his allies. It seems that the Mewatis of Rewari were doubtful about the loyalties of their ruler Rao Tula Ram. He not fully cooperated to the Emperor Bahadur Shah Zafar by sending the required money, but frequently complained against the Mewatis for their turbulence in the court of the Emperor. Hakim Abdus Shakoor writes that Rao Tula Ram was intended to occupy the Tauru pargana, that's why he complained against the Meos' resistance and wanted to seek permission of the Emperor to capture the Meo dominated area. However, the Emperor never permitted him to take action against the Mewati revolutionaries.[61]

Farrukhnagar: During the Rebellion of 1857, the ruler of Farrukhnagar principality was Nawab Ahmad Ali Khan. He was in favour of the revolutionaries and personally attended the court of Mughal Emperor Bahadur Shah Zafar on 31st July 1857. He occupied the Meo village Bahora against the wishes of Rao Tula Ram. Subsequently, Rao Tula Ram re-occupied the Bahora village and openly invited the animosity of Meos and the Nawab.[62]

Needless to say that Nawab Ahmad Ali Khan was in the Mewati influence and fully aided the Mewati revolutionaries against the British as well as against Rao Tula Ram. Not only Bahora, but other Meo villages were in support of the Nawab and constantly fought against the British until the arrest and death punishment of Nawab Ahmad Ali Khan.

Ballabhgarh: Ballabhgarh was ruled by Raja Nahar Singh during the Rebellion of 1857. He initially pleaded the British Government for help against the revolutionaries who were active in his dominion, but ultimately turned against the British. He raised troops for the Mughal Emperor, helped him with money and provisions, and actually invaded the British territory and seized Palwal. When Delhi fell and all was lost, he gave himself up, hoping to save his miserable life. Nevertheless, such compromises did not accord with the British Government. Sentence of death was passed, and he was hanged on the 9th of January 1858, and all his estates forfeited.[63]

Most certainly the revolutionaries which were the cause of anxiety for Raja Nahar Singh, which compelled him to seek British help, were the Mewatis who were from the villages of own State. The same revolutionaries and the Sepoys were formed in his army when the Raja was against the British.

References

1. Cunningham, p. 21, see also *Tahrik-e-Azadi Aur Mewat*, p. 34.
2. Raikes, Charles, *Notes on the Revolt in the North-Western Provinces of India*, London, 1858, p. 159.
3. Reginald, George, Burton, *The Revolt in Central India 1857-59*, Simla 1908, p. 14, (hereafter cited as *The Revolt in Central India*).
4. *Ibid*, p. 67.

5. Showers, Charles Lionel, *A Missing Chapter of the Indian Mutiny*, New York, 1888, pp. 89, (hereafter cited as *A Missing Chapter*) see also Kaye&Malleson, Vol. V, London, 1896, p. 44, and Malleson, George Bruce, *History of the Indian Mutiny, 1857-59*, Vol. III, London, 1880, p. 65.
6. *Ibid*, pp. 90.
7. *The Revolt in Central India*, p. 76, see also *Records of the Intelligence Department*, Vol. II, Edinburgh, 1902, p. 53.
8. *A Missing Chapter*, pp. 92-93.
9. Kaye&Malleson, Vol. V, London, 1896, p. 45, see also *The Revolt in Central India*, p. 76.
10. *Ibid*, p. 77.
11. Kaye & Malleson, Vol. V, London, 1896, p. 55.
12. *Records of the Intelligence Department*, p. 50.
13. *Social Scientist*. Vol. 26, No. 1-4 (Jan-April 1998), New Delhi, pp. 54-57.
14. *Ibid*, pp. 56-57.
15. *Records of the Intelligence Department*, p. 22.
16. *Ibid*, p. 16, see also Chick, N.A., *Annals of the Indian Rebellion, 1857-58*, London, 1974, p. 12, (hereafter cited as *Annals of the Indian Rebellion*).
17. Atkinson, Edwin Thomas, *Statistical Descriptive and Historical Account of the North Western Provinces of India*, Vol. II, Allahabad, 1875, p. 499, see also *Tahrik-e-Azadi Aur Mewat*, p. 36.
18. *Ibid*, pp. 501-502, see also *Records of the Intelligence Department*, pp. 16, 23 & 34, (The Intelligence Report says that there were a new Kotwal everyday in Aligarh, p. 16), and *Annals of the Indian Rebellion*, pp. 12-13.
19. *Dehli Urdu Akhbar*, 24 May, 1857.
20. Atkinson, Edwin Thomas, *Statistical Descriptive and Historical Account of the North Western Provinces of India*, Vol. II, Allahabad, 1875, p. 523, see also *Tahrik-e-Azadi Aur Mewat*, p. 36.
21. *Meo Qaum Aur Mewat*, p. 145, see also Malleson, George Bruce, *History of the Indian Mutiny, 1857-59*, Vol. III, London, 1880, p. 275.
22. *Tahrik-e-Azadi Aur Mewat*, p. 36.
23. *Records of the Intelligence Department*, Vol. I, Edinburgh, 1902, p. 45.
24. *Ibid*, p. 41.
25. *Ibid*, p. 73-76.
26. Shrivastawa, M.P., *The Indian Mutiny of 1857*, Allahabad, 1979, pp. 49-50.
27. *Records of the Intelligence Department*, Vol. I, Edinburgh, 1902, p. 234.

28. *Haryana District Gazetteers, Faridabad*, Chandigarh, 1993, p. 51, and *Haryana State Gazetteer*, Volume I, Chandigarh, 2001, p. 288, see also *Mathura: A District Memoire*, p. 46.
29. *Records of the Intelligence Department*, Vol. I, Edinburgh, 1902, pp. 34-35, see also *Mathura: A District Memoire*, pp. 46-47.
30. *Social Scientist*. Vol. 26, No. 296-99 (Jan-April 1998), New Delhi, p. 135, see also *Aaj Kal* (Magazine), New Delhi, 2007, p. 53.
31. Maulvi Liaqat Ali was born to Qazi Mehar Ali of Mahangaon, near Allahabad, on 5th October, 1826. Following to the word 'Mehar' in his father's name, it is a hard fact to believe that he belonged to a Meo or Mewati family. He was in the Government military service but lost his job due to his anti-British activities. He started teaching the Islamic learning in his village mosque. However, when the Rebellion started, he assumed the leadership of the revolutionaries of Allahabad as well as the governorship of the subah under the Emperor Bahadur Shah Zafar. He lost the battle against the British and after handing over the treasury to Nana Sahib fled towards Mumbai. He was arrested in 1871 and sentenced for deportation to Andaman, where he died on 17th May 1892, after twenty-years imprisonment. See for details *Aaj Kal* (Magazine), New Delhi, 2007, pp. 52-53.
32. Shrivastawa, M.P., *The Indian Mutiny of 1857*, Allahabad, 1979, pp. 73-74.
33. *Aaj Kal* (Magazine), New Delhi, 2007, pp. 52-53.
34. *Social Scientist*. Vol. 26, No. 1-4 (Jan-April 1998), New Delhi, p. 53.
35. Atkinson, Edwin Thomas, *Statistical Descriptive and Historical Account of the North Western Provinces of India*, Vol. II, Part-I, Allahabad, 1875, pp. 192-193 & 268.
36. *Meo Qaum Aur Mewat*, p. 144.
37. *Akhbar-uz-Zafar*, Delhi, 19th July, 1857, see also Powlett, p. 23, and *Tarikh-e-Meo Kshatriya*, p. 475.
38. Ibbetson, p. 179.
39. *Against History Against State*, pp. 188-189.
40. Sahai, Jwala, *History of Bharatpur*, Agra, 1912, p. 48.
41. *Records of the Intelligence Department*, p. 45.
42. *Ibid*, p. 48.
43. *Meo Qaum Aur Mewat*, p. 145.
44. *Haryana District Gazetteer, Mahendragarh*, Chandigarh, 1988, p. 48.

45. Kaye&Malleson, Vol. IV, London, 1911, p. 77.

46. *Haryana District Gazetteer, Mahendragarh*, Chandigarh, 1988, p. 49.

47. *Records of the Intelligence Department*, Vol. II, Edinburgh, 1902, p. 216, see also *Records of the Intelligence Department*, Vol. I, Edinburgh, 1902, p. 261, Innes, P. R., *History of the Bengal European Regiment, now the Royal Munster Fusiliers and How it Helped to Win India*, London, 1886, p. 496, (hereafter cited as *History of the Bengal European Regiment*), and Jaques, Tony, *Dictionary of the Battles and Seiges*, Connecticut, USA, 2007, p. 714.

48. Prince Mohammad Azam, a descendant of the Mughal family of Delhi, gave the revolutionaries an effective lead in the Hisar area. He attacked Hisar with a big force comprising 1,000 strong. Capt. Mildway who looked after Hisar could not stand for long against the Prince, and, therefore, Hisar was taken over by Azim. However, he was not destined to control it for long, because soon after General Van Cortland rushed to Hisar and drove him out. Azim gave a tough battle to the enemy at Mangali and fought bravely but lost the day and also 400 of his men. After this, he left the field with his followers, but was hotly chased by the British. On September 30, he fought the last battle at Jamalpur, where again, he met the same fate. The Prince left Hisar and moved into the Gurgaon district. There he joined Rao Tula Ram, and both fought against the British at Narnaul (Battle of Narnaul, 16 November, 1857). Nothing was heard of the Prince or his family after that. See for details *Haryana District Gazetteer, Hisar*, Chandigarh, 1987, pp. 39-40.

49. Malleson, G. B., *The Indian Mutiny of 1857*, New York, 1891, p. 319, see also *History of the Bengal European Regiment*, pp. 497-498, and *Haryana District Gazetteer, Mahendragarh*, Chandigarh, 1988, p. 49.

50. *Ibid*, p. 320, see also *History of the Bengal European Regiment*, pp. 497-498, and *Haryana District Gazetteer, Mahendragarh*, Chandigarh, 1988, p. 49.

51. *History of the Bengal European Regiment*, pp. 497-498, see also *Records of the Intelligence Department*, Vol. II, Edinburgh, 1902, p. 217, and *Haryana District Gazetteer, Gurgaon*, Chandigarh, 1983, pp. 67-68.

52. Cave-Browne, John, *The Punjab and Delhi in 1857*, Vol. II, Edinburgh, 1861, pp. 232-233, (hereafter cited as Cave-Browne).

53. *Ibid.*

54. *Akhbar-uz-Zafar*, 23 August, 1857, see also *Two Native Narratives*, p. 101.

55. Ball, Charles, *History of the Indian Mutiny*, Vol. II, London, 1863, p. 58, see also Husain, Iqbal, *1857 Ke Swatantra Sangram Me Mewatiyon Ka Balidan*, (Unpublished) AMU Aligarh, pp. 101-102.

56. *Haryana District Gazetteer, Mahendragarh*, Chandigarh, 1988, p. 51.
57. *Ibid*, p. 47.
58. *Ibid.*
59. *Ibid*, pp. 47-49.
60. *Ibid*, p. 49.
61. *Tarikh Meo Kshatri*, p. 170.
62. *Two Native Narratives*, p. 196.
63. Cave-Browne, pp. 235-236.

5

Some Drawbacks of the Mewati Rebellion

The war of independence was no doubt a boon for the martial Mewati communities, which provided them a fair chance to show their chivalry and patriotism. However, unfortunately, the side effects of this freedom movement created the lawlessness and anarchy among the Jats, Ahirs, Goojars, Rajputs and Meos of Mewat. Perhaps this was the adverse point of the Rebellion in Mewat. While the Mewati revolutionaries bravely fought for the freedom of their motherland and set free from the oppressive British rule, some of the Mewatis find it an opportunity to settle their old disputes. It must not be forgotten that the Mewati people ware basically attached to the agricultural lands and undoubtedly, there were a lot of landed feuds among them. The contradictions within the rural society of the first half of the nineteenth century came out in the open with the revolts of 1857.

The mutual animosity which continued from the decades, naturally burst when the rural people freed from the British bounds. They tried to settle the old existing disputes in the absence of the British administrative machinery. The so-called freedom created an atmosphere of anarchy and lawlessness in some areas of Mewat. Many of the Mewatis, including the revolutionaries and loyalists such as Meos, Jats, Goojars, Rajputs, Khanzadas, etc. began to settle their old disputes at the same time. Thus, the process of internal differentiation impacted on the nature of the Rebellion and affected the nature of the Rebellion. They find it fare chance to set their age-old feuds by attacking upon each other.

There were also some instances of loot and plunder of the Government treasury by the Mewati people. It was first noticed at the beginning of the Rebellion, when the revolutionaries attack on Gurgaon city. Munshi Jeewan Lal in his Roznamcha writes, "A trooper arrived and reported that as several lakhs of treasure were coming in from Gurgaon to Delhi under charge of one company of foot and several cavalry, it had been attacked by, a body of Mewatis, and he had left them, still fighting, to ask for aid. Maulvi Baki ordered two companies of foot and one troop of cavalry to rescue the treasure."[1]

In the absence of the British rule and its police force, the lawlessness and anarchy gained the ground in Mewat during the Rebellion of 1857. The whole Mewat area was burning in the revolutionary fire in July, after the departure of Major Eden. *Dehli Urdu Akhbar* reported about the condition of Mewat in its edition of 5th July 1857. The report of the newspaper is as follows:[2]

> "A person came from the Firozpur side says that the Mewatis have created the rampage. They have burnt the towns such as Nuh, Nagina, Tauru, and Firozpur. They have looted all the towns and villages of that side. The pathways are blocked. Except beggar or impoverished persons, who do not have even clothes or sheets, nobody could move anywhere. Only beggars could move in the state of begging door to door. The persons, along with the gathering of armed men, also could move on the pathways of Mewat."

However, the quotation of *Dehli Urdu Akhbar* is unable to prove its authenticity. It reports that Mewatis were looting and burning their villages but how it's possible that the Meos could loot and burn their own villages. Undoubtedly there might be some landed feuds and village-wise disputes but such a situation as reported by the newspaper only shows the hyperbole of the situation.

It is worthy to discuss some personal disputes that how the Meos, Khanzadas, Jats and Rajputs started civil war for their petty issues. These personal feuds invited the attention of the British Government and ultimately loss of their lives and property.

Kot and Baheen

After the victory over Nuh, the Mewati revolutionaries intended to chastise the loyalist of Rawat Jats of Hodal and the Rajputs of Hathin. They were attacked by a large gathering of Surot Jats of Hodal, Pathans of Seoli and the Meos. The fight continued for several months, and the loyalists suffered heavy losses. The Rawats informed the British authorities and sought their help and accordingly, a small force was dispatched from Delhi to Hodal to help their supporters.

The *Punjab Gazetteer of Gurgaon District* gives the details of the story that in Palwal, there was a tribe of Jats, known as Surot, inhabiting Hodal and the surrounding villages. They were in the alliance with the Pathan village called Seoli. Adjoining them, there were the villages owned by another Jat tribe known as Rawats. Between Rawats and Seoli there had been before 1803 a quarrel which had cost many lives on either side. The Rawats also had an old feud with the Chhriklot tribe of Meos, originating to the village of Kot. It led to a grouping of Meos, Pathans and Surot Jats on one side and the Rawat Jats on the other. The Rajputs of Hathin were also allied to the Rawats most probably due to their pro-British policies.[3]

The *Gazetteer* continued to quote that during the Rebellion, the Rawats, were attacked, on both east and west by their enemies, and allied themselves with Rajputs of Hathin, and the fight went on for months. On the whole, the Rawats triumphed and on one occasion, a runaway horse brought the leader of their enemies, a *lambardar* of Kot, into their ranks. He was killed, and his head was cut off and kept a few days in Baheen, the chief Rawat village. On this brutal episode, the Kot men inverted their war drum, and until they have had their revenge, the inverted drum remained on its position. The Meos attacked on the Rawats and caused them heavy loss. Eventually, a British force came to the assistance of the Rawats, who were supposed to be the loyalists of the Government. The allied force initially met a success, looted and plundered the Meo villages. However, the situation changed when suddenly a strong hostile force of revolutionaries appeared to aid the Meos against the British and their allies. In a fierce battle, the British troops compelled to retreat and many Rawats were surprised and killed.[4]

Hathin and Rupraka

The fight between Meos and Rajputs of Hathin was also condemnable in the same way which led to a setback of the Rebellion. Both the parties continuously fought for three days and consequently, Captain Drummond attacked at Rupraka. While advancing from Sohna to the village Rupraka, Captain Drummond burnt the villages like Pachanka, Gohpur, Malpuri, Chilli, Utawar, Kot, Mughla, Mithaka, Khilluka, Guraksar, Maluka, Jhanda, etc.[5]

A fierce battle took place at Rupraka, and the Meos lost the ground with the loss of hundreds of the Meo revolutionaries. After their victory over the revolutionaries at Rupraka, the British force burnt the other villages of Mewat such as Shikrawa, Khilluka, Ghasera, Pinangwa, Nai, Singer, Nagina, etc. If both the native groups were organized against the British by forgetting all their rivalries, the Rebellion would have gained strength rather loss of about four hundred Meo revolutionaries.

Bazidpur and Bukharka

Another example of such a civil war was in Firozpur Jhirka where two Meo chaudharies of Chhirklot clan, Chand Khan of Bazidpur and Kabir Khan of Bukharka. These men were closely related but taken different sides in a quarrel which had originated in the murder of a *lambardar* of Badarpur by a villager of Khuspuri during the rule of Nawab Ahmad Bakhsh Khan.[6]

After gaining their independence and from the British control in 1857, the quarrel broke out afresh, and all the Chhirklot and some of the other villages of the neighbourhood were divided into two factions, headed respectively by Chand Khan and Kabir Khan. Kabir Khan burnt and plundered the villages of Aterna, Shamshabad, Shadipur, Aklimpur, and Chantipur, a hamlet of Bhadas. Chand Khan in the retaliation assembled his men and burnt Bukharka and plundered Imamnagar. Finally, both parties mustered in strength, and a fight, which lasted eight days, took place on the boundary of Badarpur and Bukharaka. The result was indecisive, and the loss on each side was some fifty or sixty killed.[7]

Nuh

Another example of local dispute was the fight between the Meos and the Khanzadas. The Khanzadas were also a Mewati race and had traditional glorious past. During the Sultanate period, they were the ruling class; they were jagirdars or fief holders during the Mughal period and were highly educated and servicemen during the British rule. Naturally, due to their traditional past, the Khanzadas were more prosperous than their co-inhabitant Meos. They were having different culture and traditions. The common thing among them was their religion and residential place.

There might be some traditional enmity on agrarian or land based grounds but the loyalty of the Khanzadas for the British was the main reason behind the skirmishes. The local Government officials and the British authorities were having much hope with them as the Nuh town was the stronghold of the Khanzadas. During this Rebellion, the Khanzadas supported and fought for the British. They met a direct clash with the Meos and as soon as the Rebellion progressed, the Khanzadas suffered heavily for their loyalty. After the Rebellion, the situation reversed, and they avenged the Meos and mass level destruction and plight of the Meos followed.

The *Gurgaon District Gazetteer* also confirms that Nuh town proved very tough for the Mewati revolutionaries like Ali Hasan Khan Mewati and his fellow men. Because of the local police, the Khanzadas, loyal to the British, gave a stiff battle the Meos. However, due to his numerical strength, Ali Hasan Khan became victorious and Khanzadas suffered heavy casualties. A large number of them were treacherously put to death after their surrender. The Khanzadas along with other loyalists and British troops completely rooted out by the Meo revolutionaries. The victory of Nuh town resulted in a complete withdrawal of the British administration from Mewat.[8]

Firozpur Jhirka

The same episodes of fights were also noted from Firozpur Jhika, another stronghold of the Mewati revolutionaries. A revolutionary named Majlis Khan was very active in Firozpur Jhirka. Following the other revolutionaries of Mewat, Majlis Khan too fought against the British along with the Mewati band of revolutionaries. It was reported that Majlis Khan had also waged war against the loyalists of Mewat and killed and imprisoned many of them. He was also having the close connection with the famous revolutionary leader Rao Tula Ram of Rewari.[9]

Regarding this episode of Majlis Khan, the famous revolutionary leader Firoz Baksh reported to the Tahsildar of Firozpur Jhirka on 8th of August that a revolutionary named Majlis Khan along with his revolutionary band had killed five persons and arrested 29 persons belonging to the loyalists of the British. Firoz Baksh further reported that Majlis Khan had gone to Rewari for some hidden purpose and subsequently returned to his abode.[10]

Bahora

In the Mewat region of the Rewari area, the Meo peasants refused to acknowledge the authority of the revolutionary Ahir chief, Rao Tula Ram, who had provided protection to the Jat peasantry with whom the Meos had a direct contradiction. There was a forthright attack on the villages of the Jats, Ahirs and Brahmins by the Meo revolutionaries. The Jats were seen as having benefited the most from the canal irrigation policy of the British. Bahora pargana was the centre of the dispute, where local revolutionaries stood against each other. Here the Meos and the Jats fought not only against the British but also wasted their lives and property in each others fightings.[11]

The fight started when Rao Tula Ram extended his rule over Bahora during the Rebellion of 1857. A few Meo villages under the Bahora pargana declined to acknowledge his authority. It was perhaps due to the misunderstanding that Rao Tula Ram was having terms with the British Government. The Meos villages were plundered and burnt by the neighbouring Jat villages with the aid and assistance of the forces of Rao Tula Ram. However, mostly the Meos proved themselves heavy upon the Jats. So the Jats of the village of Bahora lived in continual dread of their powerful and turbulent Meo neighbours, and so aided Rao Tula Ram, during his short sway. When the power of Rao Tula Ram collapsed, they were at once attacked by the Meos. The conflict took place at the village Jaurasi where the Jats were assembled. For two days, the fight lasted, but the Jats were driven back on the small conical hill close to the village. In this battle, about one hundred and eleven Jats, Ahirs and Brahmans were killed while the Meo loss was eighty.[12]

Mahendragarh

Mahendragarh, earlier known as Kanaud, was under the Nawab of Jhajjar Abdur Rahman Khan. This town also witnessed a conflict which weakened the position of Nawab and his forces. Nawab was in immense pressure due to repeated demand of money from the Delhi court of Emperor Bahadur Shah Zafar. In order to save his treasury, Nawab sent seven lakh of rupees to Mahendragarh fort through Shalu Singh and Imdad Ali. After handing over the money, Shalu Singh stayed there on the pretext of the marriage of his daughter, while Imdad Ali returned to Jhajjar.[13]

Shalu Singh stayed at the residence of Nawab in the fort of Mahendragarh and enjoyed the night dance following the style of Nawab. When the soldiers raised their resistance, Shalu Singh killed one of the soldiers and dishonoured his dead body. All the soldiers revolted over this act and rushed to Kotani, the village of Shalu Singh. They looted and raised his haveli on the ground. Next day, the soldiers returned to Jhajjar. The Nawab blessed them over their act.[14]

The above-mentioned incidents definitely weakened the position of the revolutionaries in Mewat region. Surely, they would have emerged the strongest power if they had fought unitedly against the British. Their personal disputes were undoubtedly a reason of the failure of the Mewati Rebellion of 1857. The martial communities of Mewat were so strong and there is no exaggeration to say that they would have sandwiched the numerically weak British force stationed at Ridge near the wall of Delhi, if they were united and would have been provided the latest arms and ammunitions.

References

1. *Two Native Narratives*, p. 95.
2. *Dehli Urdu Akhbar*, Delhi, 5th July, 1857.
3. *Punjab Gazetteer, Gurgaon District, 1883-84*, Lahore, 1884, p. 26.
4. *Ibid.*
5. *Gurgaon District Gazetteer*, Chandigarh, 1983, pp. 63-64.
6. Malleson, George Bruce, *Indian Mutiny of 1857*, London, 1912, p. 125.
7. *Ibid*, pp. 125-126, see also, Roberts, P.E., *A Historical Geography of the British Dependencies: India*, Vol. VII, London, 1914, p. 371.
8. *Punjab Gazetteer, Gurgaon District, 1883-84*, Lahore, 1884, p. 26, see also Yadav, K.C., *Revolt of 1857 in Haryana*, New Delhi, 1977, p. 58.
9. *1857 Aur Haryana*, p. 70.
10. *Ibid.*
11. *People's Democracy, (Agrarian Uprisings and Rural Society: The 1857 Rebellion and its Aftermath-* Archana Prasad), Vol. XXXI, No. 14, April, 8, 2007.
12. *Punjab Gazetteer, Gurgaon District, 1883-84*, Lahore, 1884, p. 27, see also Channing, p. 26.
13. Husain, Iqbal, *1857 Ke Swatantra Sangram Me Mewatiyon Ka Balidan*, (Unpublished) AMU Aligarh, pp. 87-88.
14. *Ibid*, pp. 88-89.

6

Suppression of Mewati Revolutionaries

It has been stated in the previous chapter that during the siege of Delhi, on 1st July 1857, Major Eden and William Ford compelled to leave the Mewat region. It led to continue the Mewat region in the state of independence under the Mewati revolutionaries. Perhaps the British were more concerned in the Delhi affair rather than weakening their power by fighting the martial communities of Mewat. Above all, the British forces concentrated their power and energy for the re-occupation of Delhi. Mewat region enjoyed the full freedom without any British interference for three months from July to September 1857. On 20th September 1857, the British forces, with the assistance of the forces of Patiala, Nabha, Jind and Kashmir States, re-occupied Delhi and started genocide and butchery of innocent population of Delhi.

After the brutal killings of thousands of the innocents, the British turned their attention towards Mewat, the neighbouring territory of Delhi. Mewat was still under the control of the revolutionaries. The British sent large forces under their able officers and repeated the same brutality as of Delhi. The Mewati revolutionaries as well as innocents faced harsh, deadly, barbaric torture, and most heinous cruelties by the British. It was the worst example in the history that the so called most civilized community of the world had committed such a worst type of retribution, which has no parallels in the freedom struggle of India.

Villages after village were burnt or felled with cannon balls to quash the Rebellion. Hundreds of Mewati revolutionaries were hung from gallows and an equally large number were hung from trees as instant punishment. The Rebellion left a deep imprint in the minds of the common people that was very different from the scanty recorded history of that period. This was a unique history which has witnessed the Mewat region, especially the marginalised peasantry of Meo caste and other Mewati communities.

However, these types of retributions are a testimony to the significance of large-scale involvement of the Mewatis during the Rebellion of 1857. The British Government killed thousands of Mewati people and destroyed property worth many crores of rupees. They burnt over eighty villages — sixty in the Mewat region alone. The British Government in India faced the worldwide reprehension over their cruelties.[1]

In the process of re-occupation of Mewat region and retribution of the revolutionaries the British Government, without wasting time, send the military forces in Mewat region. In order to fulfill the task a force marched into the Gurgaon district, under Brigadier General Showers to suppress the Rebellion on 2nd October 1857. The Gurgaon city was easily captured and dispersed the leaders of the Rebellion. Baktar Singh, the chief of the revolutionary leader of Gurgaon, was captured and hanged. The other revolutionaries were also met the same fate. Eventually, the civil administration was resumed under orders from the Government of the Punjab, to which province the district was formally annexed on the final pacification of the country. William Ford, the Deputy Commissioner of Gurgaon, also left Delhi and resumed his duty on 13th of October 1857.[2]

After establishing their control over Gurgaon, the British forces turned towards Mewat, which still under the control of the revolutionaries. William Ford also provided every kind of assistance to the commanders to quell the Rebellion in Mewat. Sohna was the nearest station after Gurgaon, which was targeted at first by the British forces. In a letter from Charles Saunders to Sir William Muir, dated 21st October, it is mentioned that "There are a great number of Mewatis collected at Sohna and in the neighbourhood. The natives declare that their number 20,000, but that is an exaggeration. Our troops will have to be employed in dispersing them."[3]

Brigadier General Showers and Wigram Clifford

It has been mentioned earlier that at the very beginning of the Rebellion in Mewat, Major Eden tried his level best to suppress the Mewati revolutionaries. But somehow he left his task and returned to his abode, but his departure led to further deterioration in the existing situations. Even the fall of Delhi on September 20, 1857 did not affect any improvement in the situations of Mewat. Consequently, on 2nd October, a strong column of 1,500 men with a light field battery, a few 18 two-ponder-guns, and mortars were sent under Brigadier General Showers to punish the turbulent Meos, Goojars, Ranghars and Ahirs and the rebel princes. Next day the column reached at Gurgaon. The column occupied Gurgaon without any major trouble and restored the order.[4]

After gaining control over Gurgaon, the whole party moved towards Pataudi, and thereafter Rewari, the prime target of the British force. In the way, the British column met light skirmish with some Rao Tula Ram's Sawars on 5th October at Pataudi and reached Rewari on 6th October. However, the leader Rao Tula Ram moved towards Narnaul for a new coalition against the British, leaving all the ammunitions in the fort. Hodson, who was also the part of the column, shows the secret of dubious nature of Rao Tula Ram by leaving the town while abundance of arms and ammunition. Showers satyed at Rewari for a week and tried to pursue Rao Tula Ram for surrender, but he could not become successful. Brigadier General Showers along with most of his soldiers left for Kanaud, then went Chhuchakbas and arrested the Nawab of Jhajjar.[5]

Hodson, who accompanied Brigadier General Showers in this campaign, writes on 3rd October, "Today we struck off to ..... and go on to-morrow through Goorgaon to a place called Rewarree, where one Toli Ram, a farmer of Government revenue in better times, but who now "affectionate" independent authority, has collected a force round his fortlet of some 4,000 to 5,000 men, and shows fight; but again I opine we shall have a tedious march for our pains." Hodson again says that the party encamped at Gurgaon on 4th of October, and on the same day ordered to proceed to punish some refractory villages, a few miles off.[6]

Hodson again writes from Rewari on 6th October, "We arrived here, after a tediously protracted march, at eleven this morning, only to find my prediction verified, that the birds would be flown and the nest empty. Mr. Toli Ram bolted yesterday, and left only an empty fort and his guns behind him; in good hands it would have given us considerable trouble, and he was evidently a clever fellow, and had adroitly and promptly contrived so as to be first in the field, should our power have ceased. We found extensive preparations, and large workshops for the completion of military equipments of all kinds, guns, gun-carriages, gunpowder, accoutrements, and material of all kinds. He had already done much, and in a couple of months his position would have been so strong as to have given him the command of all the surrounding country, as well as the rich town and entrepot of Rewarree, close to the walls of his fort." Hodson further says, "Had our empire fallen, he would have mastered all the surrounding villages and districts, and probably extended his power on all sides, and founded a "Raj" like that of Puttiala or Jheend, to fall in its turn before the (then) newly aroused energies of the Sikhs. At the same time he was prepared, if we won the day, to profess that he had done all this solely in our interests, and to preserve the district for us from the Goojur population."[7]

After arresting Nawab of Jhajjar Abdur Rahman Khan, the column moved to Jhajjar and after looting the fort, the Nawab was sent to Delhi for trial. In the Military court, Nawab was found guilty and hanged on 23rd January 1858. After the occupation of Jhajjar, Showers sent on 19th of October one part of his column under Hodson to Kanaud, the treasury fort of Jhajjar Nawab. He himself went towards Dadri and arrested the Nawab Bahadur Jang Khan. Showers left for Delhi via Rewari Farrukhnagar, Taoru, Sohna and Ballabhgarh on 22nd of October.[8]

Showers came back to Gurgaon on 25th of October, 1857, to settle the Rebellion of the Mewati revolutionaries. About the campaign of Mewat, Hodson writes, "We march to-night towards Rewarree, and shall get there on the 24th; from thence a part goes to Goorgaon, and waits the arrival of the larger portion of the troops which are to go into the Mewattee country, and punish some rascals who have plundered the large town of Sonah. The Brigadier is planning a series of manoeuvres, by which he intends to surround and capture 4,000 Mewattees. I shall be very much surprised if we see one of that interesting race!"[9]

From Gurgaon, Showers send one of his firebrand officers Wigram Clifford, the Assistant Collector (ADC) of Gurgaon to subdue the Mewati revolutionaries. Wigram Clifford was very poisonous for the revolutionaries as his sister was killed in Delhi at the beginning of the Rebellion. It was rumored that during the revolutionary Government at Delhi, Wigram Clifford's sister was stripped naked at the Delhi palace, tied in that position to the wheels of gun carriages, and in the presence of the Emperor's son, she was cut to pieces. Wigram Clifford had it in his mind that his sister, before being murdered, was outraged by the revolutionaries. Naturally, he had a fire of revenge burning violently in his heart. He burnt villages after village and destroyed the country side. He burnt villages of Mewat from Gurgaon to Sohna. According to him, he put to death all those who came across and did not spare even women and children.[10]

Undoubtedly, the Mewati revolutionary resistance was the hard nut to crack for Brigadier General Showers. Perhaps the martial background of the Mewatis would have left a deep imprint on the mind of Brigadier General Showers and he surely sould have suffered a Mewati phobia. He reported all his experiences of Mewat to his officers stationed on the Ridge of Delhi. He writes, "From the time I entered the Gurgaon district, I was in enemies' country, that in all encampments and during every march I was exposed to the attacks of the enemies horsemen.... I had to anticipate attack from every village that I passed, where I had to be continually on the alert against an enemy..... It may well be understood that the protection of captured property was of secondary consideration."[11]

Brigadier General Showers carried fire and sword far and wide in Mewat region. Without taking any risk, he decided to completely subjugate the Mewatis by brutal massacre and burning their villages. All the villages between Dharuhera and Tauru were indiscriminately burnt, and their inhabitants were shot down ruthlessly. At the deserted town of Tauru some 30 persons were killed.[12]

About the tough resistance of the Mewati revolutionaries, Brigadier General Showers writes, "They are in numbers on Mewattis in the hills and in the villages near Sonah. Some Bandies and horsemen are associated with them, and if I were to leave this part of the country without going in among them they would come forward again and give a great deal of trouble. I have therefore decided on going to Sonah via Kasun and Taoroo."[13]

He personally reported that his men "were greatly knocked up. ....and many completely ineffective from sickness and fatigue, and ....required rest." The horses of Scott's Battery were hardly able to drag the guns. In spite of full trained force with arms and ammunitions, he was fully terrorized and himself says that "from the time I entered the Gurgaon district, I was in enemies' country, that in all encampments and during every march I was exposed to the attacks of the enemies horsemen ....I had to anticipate attack from every village that I passed, where I had to be continually on the alert against an enemy."[14]

Sir William Muir quotes the words of the Saunders, who writes that his Infantry portion musters not more than between 500 and 600. "One regiment, the Kumaonies, have only 90 effective men out in camp." "It will be necessary," Saunders adds, "for the whole Column to march into Delhi to refit, or to have other regiments substituted for those that are unable to march." This was apparently determined on Showers' visit to Delhi. However, on his return to Mewat he found that the Mewati revolutionaries were too strongly posted without having a regular expedition in force against them.[15]

Under Brigadier General Showers, the British column, in assistance of Wigram Clifford, attacked a rebellious village Raiseena. On hearing the news of British advance, a Meo revolutionary named Firoz Shah Mewati immediately called the people to fight against the British. On his call hundreds of the Meos assembled to repulse the attack of Mr. Clifford. Some of the revolutionary Sepoys were also arrayed under Firoz Shah Mewati and a fierce battle took place on 31st October 1857, and lasted for four hours. A portion of the British force led by Wigram Clifford attacked a body of the revolutionaries of Raiseena and Mohammadpur, who had taken up a position on the hill of a village named Alipur. The revolutionaries at the hills were dislodged and driven away. The infamous Wigram Clifford was killed by a shot from a revolutionary Sepoy; he died almost immediately on being wounded, as the ball passed through his head. He had apparently rode in advance of the party. The local traditions say that the total loss of the British force in the battle of Raiseena was three officers, including Wigram Clifford and 150 army men. The rest of the British force was fled away after the shameful defeat.[16]

About this battle of Raiseena *Haryana State Gazetteer* writes by quoting a British historian Charles Ball that a few kilometres short of sohna, General Shower's column met a stiff resistance at the hands of the inmates of a Meo village. They killed about 60 sepoys of General Showers' column in a hand to hand fight. Describing the strife of a brave Mewati, an eye witness observes: A Mewati, a huge fellow, armed with shield and sword, was put up half way down the *Khud* (pit) at our feet. Twenty shots were fired; but the bold fellow held steadily on, springing from rock to rock, descending to the bottom of the den and then mounting the opposite face. The braveman, who put up this heroic show for quite a long time, was ultimately put to death by the Guides.[17]

About the battle and Brigadier General Showers, Lieutenant-Colonel P. R. Innes says, "The 2nd Bengal Fusiliers had already marched, forming part of a force under Brigadier Showers, who had proceeded towards the Maywattee District, to the south and west of Delhie; where they had been doing good service in reducing some Forts, and relieving many villages, which were oppressed by the rebels; and re-establishing order in our provinces."[18]

The Mirasis of Mewat still sing the song of the bravery of the Mewati revolutionaries of Raiseena. A couplet is as follows:

"Raiseena Ke Mewan Ne, Bado Jagayo Deen,

Khakka Mare Dedh Sau, Khali Kar Di Kursi Teen"

(The Meos of Raiseena got awakened. They killed one hundred and fifty army men and three officials in the battle of Raiseena)

The same Mirasis also sung the glory of their people in the couplet as follows:

"*Raseena Hai Gaon, Raub Baro Palan Me,*

Kursi Khali Hogai Teen, Hue Charcha London Me"

(The village Raiseena carries weight among the twelve Pals. Three chairs were vacated (the matter) was discussed in London.)

It is said that the heads of the British forces were buried under the stairs of the *Chaupal* of Raiseena village. Mewati revolutionary of Raiseena roped the defeated British force and forced them to prepare the thorny thatched fencing. The rest of the British forces took shelter in the Sohna valley.[19]

The Mirasis of Mewat have prepared a story on the defeat and killings of the Englishmen. They sung the story as follows:

"*Bangla Me Man Na Lage, Sooni Dekhan Sej,*

Raiseena Ka Gor Me, Dekha Bina Sees Angrez"

(The British Madams miss their husbands in their bungalows and on their bed; they were seen without head (killed) in the village of Raiseena.)

Brigadier Showers also carried fire and sword to avenge the killing of Mr. Clifford and his army. He destroyed and burnt the Raiseena and adjoining villages. The British also confiscated the agricultural lands of the Meos of adjoining villages of Raiseena such as Naunehra, Mohammadpur, Saanp ki Nagli, Haryahera, Baiki, Hirmithla, etc. The confiscated lands were awarded to the Rajputs of Bhondsi and Kayasths of Sohna. After overpowering revolutionaries around Sohna, Hathin, Palwal and Tauru, Brigadier Showers, leaving it in the charge of a Gorkha detachment of the late 22nd Native Infantry under Captain Drummond, went towards Farrukhnagar.[20]

At Farrukhnagar, Nawab Ahmad Ali Khan surrendered without any opposition and sent to Delhi where he was tried and hanged on 22nd January 1858. Thence he marched to Ballabhgarh on 31st October, 1857. Raja Nahar Singh also surrendered and sent to Delhi and hanged on 9th January 1858. Showers returned to Delhi in the first week of November with huge booty worth 80,000 pounds, 70 guns and a large number of ammunition along with prisoner chiefs of the region.[21]

Lieutenant H. Grant

After the return of Showers' Brigade to Delhi, a new column was formed for service under Ltieutenant H. Grant and Ltieutenant Rongton. On 7th November, 1857, the English army under the command of Ltieutenant H. Grant attacked upon the villages of Barka, Rewasan and Ghasera.[22]

Lt. H. Grant and Lt. Rongton played the worst role in subjugation of the Mewati revolutionaries. They carried the fire and sword against the turbulent Mewati revolutionaries. In order to subdue them, they burnt the villages which were found in route. They heard that a huge gathering of the revolutionaries was assembled at Ghasera, and accordingly, the British force planned to attack on that village. The village Ghasera was the centre of the revolutionaries, where they were assembled in a large number under the leadership of Ali Hasan Khan Mewati.[23]

The British forces attacked the village on 8th of November from two sides. About 500 revolutionaries under Ali Hasan Khan Mewati defeated the British forces and forced to return. However, at the same time another British force advancing from Rewasan side, attacked the village Ghasera and started bombarding on both the revolutionaries and innocents.[24]

A bloody and fierce battle took place in the village on 8th November 1857. The Meo revolutionaries fought valiantly but could not stay long before the well-equipped and trained British forces. In that battle at Ghasera, about 150 Meo revolutionaries and innocent villagers lost their lives. After their victory, the British force looted and burnt the villages of Barka, Rewasan and Ghasera.[25]

The Mirasis of Mewat, while praising the Meo revolutionaries, sung the story of the battle at Ghasera in the following couplet:

"Garh Ghasero Gaon Pal Ko Bado Bharoso,

Raja Ram Chandra Awtar Raj Rawan Ka Khoso"

(The Meos of (Dahangal) Pal are proud of the fort Ghasera village. (Like) The incarnate Raja Ram Chandra seized the kingdom of Rawana.)

Colonel John Grant Gerrard

Brigadier General Showers tried his level best to subdue the revolutionaries of Mewat and Ahirwal along with the princes of these areas. However, he was unsuccessful to root out the main revolutionaries of that region. Rao Tula Ram, his cousin Kishan Singh of Rewari, General Abdus Samad Khan of Jhajjar, Mohammad Azim Beg of Bhattu, who were the nucleuses of the Rebellion, moved Shekhawati in Rajasthan and joined the rebellious force of Jodhpur Legion. They jointly moved towards Narnaul and re-occupied the entire area.[26]

The loss of the conquered territories compelled the British to re-send a strong force under Colonel Gerrard of 1st European Bengal Fusiliers. He marched from Delhi on the 10th of November, 1857, with a column of approximately 2,500 men hoping that Rao Tula Ram had recaptured Rewari, the part of the ancient Mewat region. He stayed the same night at Gurgaon and reached Rewari on 13th of November. He might have faced the Mewati turbulences while passing through the heart of the Mewat region. At Rewari, Gerrard easily occupied the city as Rao Tula Ram had left for Narnaul, another area of ancient Mewat region, much earlier on 8th of Navember. In his way Rao joined the forces of General Samad Khan, father-in-law of Nawab of Jhajjar. They jointly moved towards Narnaul along with their four or five thousand forces.[27]

Following the footsteps of Rao, Gerrard proceeded towards Narnaul. He reached at Kanaud on 15th of November and next morning he pushed on to the Narnaul and reached a little before the midday of 16th of November. He was to check the revolutionaries at Narnaul, where revolutionaries from all around gathered with a hope to fight jointly against the British.[28]

The revolutionaries at Narnaul were in the strong position and had occupied in considerable force. Gerrard find a little chance to re-arrange his force as the revolutionaries made an attack immediately after their reach. Apart from the Ahirs, the other communities also joined Rao Tula Ram in this battle. Rao Tula Ram retained the overall command of the battle but entrusted the command of the fighting troops to the most able General Samad Khan, who had full support of the Mewatis and other Muslims. Samad Khan faced the enemy bravely and ultimately killed in the direct encounter with the British forces.[29]

It was very tough for Gerrard to fight against them but the Guides, led by Kennedy, and the Carabineers by Wardlaw, fought splendidly against considerable odds. The revolutionaries too fought well, but eventually they gave way due to the defeat of their cavalry. However, the revolutionaries were in full fight and were in the hope to restore the fortunes of the day. At this crisis Gerrard, riding in front, conspicuous on his white Arab charger, was mortally wounded by a musket ball and died within two hours on the same day. The Fusiliers, however, charged and drove the revolutionaries into flight, and completed their expulsion from the fort of Narnaul. Caulfield, and subsequently Seaton, who had succeeded to the command, were called back to Delhi after few days stay.[30]

The revolutionaries lost the ground as the forces of Patiala, Nabha, Jind, Jaipur and Alwar supported the British in the very crucial phase of the battle. The losses from both the sides were heavy. General Samad Khan, Rao Tula Ram's cousin Rao Kishan Gopal, his son Ram Lal, Munshi Nizamuddin, Ghous Mohammad Khan, General Samad Khan's son, Kunwar Fateh Khan, and other top level patriots along with 400 revolutionaries lost their lives. Rao Tula Ram and Prince Mohammad Azim Beg were escaped. The total loss on the British side was 70 killed and 45 wounded. Rao Tula Ram was escaped to Iran and afterwards Afghanistan, where he died on 23rd of September 1863, due to illness at the age of thirty eight.[31]

Captain Drummond

As it has been already stated that before leaving for Delhi, Brigadier General Showers had deputed Captain Drummond for the subjugation of the Mewatis, Drummond stationed at Sohna and continued the work of retribution of Mewati revolutionaries. In the third week of November 1857, Captain Drummond received the intelligence through the native officials of Hathin and Palwal that several thousand Meos and a few hundred cavalry were congregated at villages of Kot and Rupraka, and had been attacking the loyal Rajput villages for several days. It was also said that they were also having the intention to loot the Palwal Treasury. Captain Drummond, along with 59 Tohana Horses, 50 Hodson Horses, and 102 men of Kumaon Battalion under Lt. Temple proceeded towards Rupraka. The 1st Punjab Infantry under Lt. Coke, coming from Ballabhgarh, also joined Captain Drummond in the way.[32]

While advancing from Sohna to the village Rupraka, Captain Drummond burnt the villages like Pachanka, Gohpur, Malpuri, Chilli, Utawar, Kot, Mughla, Mithaka, Khilluka, Guraksar, Maluka, Jhanda, etc.[33]

Captain Drummond reached Rupraka on 19th November 1857, where he met a huge gathering of around 3500 Meo revolutionaries under a Meo leader Sadruddin. The Meo revolutionaries fought heroically, but unfortunately lost the battle due to the superior artillery of the British forces. It followed the streat fighting but eventually that too came to an end. In this battle of Rupraka, around 400 Meos martyred on the ground.[34]

The Intelligence Department in its reports says that the casualty of the Meo revolutionaries was about 450. It reports about the Rupraka episode as follows:[35]

> "At Roopraka, 3500 of these insurgents received the detachment with a sharp discharge of matchlocks. Our troops reserved their fire till within a hundred yards, then poured into them a destructive volley, and charged with the bayonet. Fifty were killed in the village, and some four hundred by the Cavalry outside."

Gurgaon District Gazetteer, quotes the words of Captain Drummond about the action at Rupraka, saying that it was very important in the way, "not only have the Meos been defeated, their villages and property burnt and destroyed, but the friendly villages, who have hitherto been kept in a state of siege by constant aggression on the part of their enemies, are relieved."[36]

After their victory over the revolutionaries at Rupraka, the British burnt the other villages of Mewat such as Shikrawa, Khilluka, Ghasera, Pinangwa, Nai, Singer, Nagina, etc. It is said that Captain Drummond returned to Delhi considering the Mewat cleansed from the revolutionaries.

K.C.Yadav quotes the words of Brandieth, the Officiating Commissioner of Delhi about the British savagery and cruelty shown at Rupraka and adjoining villages:[37]

> "The signal punishment inflicted upon the enemy by the burning of their villages, the destruction of their stacks and loss of 400 of their number slain in the engagement at Rupraka well, I have no doubt, be productive of the best effect as well in showing the Meos the folly of resistance to the British Government."

Captain Ramsay and Mr. Macpherson

The Mewati subjugation by the forces of Captain Drummond at different areas of Mewat did not last long and after a little time span the Mewati revolutionaries again began to re-organise under a Meo leader Sadruddin. On 27th November 1857, Mewati revolutionaries under Sadruddin attacked the Pinangwan town. The British responded quickly, and a military contingent (Gurkha Regiment) from Palwal and Gurgaon was immediately dispatched under Captain Ramsay with assistance of Joint Magistrate of Gurgaon Mr. Macpherson.[38]

The British column under Captain Ramsay and Mr. Macpherson reached Pinangwan on 29th November, but they find that the revolutionaries were assembled at a different nearby village Mahun. The British force made for that village next day and reached there at 7 a.m. The revolutionaries were only 70 in the number, but given tough resistance to mighty British army. Until the noon of the 29th November, the revolutionaries didn't lose heart and fought gallantly. At last, the three Gurkha Regiments began bombarding the village from three sides and destroyed the village completely. The Meo revolutionaries were ultimately defeated with the loss of 28 men, including a son of Sadruddin. British forces killed another 42 men in the neighboring villages.[39]

The Mirasis of Mewat still sung the heroic story of the revolutionaries of the village Mahun. One of its couplets is as follows:

"Mero Mahu Tigaon, Jahaan Ka Veer Ladaka,

Kat Diyo Angrez Likhaga Naam Sada Ka"

(I belong to Mahun and Tigaon where the brave people had cut the British into pieces and got written their names in history as warriors.)

After the defeat, the revolutionary leader Sadruddin along with his loyalists fled towards Rajasthan by crossing the mountain Arawali. Sadruddin was never heard afterwards. Macpherson, the Joint Magistrate of Gurgaon, who was the chief actor in the action at Mahun, observed: "Altogether I look upon it as a most successful affair, I should say about 70 rebels killed...... The whole number of the rebels assembled was so small that their resistance was to me a subject of the greatest surprise."[40]

After the victory at Mahun, the British force went towards Firozpur Jhirka. The British force showed its extreme brutality by burning the village falling in the way. The villages of Shahpur, Kherla, Chitora, Niharika, Bai Khera, Kala Khera, Goojar Nagla, Bahri Pur, Kheri, etc., were set on fire and wiped out of existence. After some time, many more villages in the neighbourhood of Pinangwan met the same fate for assisting the revolutionary leader Sadaruddin and refusing to pay revenue to the British Government.[41]

The Nuh town in Mewat region was another centre of the revolutionaries, where they had got hold after defeating the Khanzadas, the British sympathizers. While returning the British column under Mr. Macpherson[42] from Firozpur Jhirka, they were attacked by the Mewati revolutionaries at Nuh. It is said that Chaudhary Nahar Khan was leading the Mewati revolutionaries of Nuh, Adbar and Shahpur Nagli. In a sudden attack, the Mewati revolutionaries under Nahar Khan defeated and killed Mr. Macpherson. A lot of Khanzadas, who were fighting for the British, were also killed. In retaliation, another column of the British forces attacked the revolutionaries at Nuh town and defeated them in which Chaudhary Nahar Khan was killed.[43]

The British forces combed and arrested a lot of the revolutionaries. On the instructions of Khairullah Khanzada, 52 Meos from Nuh and nearby villages were arrested and hanged. It is said that when the Meos were being hanged, Meda Khan of Meoli village requested the British to stop the hanging of the Meos. Out of 52 Meos, who were hanged, four were from Adbar, 12 from Shahpur Nagli and 36 were from Nuh town. A penalty of Rs. 3500 realised from the suspected revolutionaries. Chaudhary Ujagar Khan, Shahamat Khan, Wazir Khan, Jawahar Khan, Dhan Singh, Dhannu, etc. were the martyrs from Nuh.[44]

After setting law and order at Nuh, the British advanced towards Firozpur Jhirka, where Saadat Khan was leading the revolutionaries. He was finally killed in a battle at Doha along with a lot of Mewati revolutionaries. The British started retribution at Firozpur Jhirka and other nearby villages. In the series of retributions, the British hanged 42 Meos at Firozpur Jhirka and 18 at Gahlab.[45]

At the end of November 1857, the British Government became successful to suppress the Rebellion in Mewat region and finally in 1858 in most parts of the country. However, more chagrin to the East India Company, by the declaration of Royal Proclamation in 1858, the India's administration was taken over directly by the British Crown, abolishing the Company's rule. The Government realised the extent of people's resentment and re-examined their policy towards India. Therefore, they adopted a strategy to check the future incidents of such a revolt. Special awards were given to the loyalists who were helpful for the British during the Rebellion, but a very harsh policy was adopted against revolutionaries and other suspects. However, the most important policy adopted by the British was the policy of 'divide and rule' by tactfully utilizing caste, religious and regional identities of Indian people.

Gurgaon District Gazetteer by quoting the Governments documents mentions that in the series of retribution, the landed property of several of the villagers, chaudharis and lambardars, was confiscated in accordance with the Acts XXV of 1857 and 1858 for their rebellious acts and failure to extend any help to the British at the time of sore need. The villagers of Jharsa, Kheri, Jalalpur, and Davela in the Jharsa pargana and Shikrawa and Ghaghas Kheri in the pargana of Nuh, suffered confiscation of the entire landed property of theirs. Baktawar Singh of Jharsa and Udampur, Ilahi Baksh of Badshahpur and Dhanuspur, Mir Khan of Naurangpur and Abu of Bhora and Binola in the Jharsa pargana, Brija Nand of Shahjahanpur, Ramjas and Hamza Ali of Chhajunagar, Jaffar, Narkhan, and Ghariba of Rasulpur in the pargana of Palwal got their shares of landed property confiscated.[46]

Haryana State Gazetteer reports that about 235 persons were hanged, and many more got long term imprisonments for taking part in the Rebellion. Heavy fines were imposed on the individuals and rebel villages. The confiscated landed properties of the revolutionaries were awarded to the loyalist, who assisted the British forces in their fighting in Mewat region.[47]

Following persons were awarded in cash and kind due to their help for the British during the Rebellion of 1857:[48]

Hayat Khan s/o Bakshullah of Salaheri village; Mansukh s/o Dhan Singh of Hathin; Nasrullah Khan of Firozpur Jhirka; Ashraf Khan; lala Kishori Lal; Karim Khan Dafadar; Punda Khan Chaukidar; Mehrab Khan Meo, the Peon; Mohan Singh Sawar; and Ramdhan Jamadar.

The persons are also listed below who faced the heavy hand of the British by severe punishment, confiscation of the property and even death sentence for their help to the revolutionaries:[49]

Mahtab Lambardar of Shajahanpur, Palwal; Brijnandan Lambardar of Khajurnagar, Palwal; Ramjas Lambardar of Khajurnagar, Palwal; Hamza Ali Lambardar of Rasulpur; and Jaafar Husain Lambardar of Rasulpur were allied to the revolutionaries whose landed property was confiscated. Apart from them, there were many persons, whose involvement in the Rebellion was considered more active, were given death sentence in addition with the confiscation of their property. They were Ghareeba Tilanga of Ghagas, whose name is mentioned in Appendix IV, Shaikh Saadul of Palwal; Dunde Khan of Jhajjar; Ilahi baksh Kalla of Nuh; Wahid Khan of Gurgani, Jhajjar; Ameen Khan of of Gurgani, Jhajjar; Ameen Khan (Second) of Gurgani, Jhajjar; Wajid Khan of Fullar, Jhajjar; Fazle Khan of Komondh, Godali; Fazle Khan (Second) of Buana, Komondh; Dhangal Khan of Buana, Komondh; and Shahbaz Khan of Buana, Komondh. Burhan Khan of Fullar, Jhajjar was sentenced ten years imprisonment while Yaqub Ali of Jhajjar was given the punishment of life imprisonment.

The Mirasies and intellectuals of Mewat region gives the data that from the beginning of the Rebellion to its end at Mewat on 29th of November 1857, about 3600 Meo revolutionaries were killed while fighting against the British forces. A large number of the Meo revolutionaries, around 102 were also captured and sent to Delhi, where they were tried and hanged. It was the worst example in the history that the so-called most civilized community of the world had committed such a worst type of retribution, which has no parallels in the freedom struggle of India.

Famine of 1860-61

After a short period of about three years to the Rebellion of 1857, the region of south-east Punjab, including the districts of Ambala, Thanesar, Delhi, Hisar, Sirsa, Panipat and Gurgaon, was badly affected by the famine of 1860-61. Mewat was also one of the regions of Gurgaon district, which was severely affected by a famine during the years 1860-61. This famine gave a death blow to the people of Mewat after the curse of retribution by the British after 1857. This famine was due to the failure of rains. The rains of 1859-60 were poor and in 1860-61 the rain failed almost entirely so that many jhils of the region were dried. This famine was popularly known as *Sattaraha* famine (Samvat 1917 or1860-61AD), which was harsher than the *Chalisa* famine (Samvad 1840 or 1782-83AD).[50]

As Powlett mentions, the year and name of the following famines as given below:[51]

Sr. No.	Year in Samvat Calendar	Year in Gregorian Calendar	Description of the Famine
1.	1810	1753-54	Dasotia
2.	1840	1783-88	Chalisa
3.	1860	1803-4	Satha
4.	1869	1812-13	Unhattara
5.	1874	1817-18	Chauhattara
6.	1890	1833-34	Nawra
7.	1894	1837-38	Chaurtanwara
8.	1910	1853-54	Dasma
9.	1917	1860-61	Sattaraha
10.	1925	1868-69	Pachisra

Thousands of people were dead by the gradual starvation in the scarcity of food during the famine of 1860-61. Besides that the other causes of deaths were also on account of subsequent diseases, malnutrition and consumption of unwholesome herbs, vegetables and fruits. In the famine years, the people were depended for food on the berries of *Kair* bushes and *Jal* trees. The people lived largely on these fruits for weeks.[52]

Undoubtedly, the main reason of the famine was the failure of rains, but a number of factors contributed towards the occurrence of the famine. Failure of the Rebellion was considered by the people as one of the most important causes. The others were the persistent of low prices of agriculture produce since 1849 and even before, the changed mode of payment of land revenue and its consequences. Besides, the land revenue demand, however, was lowered but made fixed and regular. The considerable fall of the prices of agricultural produce also added another reason of the famine. This cheapness of the products rendered it difficult for the agriculturists to obtain cash for their produce when they required it for paying their new assessments. The situation became extremely grave and zamindars were ultimately forced to borrow money from the moneylenders to be able to meet revenue demands.[53]

Mr. Wilson reported to the famine commission that the Meos owned some 850 villages in the two southernmost tahsils of Nuh and Firozpur. Without the excuse of a barren soil or excessive revenue, they live so closely up to their income, are so negligent in developing the resources of their land, and indulge so in unwarranted expenditure, that the failure of one harvest plunges them irretrievably into debt. Last year's scarcity found many of them still burdened with debt contracted in the famines of 1860-61 and 1868-69, and has left them with 17 per cent of their land heavily mortgaged, and much floating debt hanging over them besides. Wilson also complained for their growth of population and extravagance in their marriages, births and deaths.[54]

In almost all of his statements, Mr. Wilsom has tried to prove that the Meos themselves were responsible for their misery and suffering during the famine. Nevertheless, the reality was somewhat else for which neither the people, nor the Government was responsible. Certainly, the Government could have saved the life of thousands of people, who suffered the death, by their relief measures. However, unfortunately, no action was taken by the Government for gratuitous relief for the people of Mewat. This caused severity of the famine and subsequently thousands of deaths of the Mewat region. The following saying reminds the sufferings and deaths, when the intensity of famines was felt greater:[55]

"Parte Kal Jullahe Mare, Aur Beech Mey Mare Teli,

Utarte Kal Baniya Mare, Rupiye Ki Rah Gai Dheli,

Chana Chirongi Ho Gaya, Aur Gehun Ho Gae Dakh,

Sattrah Bhi Aisa Para Chalisa Ka Bap"

(In the beginning of the famine died weavers, in the middle the Oilmen, at the end the traders. A rupee reduced to a few pices, gram was sold at the price of pista -nuts, and wheat at the price of raisin. The famine of seventeen was more severe even to that of forty.)

References

1. *People's Democracy*, Vol. XXXI, No. 21, May 27, 2007.
2. *Records of the Intelligence Department*, Vol. II, Edinburgh, 1902, p. 295, see also Husain, Iqbal, *1857 Ke Swatantra Sangram Me Mewatiyon Ka Balidan*,(Unpublished) AMU Aligarh, p. 94.
3. *Ibid.*
4. *Haryana District Gazetteers, Faridabad*, Chandigarh, 1993, p. 52, see also *Gurgaon District Gazetteer*, Chandigarh, 1983, p. 62.
5. Hodson, William Stephen Raikes, *Twelve Years of a Soldiers Life in India: Being Extracts from the Letters of the Late Major W. S. R. Hodson*, (edited by George H. Hodson), Boston, 1860, pp. 369-375, (hereafter cited as Hodson), see also *The Role of Punjab Haryana and Himachal Pradesh*, p. 174 (K.C. Yadav while favouring the movement of Tula Ram quotes the words of the *Illustrated London News* that a fight with the British forces in the mud-fort of Rampura, in the changed circumstances after the fall of Delhi, would have resulted in complete destruction of his army without any serious loss to the British. So he left his mud fort in a hurry, a few moments before Shower's arrival. *The Role of Punjab Haryana and Himachal Pradesh*, p. 175).
6. *Ibid*, p. 366.
7. *Ibid*, pp. 368-369.
8. *The Role of Punjab Haryana and Himachal Pradesh*, p. 176.
9. Hodson, p. 375.
10. *Gurgaon District Gazetteer*, Chandigarh, 1983, p. 62, see also *The Meos of Mewat*, p. 28, *Haryana State Gazetteer*, Volume I, Chandigarh, 2001, p. 288, and *Meo Qaum Aur Mewat*, p. 140, (In an inscription of a memorial at Delhi it has been inscribed that, "Sacred to the memory of M.J.A. Clifford, daughter of Captain R.M. Clifford, Carn Cottage, County Cavan, aged 24 years who was cruelly murdered on the 11th May 1857 in the palace of Delhie when on a visit at the Revd. J. Jennings also to the memory of Wigram Clifford brother of the above, Bengal Civil Service, aged 23 years who after having shared in all the dangers of the siege of Delhie fell in an attack on the outpost of the Mewatties near the village of Alipoor in the Goorgaon district on the 31st October 1857.").
11. Ball, Charles, *History of the Indian Mutiny*, Vol. II, London, 1863, p. 59, see also *Gurgaon District Gazetteer*, Chandigarh, 1983, p. 63. See also *Meo Qaum Aur Mewat*, pp. 141-142.

12. *Gurgaon District Gazetteer*, Chandigarh, 1983, p. 62, (Showers subjugation and massacre of the Meos was due to the impact of martial background of the Mewatis on his mind. Perhaps he was aware of the local proverb, "*Meo Mara Tab Jaaniyo, Jab Teeja Ho Jaaye*", (A Meos should be considered as dead when the third day ceremony of his death had been completed.) The complete destruction of the Meo revolutionaries was the only way to save his life and the lives of his force.)
13. *Records of the Intelligence Department*, Vol. I, Edinburgh, 1902, p. 243.
14. *Ibid*, see also *Haryana State Gazetteer*, Volume I, Chandigarh, 2001, p. 289.
15. *Ibid*, p. 244.
16. *Ibid*, p. 243, see also *Haryana State Gazetteer*, Volume I, Chandigarh, 2001, p. 288, and *Tahrik-e-Azadi Aur Mewat*, pp. 20-21.
17. *Haryana State Gazetteer*, Volume I, Chandigarh, 2001, p. 289, see also *Meo Qaum Aur Mewat*, p. 141.
18. *History of the Bengal European Regiment*, p. 496.
19. *1857 Aur Haryána*, p. 142, see also *Tarikh-e-Meo Kshatriya*, p. 460.
20. *Gurgaon District Gazetteer*, Chandigarh, 1983, p. 62, see also *Haryana State Gazetteer*, Volume I, Chandigarh, 2001, pp. 288-289, *Tahrik-e-Azadi Aur Mewat*, pp. 21-22, *Tarikh-e-Meo Kshatriya*, p. 460, *Meo Darpan*, August, 1997, p. 18, and *Haryana District Gazetteers, Faridabad*, Chandigarh, 1993, p. 53.
21. Malleson, G. B., *The Indian Mutiny of 1857*, New York, 1891, p. 319, see also *The Role of Punjab Haryana and Himachal Pradesh*, pp. 177-178.
22. *Against History Against State*, p. 195.
23. *History of the Bengal European Regiment*, p. 496.
24. *1857 Aur Haryana*, p. 144, see also *Against History Against State*, p. 195.
25. *Tahrik-e-Azadi Aur Mewat*, p. 59.
26. *The Role of Punjab Haryana and Himachal Pradesh*, p. 178.
27. Malleson, G. B., *The Indian Mutiny of 1857*, New York, 1891, p. 319, see also *Followers of Krishna*, p. 60.
28. Rice Holmes, T., *A History of the Indian Mutiny and of the Disturbances which Accompanied it among the Civil Population*, New York, 1898, pp. 396-397, see also *Followers of Krishna*, p. 60.
29. *Followers of Krishna*, p. 60.

30. Malleson, G. B., *The Indian Mutiny of 1857*, New York, 1891, pp. 319-320, see also Rice Holmes, T., *A History of the Indian Mutiny and of the Disturbances which Accompanied it among the Civil Population*, New York, 1898, pp. 396-397.
31. *Followers of Krishna*, pp. 61-62, see also *The Role of Punjab Haryana and Himachal Pradesh*, pp. 182-183.
32. *Haryana District Gazetteers, Faridabad*, Chandigarh, 1993, p. 53, see also *Gurgaon District Gazetteer*, Chandigarh, 1983, p. 63, *Haryana State Gazetteer*, Volume I, Chandigarh, 2001, p. 289, and *Tarikh-e-Meo Kshatriya*, pp. 463-465 (quoted from the letter of Captain Drummond to the Commissioner Mr. Ford Smith).
33. *Gurgaon District Gazetteer*, Chandigarh, 1983, p. 63.
34. *Haryana State Gazetteer*, Volume I, Chandigarh, 2001, pp. 289-90.
35. *Records of the Intelligence Department*, Vol. II, Edinburgh, 1902, p. 220, see also *Records of the Intelligence Department*, Vol. I, Edinburgh, 1902, p. 283.
36. *Gurgaon District Gazetteer*, Chandigarh, 1983, p. 64, see also *Haryana State Gazetteer*, Volume I, Chandigarh, 2001, p. 290.
37. *The Role of Punjab Haryana and Himachal Pradesh*, p. 183.
38. *Gurgaon District Gazetteer*, Chandigarh, 1983, p. 64, see also *Haryana District Gazetteers, Faridabad*, Chandigarh, 1993, p. 53, and *Haryana State Gazetteer*, Volume I, Chandigarh, 2001, p. 290.
39. *Gurgaon District Gazetteer*, Chandigarh, 1983, p. 64, see also *Haryana District Gazetteers, Faridabad*, Chandigarh, 1993, p. 53, and *Haryana State Gazetteer*, Volume I, Chandigarh, 2001, p. 290.
40. *1857 Aur Haryana*, p. 146, see also *Haryana State Gazetteer*, Volume I, Chandigarh, 2001, p. 290.
41. *Gurgaon District Gazetteer*, Chandigarh, 1983, pp. 64-65, see also *Haryana State Gazetteer*, Volume I, Chandigarh, 2001, p. 290.
42. The Englishman who was killed at Nuh by the revolutionaries under Nahar Khan was not Mr. Macpherson, the Joint Magistrate of Gurgaon district. Macpherson was alive in 1858 and his reports of 1858 about the Rebellion are available in the Delhi Division Records, Haryana State Archives Panchkula. It is also being told that the name of the Englishman who was killed at Nuh was Captain Nixon. However, Captain Nixon was the Political Agent of Bharatpur State and he never came at Nuh, and moreover, he was alive following the years of the Rebellion. Some Scholars also says that the name of the same Englishman was Mixon. Nevertheless, the author is frustrated

to say that there was no Englishman of such a name who had participated in the suppression of the Rebellion.

43. *Tarikh-e-Meo Kshatriya*, p. 462, see also *Tahrik-e-Azadi Aur Mewat*, p. 81.
44. *Ibid*, see also *Tahrik-e-Azadi Aur Mewat*, p. 132.
45. *Tahrik-e-Azadi Aur Mewat*, pp. 23, 81.
46. *Gurgaon District Gazetteer*, Chandigarh, 1983, p. 65, see also *Haryana State Gazetteer*, Volume I, Chandigarh, 2001, pp. 290-291.
47. *Haryana State Gazetteer*, Volume I, Chandigarh, 2001, p. 291.
48. *File No. 8, and R/168*, Deputy Commissioners office, Gurgaon.
49. *File No. 1, R/193, R/143, R/184, R/143*, and *R/194*, Deputy Commissioner's Office, Gurgaon.
50. *Haryana State Gazetteer*, Volume II, Chandigarh, 2005, p. 10.
51. Powlett, p. 99.
52. *Haryana State Gazetteer*, Volume II, Chandigarh, 2005, p. 10.
53. *Shodh Samiksha Aur Mulyankan*, International Referred Research Journal, Jaipur, July, 2011 Vol. III, Issue- 30.
54. Channing, p. 40.
55. *Haryana State Gazetteer*, Volume II, Chandigarh, 2005, p. 10.

7
Conclusions

In the above narrative of the role of Meos and other Mewatis in the Rebellion of 1857, I have endeavoured to honestly give an account of their chivalry, courage, patriotism and fights against the British. Every single event of that period has been covered with full details. Their sacrifices of lives and property also have been given the proper place. The Mewati participation in the Rebellion of different states beyond Mewat has also been described in short. Even the drawbacks of the Mewati revolutionaries also have been analysed with intense care.

The Rebellion 1857 is one of the most momentous events in the history of modern India. Due to multi-dimensional aspects and nature of the events, it remains the most written history in India. The participation of the Mewati people in the Rebellion is one of the viewpoints, which has been deeply researched in this book. I have discussed almost all the issues related to the Mewati Rebellion in Mewat region and other parts of north and central India. Through different chapters, I have tried to prove that how the British East India Company during its rule of about half-century in north India, had threatened the religion, changed the political system and ruined the socio-economic setup of almost all classes of Indian society, including the Mewatis.

As the region of Mewat was mostly rural, the Rebellion of 1857 was mainly confined to the peasants and Sepoys at the village level. Nevertheless, the events mostly were undocumented and unrecorded. The events at the town and city level were, to some extent, recorded by the British officers in their memoirs. It provided the researchers an ample space to search for the local Mewati heroes of this revolt and posit them alongside mainstream nationalist heroes. Moreover, in this work the peasantry as a whole has been focused especially the Meos or Mewati peasantry of Mewat and various parts of north and central India. Their role in the Rebellion has been highlighted by giving the examples of their various grievances and fights against the British.

There are a lot of analysis, research and writings about the events, nature, causes and consequences of the Rebellion of 1857, as one of the most significant events of the history of India. The historians of various thoughts of historiography have drawn conclusions from diverse perspectives of the Rebellion. Its significance also been widely discussed as for the first time, it brought together the people having different ethnic, religious and class in a unified movement against the British rule. Much stress has been given to the perspective of the peasantry uprising. However, the debates still not finished and continued for the researchers that whether the Rebellion should be called merely a mutiny or military insurrection, war of religion, first war of independence or its leanings towards the mobilization of peasantry.

Although the people of Mewat were having the grievances of their own as their social setup was different to those other people of India. Like the other people of India, the Mewatis were also having a lot of grievances from the British rule. These grievances were the chief causes of their participation in the Rebellion of 1857. As the Mewatis were basically the agrarian community, their first and foremost cause was the change of agrarian setup due to British occupancy of the Mewat region.

There were a lot of causes for the Mewati insurrection, including feelings of insecurity of the Indian masses, destruction of the village communities, the economic policies of exploitation, the work of the Christian Missionaries. The frequent famines and recurring epidemics made the position of the people more miserable and the masses suspect the policies of the British administration. Under such a strained condition, the needed spark was supplied by the Sepoys of the Meerut cantonment. The people mobilized themselves against the British Government which burst out in the year of 1857.

The causes of the Mewati insurrection were multi faceted; the most important of them was the land revenue policy of the British Government. The agrarian Mewati community suffered a lot due to the land revenue settlements of the British Government. A number of land revenue experiments were made, which caused sufferings to cultivators in Mewat region. The British Government by introducing changes in the land revenue system and in the administrative structure made its rule unacceptable to the majority of the local Mewati population. The new revenue policy was basically aimed at increasing the Government's revenue earnings and consequently reducing landed farmers into the tenants. Money lending and auction of property further added to the hardship of the peasantry. It gave the direct benefit to the money lenders who were the close alies of the British Government.

Certainly, there was laxity in the tax collection during the hardships, the local administration, however, failed to provide relief and natural justice to people of the rural Mewat. Consequently, millions of peasants, artisans and soldiers fought heroically for over a year and by their exemplary courage wrote a glorious chapter on the history of Indian people. After reading the text it becomes clear that how the peasantry and tribal people suffered under the colonial administration and why they resorted to revolts.

The glorious history of Mewati community witnesses their freedom-loving habits and martial background, which was another cause of Mewati Rebellion. The Mewatis were in full passion for their bravery and their love of warfare. They played most important role in the history right from the establishment of the Muslim rule in Delhi and subsequently, the domination of the British. It is well known that their animosity with the rulers of Delhi was due to the land revenue dispute. Due to the failure of crops and low yielding agricultural lands, the Mewatis were unable to regularly pay the revenue to the Delhi rulers. Consequently, the Delhi rulers more frequently invaded the Mewat region and indirectly trained the Mewatis as better fighters. The Mewatis never made any compromise on the cost of their independence. After hundreds of years, the Rebellion provided them a chance to show their chivalry and martial art against the British.

The annexation of Firozpur Jhirka was another cause of unrest to the Mewati people. The Meo community was naturally very loyal to their motherland Mewat and its rulers. A little bit humiliation was never tolerable to the Meos, on any conditions. In this connection, the humiliation, dethronement and execution of Nawab Shamsuddin Khan of Firozpur Jhirka and its annexation to the British territory was foremost. This infamous and humiliating episode added more fuel on the burning episode of heavy taxation policy of the British Government in Mewat.

The British interference in the famous Mewati village communities was another cause, which goaded the Meo population to rise against the British. It was the long established tradition of the Mewati people to settle their disputes through their panchayat system. Nevertheless, after assuming the power in this region, the British introduced a new machinery to run the administration. However, process of their so-called improvements directly or indirectly disturbed the social set-up of the Mewatis. The village community system in Mewat was a small republic governed by the panchayats. The British interference into their system deeply hearted their feelings and they were alarmed of the destruction of their age-old customs and traditions and more especially the social setup.

All these changes dealt a serious blow to the rural society, particularly the cultivators and tribes of Mewat region. For the peasant, the new changes in agrarian economy and social structure meant more intensive and systematic exploitation. The people did not find the British system to their taste and always regarded the British as no better than usurper and plunderer. The British system of administration greatly affected the martial races of that tract such as Meos, Goojars, Ahirs, Jats and Ranghars, who lost no chance in resisting the British whenever and wherever they could. During the Rebellion of 1857, these Mewatis rose unanimously against the British in order to save their social set-up, honour and dignity.

In Mewat region the religious factor also did a lot in raising the Mewati people against the British. The Muslim Ulema did a great job in this regard. They adopted the Wahabi ideology and mobilized the people to fight against the British. They thought that the introduction of English medium of instruction in the schools, changing of court language, propagation of Christianity, were the direct attacks on their religion. The introduction of the cartridges greased in the fat of cow and swine played the role of fuel in the fire. The people rushed to fight against the British on the call of the Ulema. During the Frontier war, the Maulvi class of the Mewati society was in constant touch with the other Maulvi *Mujahideen* of the Frontier region, who was constantly fighting against the British. When the Rebellion started at Delhi, the revolutionaries from Frontier areas arrived at Delhi to fight for the nation. Most of them were having close connection from the region of Mewat. After the suppression of the Rebellion at Delhi, they came to Mewat and fought against the British in different areas of Mewat. Among these *Mujahideen*, Maulvi Noor Ali, Maulvi Mohammad Mureed, Maulvi Abul Hasan Afghani, Huzoor of Kheti, Dr. Nazar Mohammad of Badshahpur, etc. were in fore.

Destruction of cottage industries in Mewat region was another cause of Mewati rebellion. Following their policy of all India de-industrialisation, the British also adopted the same in Mewat region. Due to the Industrial Revolution in England, there was a heavy demand of the raw materials from India and market for their finished products. The de-industrialisation policy of the British Government closely affected the petty industries of Mewat region. The import of Europeans clothes and objects to India rendered traditional artisan communities like weavers, carpenters, ironsmiths, shoe smiths and so on, jobless and without any alternative sources of income except begging. Thus, most of them actively joined in the Rebellion against the British as a protest against this social and economic injustice. During the Rebellion, they find a fair opportunity to avenge the oppressor by murder, loot and plunder.

The unrest of Meo Sepoys serving under British and native princely states was also one of the reasons of Mewati unrest. The British Government recruited native volunteers in large numbers because of the vast British territory in north India, large resources of manpower that various Indian populations offered, and as the native soldiers were less expensive, better disciplined, and healthier than their European counterparts. The Mewati youths were not only employed in the Bengal army, but in the Contingents of the principalities such as Gwalior and Kota Contingent, as well as the native governments of Alwar, Bharatpur, Gwalior, Dhaulpur, Rewari, Ballabhgarh, Jhajjar etc. They proved themselves a better fighter for their employer.

The introduction of the new Enfield Rifles and rumor of the cartridges greased in swine and cow fats, surely would have affected the Mewati Sepoys like the other Sepoys serving under the British Government. It is said that the rural panchayats issued the decree that the Sepoys using the greased cartridges would be treated as outcastes and expelled from all communion. The instances of such decrees were firstly noticed at Ambala. It was more probable that the Mewati panchayats would have also issued such decrees. Besides that the Sepoys were unhappy for low pay and racial discrimination in matters of promotion, pension and terms of service. As far as Mewat region is concerned, most of the soldiers who were basically hailing from the peasant families were also unhappy with the new land revenue settlements introduced by the British Government.

The Sepoy mutiny started from Meerut and Ambala in May 1857, immediately gained the position of national war in Delhi and subsequently in the other areas of north India. It also proved catalyst in laying open the crisis of the old feudal order whose rulers made a last attempt to defend their lost power and authority. The Rebellion gained support of the landed class, including peasantry and working class in bulk due to the contradictions within the rural society of the first half of the nineteenth century. Unfortunately, the revolutionaries did not have a future plan beyond the restoration of the old order. Nevertheless, in spite of their limited objective and narrow vision, the revolutionaries definitely exposed the unpopular character of the British rule.

The worst of all for the British, that the fire of Rebellion soon cached the neighbouring area of Mewat immediately after the Gurgaon victory by the revolutionaries. The whole month of May in Mewat was full of burning episodes such as setting free to the villages of Mewat from British tyranny; regular attack on the towns of Mewat where local police and some loyalists were giving tough fights. Interestingly, the Mewat region, where there was no ruling family, the Meos and other Mewati farmers and peasants came out in the open revolt against the British.

In spite of the least process of mobilisation in Mewat, most of the population joined the war against the British. The Mewat region totally fell into the hands of the Mewati revolutionaries, including the important towns and villages such as Nuh, Tauru, Sohna, Firozpur Jhirka, Punhana, Pinangwan, Hathin, Nagina, Rupraka, Ghasera, Mahu, Tigaon, Raiseena, Doha and Raoli, including Hodal Kosi, Mathura, Kaman Dhausa, Deeg, Bharatpur, Alwar, etc. These areas were controlled by the chaudharies of their respective villages through the age-old panchayat system. They accepted subordination of the Mughal Emperor Bahadur Shah Zafar and paid homage by sending the revenue collected by them.

The most important leaders, who led the revolutionaries of Mewat, were Sharfuddin Mewati, Saadat Khan, Sadruddin, Chaudhary Firoz Shah Mewati, Ali Hasan Khan Mewati, Maulana Mehrab Khan Mewati, etc. They were all experienced leaders, fought bravely and toured the village after village to encourage the Mewatis to fight against the British. They not only fought in Mewat region but sent a column of about 400 revolutionaries under Alif Khan Mewati to fight in Delhi for the Emperor.

The Meos beyond Mewat region were simply called as Mewatis and were also having the same martial spirit and love for independence. There was not a single example which witnesses the non-participation of Mewati in all over north and central India. If there was a Mewati, definitely he was a revolutionary. The hard nut Mewatis whether they were the civilian, military men or religious cleric, they fought against the British and sacrificed their lives and property. By the thorough study of the Rebellion, it surely can be concluded that the term Mewati was a source of inspiration to the other revolutionaries and for the British this was a phobic term.

In Madhya Pradesh, the Mewatis rebelled in the areas of Satwas, Jaoras, Mandsaur, Dhar, Indore, Gwalior, etc. In Uttar

Pradesh, the Mewatis were active in Mainpuri, Aligarh, Pilibhit, Farrukhabad, Hathras, Shikohabad, Fatehpur Sikri, Etawa, Mathura, Hodal, Kosi, Allahabad, Muzaffarnagar, Kanpur, etc. In Rajasthan, the Mewatis fought against the British from the regions of Alwar, Bharatpur, Dhaulpur, etc. In Haryana, the Mewatis, apart from the Mewat region including Gurgaon, fought in the areas of Hisar, Mahendergarh, Narnaul, Jhajjar, Rewari, Farrukhnagar, Ballabhgarh, etc.

A setback to the Mewati struggle during the Rebellion also has been discussed with proper care. Being a martial community, the Meos or Mewatis could not control themselves to fight against each other even during the crucial phase of the Rebellion. The Meos, Jats, Goojars Ahirs, Khanzadas and Rajputs tried to settle their age-old disputes in the absence of proper law and order. The instances of the fights between Meos against Meos and Jats against Jats surely show the lawlessness of these communities. Sometimes it took the communal turn, and surely it was a deviation from their right path for which they had been beholden the arms. It was definitely a setback to the national struggle of a freedom loving community which sacrificed their lives, property and even power since centuries.

When the Mewatis were enjoying the changed and independent atmosphere, a British force under Major Eden with the assistance of William Ford tried to quell the Rebellion. They jointly inflicted the unimagined heinous cruelties, which was undoubtedly a blot for such a so-called civilized community. Nevertheless, they could not become successful and eventually fled towards Delhi. When the revolutionaries at Delhi were defeated and the historic city was re-occupied by them, the British turned their attention towards other areas. The British Government after establishing their full control over Delhi, turned its attention towards the neighbouring region of Mewat, which was still independent. They sent military columns against the Mewati revolutionaries which were most harsh, deadly, barbaric and inhuman for the Mewatis.

A force under Brigadier General Showers with assistance of Wigram Clifford, the Assistant Collector (ADC) of Gurgaon, arrived in Mewat to punish the turbulent Meos, Goojars, Ranghars and Ahirs and the rebel princes. Showers seized the Nawabs of Jhajjar, Dadri, Farrukhnagar and the Raja of Ballabhgarh, dispersed their troops and took their forts. In Mewat, they burnt villages after village, destroyed the country side and put to death all those who came across and did not spare even women and children. However, Mewat proved tough for them as the firebrand Wigram Clifford was killed in a battle at Raissena near Alipur hills.

Another column under Ltieutenant H. Grant and Ltieutenant Rongton was sent to Mewat from Delhi. They carried the fire and sword against the turbulent Mewati revolutionaries. In order to subdue them, they burnt the villages which were found en route. They attacked upon the Ghasera village which was the centre of the revolutionaries, where they were assembled in a large number under the leadership of Ali Hasan Khan Mewati. A bloody and fierce battle took place in the village but due to the well-equipped and trained British forces, the revolutionaries lost the ground. After their victory, the British force looted and burnt the villages of Barka, Rewasan and Ghasera.

The next British force under Colonel John Grant Gerrard arrived in Mewat and moved Narnaul via Rewari and Kanaud. At Narnaul, all the revolutionaries were arrayed under their respective leaders such as General Samad Khan, Rao Tula Ram, his cousin Rao Kishan Gopal, his son Ram Lal, Munshi Nizamuddin, Kunwar Fateh Khan, etc. The overall command was under Rao Tula Ram. A fierce battle took place at Narnaul and the nearby village Nasibpur, where the revolutionaries lost the ground, but they killed the British commander Colonel John Grant Gerrard along with many others.

The next column which rushed in Mewat was under Captain Drummond. He along with a large army proceeded towards Rupraka, which was the centre of the revolutionaries at that time. He burnt the villages like Pachanka, Gohpur, Malpuri, Chilli, Utawar, Kot, Mughla, Mithaka, Khilluka, Guraksar, Maluka, Jhanda, etc. in the way. He met a huge gathering 3500 revolutionaries under a Meo leader Sadruddin at Rupraka. It was certainly the largest gathering which the British forces met until now. The Meo revolutionaries fought heroically, but unfortunately lost the battle due to the superior artillery of the British forces. In this battle of Rupraka, around 400 Meos were martyred on the ground.

Another British force which moved towards Mewat was under Captain Ramsay in assistance of Mr. Macpherson, the Joint Magistrate of district Gurgaon. This time the Mewatis again assembled at the village Mahun under the same Rupraka hero Sadruddin. The revolutionaries were only 70 in the number, but given tough resistance to mighty British army. The Meo revolutionaries were ultimately defeated with the loss of 28 men, including a son of Sadruddin. British forces killed another 42 men in the neighboring villages.

After the victory at Mahun, the British force went towards Firozpur Jhirka. The British force showed its extreme brutality by burning the village falling in the way. The villages of Shahpur, Kherla, Chitora, Niharika, Bai Khera, Kala Khera, Goojar Nagla, Bahri Pur, Kheri, etc., were set on fire and wiped out of existence. After some time, many more villages in the neighbourhood of Pinangwan met the same fate for assisting the revolutionary leader Sadaruddin and refusing to pay revenue to the British Government. It is also said that Mr. Macpherson was killed at Nuh by Nahar Khan while moving towards Delhi. However, the records do not prove the story as Mr. Macpherson was alive in succeeding years of the Rebellion. The British officer, who was killed at Nuh is still not known but the population at Nuh and from the neighbouring villages were brutally crushed. Fifty two Meos were hanged and a penalty of Rs. 3500 realised from the suspected revolutionaries.

After setting law and order at Nuh, the same British force under Captain Ramsay advanced towards Firozpur Jhirka, where Saadat Khan was leading the revolutionaries. He was finally killed in a battle at Doha along with a lot of Mewati revolutionaries. The British started retribution at Firozpur Jhirka and other nearby villages. In the series of retributions, the British hanged 42 Meos at Firozpur Jhirka and 18 at Gahlab.

The Rebellion left a deep imprint in the minds of the common people that was very different from the scanty recorded history of that period. This was a unique history which has witnessed the Mewat region, especially the marginalised peasantry of Meo caste and other Mewati communities. However, these types of retributions are a testimony to the significance of large-scale involvement of the Mewatis during the Rebellion of 1857 in the eyes of the British Government. They killed thousands of Mewati people and destroyed property worth many crores of rupees.

The Mewati people suffered a constant neglect from the British Government due to their active participation in the Rebellion. The negligence exposed in the famine years of 1860-61, which further crushed the Mewats. The British Government could have saved the people by relief measures. However, unfortunately, no action was taken by the British Government for gratuitous relief for the people of Mewat. This caused severity of the famine and subsequently thousands of deaths of the Mewat region.

Although the Rebellion did not produce the desired effect of overthrowing the British Government, it shook the very foundations of British Empire in India. Although the Rebellion was brutally suppressed, nevertheless, it led to the beginning of a new era in the history of British India that ended in 1947. Above all, the Mewatis regarded the foreign rule as painful and nefarious and could not be the substitute of the self-rule, no matter how wise or good it claimed. It was always degraded and sometimes forcibly resisted even by the unrecovered loss of men and property.

In spite of the unforgettable efforts of Sir Syed Ahmad Khan, an era of Muslim persecution was also started as the British regarded the Muslims the mainspring of Rebellion. Keeping in view of the previous role of the Muslims, the British started decreasing the Muslims as soldiers and administrators and also began the neglect of modern higher education by the Muslims out of both frustration and hatred on religious and cultural grounds. Being the part of the Muslim community, the Meo also met the same fate of persecution.

After the suppression of the Rebellion to the gaining of final independence, the Mewatis suffered a lot like the other Muslim communities of India. Mewati peasants remained as tenants throughout hundred developing years after the suppression of the Rebellion. More surprisingly after the independence of India the Mewatis still suffer the discriminating policies of the government. Thus, the memory of the Rebellion of 1857 is still being kept alive in the collective psyche of the Meos and other Mewati people which is helping to inspire them in their struggle against the social, economic and political exclusion and discrimination in their daily lives.

After successfully suppressing the Rebellion, the British Crown took over the India's administration and abolished the rule of the East India Company by the declaration of Royal Proclamation in 1858. The British Government adopted the new administrative and military policy. These changes made after the revolts were all intended to prevent such an outbreak in future and peacefully rule over the people of India.

One of their important policies, which the British Government most successfully adopted, was the policy of 'divide and rule' by tactfully utilizing caste, religious and regional identities of Indian people. Although the Rebellion failed, but their heroic struggle against the British Government left a deep impression in people's mind. This impression created a spirit of Indian nationalism in spite of the divide and rule policy of the government. However, the deadliest result of this policy of divide and rule was the division of the country, which was a death blow to the Mewatis who actually divided to never meet again.

Annexure-I

List of the Officers in Gurgaon District[1]

S.No.	Name of the Officers	Date of Taking Charge
1.	Honourable R. Canvendish	April 1819
2.	G. R. Campbell, Esquire	June 1922
3.	Honurable R. Canvendish	29th March, 1824
4.	G. R. Campbell, Esquire	9th October, 1826
5.	J. P. Gubbins, Esquire	17th April, 1828
6.	G. R. Campbell, Esquire	12th October, 1828
7.	J. C. Grant, Esquire	25th May, 1829
8.	G. R. Campbell, Esquire	7th October, 1829
9.	J. C. Grant, Esquire	15th April, 1830
10.	G. R. Campbell, Esquire	21st November, 1830
11.	G.W. Bacon, Esquire	4th March, 1831
12.	W.P. Masson, Esquire	15th April, 1835
13.	G.W. Trisoott, Esquire	June 1835
14.	C. Gubbins, Esquire	9th September, 1835
15.	W.P. Masson, Esquire	24th November, 1836
16.	J.M. Lawrence, Esquire	4th December, 1836
17.	M. R. Gubbins, Esquire	1st December, 1838
18.	C. Gubbins, Esquire	15th February, 1839

19.	C. Le. Bass, Esquire	15th January, 1840
20.	W. De H, Routh, Esquire	27th March, 1840
21.	C. Gubbins, Esquire	17th December, 1840
22.	F.B. Gubbins, Esquire	4th February, 1841
23.	S.G. Smith, Esquire	9th April, 1841
24.	A. Frazer, Esquire	3rd June, 1843
25.	W. Ford, Esquire	For several years up to 1862

References

1. *Punjab Gazetteer, Gurgaon District, 1883-84*, Lahore, 1884, p. 30.

Annexure-II

Tahsils and Parganas of Gurgaon District after 1857 (1861)[1]

Tehsils	Parganas
Gurgaon	Farrukhnagar, Jharsa, Parts of Sohna and Bahora
Rewari	Rewari, Shahjahanpur
Nuh	Nuh, Hathin, Tauru, Parts of Sohna and Bahora
Palwal	Palwal, Hodal, Parts of Sohna
Firozpur Jhirka	Firozpur Jhirka, Punhana

References

1. *Punjab Gazetteer, Gurgaon District, 1883-84*, Lahore, 1884, p. 28.

Annexure-III

Transfer of Villages To and From Gurgaon District after 1857[1]

Villages Transferred from Gurgaon to Delhi in 1863	Villages Transferred to Gurgaon from Rohtak in 1861	Villages Transferred from Delhi to Gurgaon in 1863
Bajri, Pali, Ranhera, Sakrawa, Firozpur, Karnerah, Kheri, Madalpur, Majesar, Naglah, Juan, Jajru, Bahalpur, Aterna, Harphala, Shahpur, Kilgaon, Malaira, Lotai, Sikri, Panehra Kalan, Panehra Khurd, Naraholi, Fatahpur, Biloch, Narela, Hirapur, Mohna, Shajahanpur, Oli, Bijjepur.Pakal, Paota, Tikri Khera, Dhauj, Zakupur, Tarohi, Salokri, Alampur, AIawalpur,Kot, Kharkhara, Khosi Jamalpur, Gotra Mohabbatabad, Mangar, Nurpur, Dhamaspur, Sanpar, Mahola, Mohyapur	Mubarikpur, Sultanpur, Kaliawas, Akbarpur, Jhanjaula, Khalikpur, Khurrampur, Duman, Gharbi Dabola, Alimuddinpur, Palri, Musbaidpur, Jaraun, Shekhpur Majre, Birhera, Karaula, Rajupur, Gugana, Khandsa, Bakainka, Faridpur, Mahchana, Basaunda, Tirpari Juniawas, Fazilpur	Chapraula, Pirthala, Taranpur, Daula, Chandu, Budhera, Makraula

References

1. *Punjab Gazetteer, Gurgaon District, 1883-84*, Lahore, 1884, p. 28.

Annexure-IV

Destruction of life and Property in Mewat Region[1]

Sr. No.	Name of the District	No. of Persons Killed	Villages Burnt/Destroyed/Penalised
1.	Mewat	1091	Total 42: Adbar, Ata Badli, Barka, Barota, Basai Khanzada, Bhanguri, Buraka, Chharora, Chilli Chitora, Doha, Ghasera, Gohpur, Mithaka, Gujar Nagla, Guraksar, Guarka, Jhanda, Khera, Kherla, Khilluka, Khori, Kot, Mahun, Malai, Malaka, Malpuri, Mandikhera, Raoli, Naharika, Nagli, Pachanka, Pachgawan, Pinangwan, Rahpwa, Rewasan, Rupraka, Sahsola, Shahpur Nagli, Tigaon, Utawar
2.	Gurgaon	474	Total 9: Badshahpur, Harchandpur, Hariahera, Kherli, Mohammadpur, Nunera, Raiseena, Sancholi, Sohna
3.	Faridabad	180	Total 21: Ahrwan, Badha, Bahadurpur, Chhajju Nagar, Dhamaka, Gopi Khera, Gudhrana, Gurwari, Hodal Garhi, Khajurka, Khetla, Lulwari, Maheshpur, Marauli, Nangli, Pahladpur, Phulwari, Rasulpur, Sarai, Seoli, Solaka
4.	Rewari	128	—
5.	Mahendragarh (Kanaud)	485	Total 01: Narnaul (Partially destroyed)

References

1. Yadav, K.C., *Roll of Honour: Haryana's Martyrs of 1857*, Gurgaon, 2008, pp. 22, 57-58, 40, 68, 76.

Annexure-V

List of the Revolutionaries Martyred and Accused from Mewat District[1]

Sr. No.	Name of the Village with Details	Name of the Traceable Martyrs	Name of Revolutionaries Accused But went Underground	Caste/ Religion	Punishment
1.	Nuh (Total Martyrs-30, Traceable-3, Went Underground -3)	Azim	———	Meo	Hanged in Feb. 1858
2.	,,	Nudgar	————	,,	,,
3.	,,	Anwar Khan	————	,,	,,
4.	,,	———	Nadir Ali s/o Hyder Ali	,,	'Wanted' Prominent Rebels (WPR)
5.	,,	———	Toye Khan s/o Zabardast Khan	,,	,,
6.	,,	———	Ahmad Baksh s/o Imam Baksh	,,	,,
7.	Adbar (Total Martyrs-8)	Chatru	————	,,	Hanged in Feb. 1858

8.	,,	Usta	———	,,	,,
9.	,,	Samat	———	,,	,,
10.	,,	Surah	———	,,	,,
11.	,,	Jagrup	———	,,	,,
12.	,,	Piru	———	,,	,,
13.	,,	Nehdi	———	,,	,,
14.	,,	Dalel	———	,,	,,
15.	Tauru including Chila, Panchgawan, Jorasi, Sahsola Patti etc. (Total Martyrs-30 Traceable-5)	Firoz Khan	———	,,	Hanged in Jan. 1858
16.	,,	Haus Khan	———	,,	,,
17.	,,	Sikandar Baksh	———	,,	,,
18.	,,	Gulhar	———	,,	,,
19.	,,	Rasul Khan	———	,,	,,
20.	Ghasera including several villages in hills (Total Martyrs-20, Traceable-4)	Asila	———	,,	Hanged
21.	,,	Dhundhal	———	,,	,,
22.	,,	Bane Singh	———	,,	,,
23.	,,	Murad Khan	———	,,	,,
24.	Barka (Total Martyrs-7)	Khushal	———	,,	Hanged in Jan. 1858
25.	,,	Kishan (Khushi)	———	,,	,,

26.	,,	Ranbaz s/o Malkhan	———	,,	,,
27.	,,	Rambhaj	———	,,	,,
28.	,,	Amir	———	,,	,,
29.	,,	Ratiya s/o Mukkha	———	,,	,,
30.	,,	Udai Chand	———	,,	,,
31.	Hathin including Dhiranka, Lakhnaka, Bhimsika, Jalalpur, Mankaka etc. (Total Martyrs -20 Traceable -4)	Rizwan	———	,,	Hanged
32.	,,	Samara	———	,,	,,
33.	,,	Bahadari	———	,,	,,
34.	,,	Leela	———	,,	,,
35.	Jarari (Total Martyrs-3)	Shah Mohammad	———	,,	Hanged in November 1857
36.	,,	Mansa Ram	———	Badhai	,,
37.	,,	Udai Singh	———	,,	,,
38.	Dhiranka (Total Martyrs-11, Traceable-1)	Johri	———	Meo	Hanged in November 1858

39.	Chilli (Total Martyrs-1)	Bhuria Chaudhary	———	,,	Hanged in November 1858
40.	Utawar (Total Martyrs-56, Traceable-1)	Mahabi Rabia (Woman), After her three brothers were killed, she took up sword and killed several enemy soldiers.	———	,,	Killed in Action
41.	Malpuri (Total Martyrs-1)	Mal Singh	———	,,	Killed in Action (19.11.1857)
42.	Rupraka (Total Martyrs-400, Traceable-70), Many martyrs were buried in mass graves. Recently a grave discovered having 18 bodies.	Khaira	———	Qureshi	,,

43.	,,	Lal Mian	———	,,	,,
44.	,,	Hinni	———	Meo	,,
45.	,,	Ranjit	———	,,	,,
46.	,,	Uzhar Mirasi	———	Mirasi	,,
47.	,,	Imami	———	Faqir	,,
48.	,,	Peeru	———	Jogi	,,
49.	,,	Sulhar	———	,,	,,
50.	,,	Amar Singh	———	,,	,,
51.	,,	Amar Nath	———	,,	,,
52.	,,	Raj Shah	———	Meo	,,
53.	,,	Samad Khan	———	,,	,,
54.	,,	Danshah	———	,,	,,
55.	,,	Arjun	———	,,	,,
56.	,,	Fateh Singh	———	,,	,,
57.	,,	Raj Khan	———	,,	,,
58.	,,	Bisambhar	———	,,	,,
59.	,,	Ilahi Baksh	———	,,	,,
60.	,,	Ananta	———	,,	,,
61.	,,	Lahru	———	,,	,,
62.	,,	Lahana	———	,,	,,
63.	,,	Ruza	———	,,	,,
64.	,,	Chaina	———	,,	,,
65.	,,	Mangal	———	,,	,,
66.	,,	Ghatak	———	,,	,,
67.	,,	Usata	———	,,	,,
68.	,,	Badulla	———	,,	,,
69.	,,	Ratan Singh	———	,,	,,
70.	,,	Kallu	———	,,	,,
71.	,,	Nasir	———	,,	,,
72.	,,	Bulla	———	,,	,,
73.	,,	Dhanwat	———	,,	,,
74.	,,	Kehra	———	,,	,,
75.	,,	Ruda	———	,,	,,
76.	,,	Ilahi Baksh s/o Meda	———	,,	,,

77.	,,	Khanka	———	,,	,,
78.	,,	Mukhrah	———	,,	,,
79.	,,	Khairati	———	,,	,,
80.	,,	Pir Khan	———	,,	,,
81.	,,	Shah Beg	———	,,	,,
82.	,,	Budha	———	,,	,,
83.	,,	Noor Baksh	———	,,	,,
84.	,,	Ratna s/o Chhajju	———	,,	,,
85.	,,	Mohammad Ali	———	,,	,,
86.	,,	Laharo	———	,,	,,
87.	,,	Nabi Baksh	———	,,	,,
88.	,,	Mahru	———	,,	,,
89.	,,	Dulla	———	,,	,,
90.	,,	Hasna	———	,,	,,
91.	,,	Murtaz Khan	———	,,	,,
92.	,,	Akbar	———	,,	,,
93	,,	Rulla	———	,,	,,
94.	,,	Jaggu	———	,,	,,
95.	,,	Imam Baksh	———	,,	,,
96.	,,	Asalat Khan	———	,,	,,
97.	,,	Bhul Khan	———	,,	,,
98.	,,	Dhan Singh	———	,,	,,
99.	,,	Azim Ali	———	,,	,,
100.	,,	Nasira Khan	———	,,	,,
101.	,,	Rasula	———	,,	,,
102.	,,	Zaina	———	,,	,,
103.	,,	Rugdha	———	,,	,,
104.	,,	Mudgar	———	,,	,,
105.	,,	Dulha Baksh	———	,,	,,
106.	,,	Jahaji	———	,,	,,
107.	,,	Mehrab	———	,,	,,
108.	,,	Mamraj	———	,,	,,

109.	Bhudpur (Total Martyrs-1)	Biddhu	———	Sakka	Hanged in November 1857
110.	Suraka (Total Martyrs-1, Went Underground -3)	Imam Ali	———	Meo	Hanged (4.12.1857)
111.	,,	———	Imam Ali	,,	WPR
112.	,,	———	Kokab Ali s/o Ghulam Qadir	,,	,,
113.	,,	———	Qutab Ali s/o Ghulam Qadir	,,	,,
114.	Sadra (Total Martyrs-1)	Mehdu Khan	———	Pathan	Hanged in Feb. 1858
115.	Sarouli (Total Martyrs-1, Went Underground -3)	Usman Khan s/o Zahur Khan	———	Meo	Hanged in December 1857
116.	,,	———	Bakhas Khan s/o Khairati Khan	,,	WPR
117.	,,	———	Sikandar s/o Khudayar Khan	,,	,,
118.	,,	———	Ahmad Khan s/o Johar Khan	,,	,,

119.	Firozpur Jhirka (Total Martyrs-35, Traceable-9, Went Underground -4)	Israil	———	Meo	Hanged in April 1858
120.	,,	Kewal Khan	———	,,	,,
121.	,,	Nawal Khan	———	,,	,,
122.	,,	Nahar Singh	———	,,	,,
123.	,,	Rai Khan	———	,,	,,
124.	,,	Lodha	———	,,	,,
125.	,,	Jodha	———	,,	,,
126.	,,	Jorawar	———	,,	,,
127.	,,	Hayat Khan	———	,,	,,
128.	,,	———	Fateh Khan	,,	WPR
129.	,,	———	Mohammad Ismail	,,	,,
130.	,,	———	Ram Ratan	Hindu, Caste not known (CNK)	,,
131.	,,	———	Shadi Ram	,,	,,
132.	Gujar Nagla (Total Martyrs -4)	Fazal Ali	———	Sayyed	Hanged in Feb. 1858
133.	,,	Jwala Singh	———	Meo	,,
134.	,,	Alamgir	———	,,	,,
135.	,,	Mahabali	———	,,	,,
136.	Jargali (Total Martyrs-1)	Kabul Khan	———	,,	Hanged in March 1858

137.	Mandi Khera (Total Martyrs-10, Traceable -5)	Mushtaq Ali	———	Khanzada	Hanged in November 1857
138.	,,	Muqaddar Ali	———	,,	,,
139.	,,	Rayuddin	———	,,	,,
140.	,,	Sujaat Ali	———	,,	,,
141.	,,	Faryad Ali	———	,,	,,
142.	Mahun including Hajanpur, Kalaka, Gujar Nagla, Naharika, Naryali, Tigaon, Chittora (Total Martyrs-70, Traceable-1)	Badruddin s/o Sadruddin	———	Meo	Killed in Action
143.	Mahun-Ka-Chaupta (Total Martyrs-30, Traceable -13)	Sharfuddin Khan	———	,,	Hanged in January 1858
144.	,,	Aslam Beg	———	,,	,,

145.	,,	Nusrat Ali	———	,,	,,	
146.	,,	Imami	———	,,	,,	
147.	,,	Kheru	———	,,	,,	
148.	,,	Mahbub Baksh		———	,,	,,
149.	,,	Sher Singh	———	,,	,,	
150.	,,	Bhanwar	———	,,	,,	
151.	,,	Lahri Baksh	———	,,	,,	
152	,,	Muqaddar Baksh		———	,,	,,
153.	,,	Mal Singh	———	,,	,,	
154	,,	Bhajat Ali	———	,,	,,	
155	,,	Nannu	———	,,	,,	
156.	Doha (Total Martyrs-30, Traceable-6)	Kehar Singh	———	,,	Hanged	
157.	,,	Mehra	———	,,	,,	
158.	,,	Fatauli	———	,,	,,	
159.	,,	Buzzagar	———	,,	,,	
160.	,,	Dhanmat	———	,,	,,	
161.	,,	Laru	———	,,	,,	
162.	Rawli (Total Martyrs-10, Traceable-4)	Ghisa	———	,,	,,	
163.	,,	Sher Singh	———	,,	,,	
164.	,,	Hasmat	———	,,	,,	
165.	,,	Zaikam	———	,,	,,	
166.	Shadipur (Total Martyrs-1)	Sulhar	———	,,	Hanged in Jan. 1858	
167.	Punhana (Total Martyrs-40, Traceable -2)	Malika Lambardar	———	,,	Hanged in March 1858	

168.	,,	Dhiri	———	,,	,,
169.	Basai Khanzada (Total Martyrs-4)	Nusrat Alir	———	Khanzada Dec. 1857	Hanged in
170.	,,	Ikram Ali	———	,,	,,
171.	,,	Hakim Baksh	———	,,	,,
172.	,,	Intzar Khan	———	,,	,,
173.	Nangla (Total Martyrs-3)	Jawala Singh	———	Meo	Hanged
174.	,,	Alamgir	———	,,	,,
175.	,,	Mahabali	———	,,	,,
176.	Nahrika (Total Martyrs-6)	Zumrat	———	,,	,,
177.	,,	Nihaala	———	,,	,,
178.	,,	Shikari	———	,,	,,
179.	,,	Lehna	———	,,	,,
180.	,,	Khuda Baksh	———	,,	,,
181.	,,	Nazba	———	,,	,,
182.	Khanpur (Total Martyrs-4)	Nusrat Ali	———	,,	,,
183.	,,	Ikram Ali	———	,,	,,
184.	,,	Hakam Baksh	———	,,	,,
185.	,,	Intzar Khan	———	,,	,,
186.	Sakras (Total Martyrs-13)	Ruksar	———	,,	,,
187.	,,	Tikam Khan	———	,,	,,
188.	,,	Meo Khan	———	,,	,,
189.	,,	Kaluta	———	,,	,,
190.	,,	Ghuspari	———	,,	,,

191.	,,	Ruzmma	———	,,	,,
192.	,,	Harchand	———	,,	,,
193.	,,	Suhaga	———	,,	,,
194.	,,	Madal	———	,,	,,
195.	,,	Nakaya	———	,,	,,
196.	,,	Baghera	———	,,	,,
197.	,,	Ugra	———	,,	,,
198.	,,	Khyali	———	,,	,,
199.	Sultanpur (Total Martyrs-8)	Amanat Ali	———	,,	Hanged in January 1858
200.	,,	Zamir Ali s/o Nusrat Ali	———	,,	,,
201.	,,	Khirajat Ali	———	,,	,,
202.	,,	Amanat Ali	———	,,	,,
203.	,,	Zamin Ali	———	,,	,,
204.	,,	Mahfuz Ali	———	,,	,,
205.	,,	Ghazanfar Ali	———	,,	,,
206.	,,	Bunde Ali	———	,,	,,
207.	Khera (Total Martyrs-1, Went Underground -11)	Fateh Ali Lambardar	———	,,	Hanged in Nov. 1857
208.	,,	———	Ghasi Khan s/o Aiz Khan	CNK (Muslim)	WPR
209.	,,	———	Farhad Khan	,,	,,
210.	,,	———	Shamsuddin s/o Azizuddin	,,	,,
211.	,,	———	Hisamuddin s/o Azimuddin	,,	,,

212.	,,	———	Sagar Beg	,,	,,
213.	,,	———	Namdar s/o Kamdar Khan	,,	,,
214.	,,	———	Rahimuddin	,,	,,
215.	,,	———	Ilahi Baksh s/o Mohammad Khan	,,	,,
216.	,,	———	Khuda Baksh s/o Khairati	,,	,,
217.	,,	———	Ahmad Khan s/o Majid Khan	,,	,,
218.	,,	———	Didar Baksh	,,	,,
219.	Nangli (Total Martyrs-47, Traceable-36)	Rattan Singh	———	Meo	Hanged in Feb. 1858
220.	,,	Kallu	———	,,	,,
221.	,,	Naseer	———	,,	,,
222.	,,	Bhulla	———	,,	,,
223.	,,	Dhanwant	———	,,	,,
224.	,,	Kehra	———	,,	,,
225.	,,	Ruda	———	,,	,,
226.	,,	Illaha baksh	———	,,	,,
227.	,,	Khauka	———	,,	,,
228.	,,	Mukhra	———	,,	,,
229.	,,	Khairati	———	,,	,,
230.	,,	Peer Khan	———	,,	,,
231.	,,	Shah Beg	———	,,	,,
232.	,,	Buddha	———	,,	,,
233.	,,	Noor Baksh	———	,,	,,
234.	,,	Ratan	———	,,	,,
235.	,,	Mohammad	———	,,	,,

236. „	Wazir	———	„	„
237. „	Laro	———	„	„
238. „	Nabi Baksh	———	„	„
239. „	Ilahi Baksh	———	„	„
240. „	Khuda Baksh	———	„	„
241. „	Matru	———	„	„
242. „	Chena	———	„	„
243. „	Dula	———	„	„
244. „	Ruda	———	„	„
245. „	Hasna	———	„	„
246. „	Murtaza Khan	———	„	„
247. „	Akbar	———	„	„
248. „	Rulla	———	„	„
249. „	Jaggu	———	„	„
250. „	Imam Baksh	———	„	„
251. „	Kanwar Chand	———	„	„
252. „	Azam Ali	———	„	„
253. „	Wazir Chand	———	„	Hanged in January 1858
254. „	Dhan Singh s/o Dhanwant	———	„	Hanged in Feb. 1858
255. Raunpur (Total Martyrs-1)	Khuda Baksh	———	„	„
256. Chitora (Total Martyrs-9, Traceable -3)	Lehna	———	„	Hanged in January 1858
257. „	Kund baksh	———	„	„
258. „	Najba	———	„	„

259.	Nagina (Total Martyrs-6, Traceable-4, Went Underground -3)	Udai Singh	———	,,	Hanged in March 1858
260.	,,	Makkar	———	,,	,,
261.	,,	Kanwal Khan	———	,,	,,
262.	,,	Udai Singh	———	,,	,,
263.	,,	———	Shamsuddin s/o Nazibuddin	,,	WPR
264.	,,	———	Valant Ali s/o Ismail Ali	,,	,,
265.	,,	———	Kuber Ali s/o Valant Ali	,,	,,
266.	Chitora (Total Martyrs-1, Went Underground -1)	Ramju	———	,,	Hanged in January 1858
267.	,,	———	Sabat Khan s/o Sadat Khan	,,	WPR
268.	Pinangwan including Katpuri, Mohammadpur, Tek, Chokha, Lalabas, Dhana, Bubalheri,				

Rehatwa, Jhimrawat (Total Martyrs-50, Traceable -5)	Wazir Khan	———	,,	Hanged in January 1858
269. ,,	Gulkha	———	,,	,,
270. ,,	Tehrrum	———	,,	,,
271. ,,	Wazir	———	,,	,,
272. ,,	Lahak	———	,,	,,
273. Ghagas Kansali (Total Martyrs-4)	Leela	———	,,	Hanged in April 1858
274. ,,	Ashila	———	,,	,,
275. ,,	Zuggar	———	,,	,,
276. ,,	Gariba s/o Channa	———	,,	,,
277. Sariral or Sail (Total Martyrs-5, Traceable-4)	Hannu	———	,,	,,
278. ,,	Nanda Khan	———	,,	,,
279. ,,	Kewal Khan s/o Saap Khan	———	,,	,,
280. ,,	Ram Singh	———	,,	,,
281. Akera (Total Martyrs-4, Went Underground -6)	Hasti	———	Meo	Hanged in Jan. 1858

282. ,,	Sukkan	———	,,	,,
283. ,,	Ajmal	———	,,	,,
284. ,,	Dhiri Khan	———	,,	,,
285. ,,	———	Ilahi Baksh	,,	WPR
286. ,,	———	Garibullah s/o Rahimullah	,,	,,
287. ,,	———	Imam Ali s/o Alisan Ali	,,	,,
288. ,,	———	Rastaq Beg s/o Sarfaraz Beg	Muslim, CNK	,,
289. ,,	———	Ali Baksh s/o Khwaja Baksh	,,	,,
290. ,,	———	Rahim Baksh s/o Ilahi Baksh	,,	,,

References

1. Yadav, K.C., *Roll of Honour: Haryana's Martyrs of 1857*, Gurgaon, 2008, pp. 31-32, 41-57.

Annexure-VI

List of the Revolutionaries Martyred and Accused from Gurgaon District[1]

Sr. No	Name of the Village with Details	Name of the Traceable Martyrs	Name of Revolutionaries Accused But went Underground	Caste/ Religion	Punishment
1.	Gurgaon (Total Martyrs-50, Traceable-37)	Nawab Ahmad Mirza	———	Mughal	Shot on 15.12. 1857
2.	,,	Nawab Akbar Khan	———	,,	,,
3.	,,	Nawab Ameer Khan	———	,,	,,
4.	,,	Nawab Duleh Jan	———	,,	,,
5	,,	Mirza Ghayasuddin	———	,,	,,
6.	,,	Ali Bahadur	———	,,	,,
7.	,,	Alladad Khan	———	,,	,,
8.	,,	Alauddin Khan	———	,,	,,
9.	,,	Muza ffaruddaulah	———	,,	,,
10.	,,	Mirza Peer Ali	———	,,	,,

11.	,,	Chhote Mirza	———	,,	,,
12.	,,	Mirza Bulaqi Khan	———	,,	,,
13.	,,	Mirza Azizuddin	———	,,	,,
14.	,,	Mirza Kallan	———	,,	,,
15.	,,	Mirza Khaibar	———	,,	,,
16.	,,	Mirza Mughal	———	,,	,,
17.	,,	Mirza Jalali	———	,,	,,
18.	,,	Mirza Itabuddin	———	,,	,,
19.	,,	Mirza Ramzani	———	,,	Hanged in 15.12 1857
20.	,,	Yaqub Bakht	———	Shaikh	,,
21.	,,	Badullah Khan	———	,,	,,
22.	,,	Mohammad Ibrahim	———	,,	,,
23.	,,	Mohammad Yousuf	———	,,	,,
24.	,,	Sahabuddin	———	,,	,,
25.	,,	Ali Gauhar)	———	,,	Hanged on 22.2.1858
26.	,,	Azimullah	———	Meo	Hanged on 13.11.1857
27.	,,	Ghisa Ram	———	Bania	,,
28.	,,	Bahadur Singh	———	Rajput	Shot on 15.12.1857
29.	,,	Bhawani Singh	———	,,	,,
30.	,,	Dalip Singh	———	,,	,,

31.	,,	Gopal Singh	———	,,	,,
32.	,,	Gurdayal Singh	———	,,	,,
33.	,,	Harnam Singh	———	,,	Hanged on 15.12.1857
34.	,,	Narain Singh	———	,,	,,
35.	,,	Kahan Singh	———	,,	,,
36.	,,	Reoti Ram	———	Saini	,,
37.	,,	Sahaj Ram s/o Harchand	———	,,	,,
38.	Jharsa (Total Martyrs-8, Traceable-2, Went Underground -1)	Bakhtawar Singh	———	Jat	Hanged on 12.10.1857
39.	,,	Imran Ali	———	Shaikh	Hanged in Dec. 1857
40.	,,	———	Hoshiyar Khan s/o Sabar Khan	,,	WPR
41.	Khera-Jharsa (Total Martyrs-2)	Fateh Ali s/o Zabardast Khan	———	,,	Shot in November 1857
42.	,,	Ghisa s/o Dalel Singh	———	Jat	,,
43.	Badshahpur (Total Martyrs-45, Traceable-33,				

	Went Underground -16)	Sukh Ram	———	Bania	Hanged in November 1857
44.	,,	Bakhta	———	,,	,,
45.	,,	Bihari	———	,,	,,
46.	,,	Khushale	———	,,	,,
47.	,,	Ilahi Baksh Khan	———	Baloch	,,
48.	,,	Rahim Baksh	———	,,	,,
49.	,,	Jan Mohammad	———	Shaikh	,,
50.	,,	Medi	———	Meo	Hanged in Feb. 1857
51.	,,	Ikki Baksh	———	,,	,,
52.	,,	Ajmeri	———	,,	,,
53.	,,	Ghulam Nabi	———	Shaikh	Shot on 15.12.1857
54.	,,	Ghulam Mohiuddin	———	,,	,,
55.	,,	Kokab Baksh	———	,,	,,
56.	,,	Kabiruddin	———	,,	,,
57.	,,	Ummed Baksh	———	,,	,,
58.	,,	Mohammad	———	,,	,,
59.	,,	Khusru	———	,,	,,
60.	,,	Khurram Bakht	———	,,	,,
61.	,,	Mohammad Kabir	———	,,	,,
62.	,,	Faiz Shah	———	,,	,,
63.	,,	Shahabuddin	———	,,	,,
64.	,,	Khuda Baksh	———	,,	,,
65.	,,	Deshpati	———	Hindu, CNK	,,

66.	,,	Jeet Singh	———	,,	,,
67.	,,	Nihal Singh	———	,,	,,
68.	,,	Ram Dutt	———	,,	,,
69.	,,	Shankar	———	,,	,,
70.	,,	Sita Ram	———	,,	,,
71.	,,	Luxman	———	,,	,,
72.	,,	Ishari	———	,,	,,
73.	,,	Matadin	———	,,	,,
74.	,,	Surat Singh	———	,,	,,
75.	,,	Kundan	———	,,	,,
76.	,,	Naurang	———	Gujar	Hanged in April 1858
77.	,,	Karima	———	Julaha	,,
78.	,,	———	Ram Sahai s/o Daulat Ram	Ahir	WPR
79.	,,		Gulab Khan s/o Ahmad Khan	Muslim, CNK	,,
80.	,,	———	Badruddin	,,	,,
81.	,,	———	Karam Baksh s/o Namdar	,,	,,
82.	,,	———	Kudrah Khan	,,	,,
83.	,,	———	Mehrab Ali	,,	,,
84.	,,	———	Boedi Ali	,,	,,
85.	,,	———	Isdar Khan s/o Wazir Khan	,,	,,
86.	,,	———	Ameer Baksh s/o Mohammad Shah	,,	,,
87.	,,	———	Amanat Ali s/o Nazib Ali	,,	,,
88.	,,	———	Alladad Khan s/o Kale Khan	,,	,,
89.	,,	———	Amir Ali	,,	,,
90.	,,	———	Rustam Ali	,,	,,

91.	,,	———	Husain Khan	,,	,,
92.	,,	———	Bahadur Khan	,,	,,
93	,,	———	Gulab Khan s/o Ahmad Khan	Baloch	,,
94.	Raiseena (Total Martyrs-50, Traceable-15, Went Underground -3)	Mir Khan	———	Meo	Hanged in Feb. 1858
95.	,,	Sikandar Khan	———	,,	,,
96.	,,	Ithad	———	,,	,,
97.	,,	Medu	———	,,	,,
98.	,,	Kanhau	———	,,	,,
99.	,,	Zulfiqar	———	,,	,,
100.	,,	Petla	———	,,	,,
101.	,,	Dhithar	———	,,	,,
102.	,,	Zahura	———	,,	,,
103.	,,	Faqira	———	,,	,,
104.	,,	Muneer Kham s/o Nasir Khan	———	,,	,,
105.	,,	Dulla	———	,,	,,
106.	,,	Birju	———	Jat	,,
107.	,,	Suraj	———	,,	,,
108.	,,	Dhanna	———	,,	,,
109.	,,	———	Mir Khan s/o Salabat Khan	Meo	WPR
110.	,,	———	Bakshi Khan s/o Hatim Khan	,,	,,
111.	,,	———	Sikandar Khan	,,	,,

112.	Farrukhnagar (Total Martyrs-7, Traceable-2, Life Imprisonment -1, Went Underground -57)	Nawab Ahmad Ali Khan	———	Pathan	Hanged on 23.1.1858
113.	,,	Bahadur	———	Baloch	Hanged in Dec. 1857
114.	,,	Dilawar Khan	———	Pathan	Life Imprisonment
115.	,,	———	Faiz Mohammad	Muslim, CNK	WPR
116.	,,	———	Khwaja Baksh	,,	WPR
117.	,,	———	Khuda Baksh	,,	,,
118.	,,	———	Fazluddin	,,	,,
119.	,,	———	Shibat Khan s/o Bakshullah Khan	,,	,,
120.	,,	———	Sikandar Khan	,,	,,
121.	,,	———	Karim Baksh s/o Qalandar Baksh	,,	,,
122.	,,	———	Ganeshi Khan	,,	,,
123.	,,	———	Awad Khan s/o Fateh Ali	,,	,,
124.	,,	———	Taj Mohd s/o Dara Khan	,,	,,
125.	,,	———	Ahmad Beg s/o Mohd Beg	,,	,,
126.	,,	———	Ghulam Rasul	,,	,,
127.	,,	———	Chhote Khan	,,	,,

128.	,,	———	Nizabat Khan	,,	,,
129.	,,	———	Mohammad Ali Khan	,,	,,
130.	,,	———	Majiduddin Khan	,,	,,
131.	,,	———	Imam Khan s/o Peer Khan	,,	,,
132.	,,	———	Sardar Khan s/o Sarfaraz Khan	,,	,,
133.	,,	———	Shujat Khan s/o Fateh Ali	,,	,,
134.	,,	———	Musahib Khan	,,	,,
135.	,,	———	Ahmad s/o Mukhtar Khan	,,	,,
136.	,,	———	Ghulam Husain	,,	,,
137.	,,	———	Mohammad Ali	,,	,,
138.	,,	———	Rahim Ali Khan	,,	,,
139.	,,	———	Niwazur Khan	,,	,,
140.	,,	———	Turrebaz Khan	,,	,,
141.	,,	———	Umed Khan	,,	,,
142.	,,	———	Sikandar Khan	,,	,,
143.	,,	———	Yusuf Ali Khan	,,	,,
144.	,,	———	Imatuddin	,,	,,
145.	,,	———	Fateh Khan s/o Sadat Khan	,,	,,
146.	,,	———	Sahmat Khan s/o Mohammad Khan	,,	,,
147.	,,	———	Maula Baksh s/o Bakshi Khan	,,	,,
148.	,,	———	Karim Khan s/o Mohammad Khan	,,	,,
149.	,,	———	Rahim Khan	,,	,,
150.	,,	———	Bahadur Khan	,,	,,

151. ,,	———	Husain Khan	,,	,,
152 ,,	———	Ahmad Khan s/o Mohammad Khan	,,	,,
153 ,,	———	Qalandar Khan s/o Karim Khan	,,	,,
154. ,,	———	Rahamdad Khan	,,	,,
155. ,,	———	Mohammad Khan s/o Khuda Baksh Khan	,,	,,
156. ,,	———	Nathe Khan	,,	,,
157. ,,	———	Fazluddin	,,	,,
158. ,,	———	Ilahi Baksh	,,	,,
159. ,,	———	Abdur Rahman Khan	,,	,,
160. ,,	———	Dilawar Khan	,,	,,
161. ,,	———	Hyder Baksh s/o Mohd Miya Jaan	,,	,,
162. ,,	———	Mohd Yar Khan s/o Khairati Khan	,,	,,
163. ,,	———	Imam Khan s/o Gulab Khan	,,	,,
164. ,,	———	Sahab Khan s/o Gulab Khan	,,	,,
165. ,,	———	Isa Khan s/o Wazir Khan	,,	,,
166. ,,	———	Faiz Mohammad	,,	,,
167. ,,	———	Khwaja Baksh s/o Husain Baksh	,,	,,
168. ,,	———	Ganeshi Khan	,,	,,
169. ,,	———	Karim Baksh s/o Qalandar Baksh	,,	,,
170. ,,	———	Taj Mohammad Khan	,,	,,

171.		———	Qadar Khan	Baloch	,,
172.	Sohna (Total Martyrs-56, Traceable-5, Went Underground -19)	Ahmad Baksh	———	Meo	Hanged in December 1857
173.	,,	Imam Ali	———	,,	,,
174.	,,	Azam Beg	———	,,	,,
175.	,,	Muddat Ali	———	,,	,,
176.	,,	Ahmad Baksh	———	,,	,,
177.	,,	———	Shahzad Khan s/o Mehtab	Muslim Rajput	WPR
178.	,,	———	Wazir Ali	Shaikh	,,
179.	,,	———	Isa Khan	,,	,,
180.	,,	———	Wazir Khan	,,	,,
181.	,,	———	Ghulam Mohammad Khan	Muslim, CNK	,,
182.	,,	———	Ali Baksh s/o Khwaja Baksh	,,	,,
183.	,,	———	Rahim Baksh	,,	,,
184.	,,	———	Hyder Beg s/o Ilahi Beg	,,	,,
185.	,,	———	Munim Beg s/o mukim Beg	,,	,,
186.	,,	———	Mohammad Baksh s/o Niamatullah	,,	,,
187.	,,	———	Rahim Beg s/o Khuda Beg	,,	,,

188.	,,	———	Husain Ali	,,	,,
189.	,,	———	Umed Beg s/o Babar Beg	,,	,,
190.	,,	———	Isa Khan	,,	,,
191.	,,	———	Qadar Baksh s/o Ahmad Baksh	,,	,,
192.	,,	———	Fateh Mohammad s/o Shah Mohammad	,,	,,
193.	,,	———	Ammir Khan s/o Zorawar Khan	,,	,,
194.	,,	———	Khwaja Baksh s/o Bedar Baksh	,,	,,
195.	,,	———	Rustam Ali s/o Husain Ali	,,	,,
196.	Kasan (Total Martyrs-17, Traceable-12, Went Underground -1)	Shah Jahan	———	Pathan	Hanged
197.	,,	Afzal	———	,,	,,
198.	,,	Miran	———	Jat	,,
199.	,,	Jaimal	———	,,	,,
200.	,,	Kalu Beg	———	Mughal	,,
201.	,,	Kalu	———	Ahir	,,
202.	,,	Naurang	———	Gujar	,,
203.	,,	Noor Baksh	———	Shaikh	,,
204.	,,	Sijjat	———	,,	,,
205.	,,	Zalim	———	,,	,,
206.	,,	Tulla	———	Hindu, CNK	,,
207.	,,	Ramphal	———	,,	,,
208.	,,	———	Nadir Khan	Muslim, CNK	WPR

209.	Hasanpur (Total Martyrs-23, Went Underground -16)	Taj Khan	———	Baloch	Hanged in January 1858
210.	,,	Mohammad Khan	———	Muslim Rajput	,,
211.	,,	Amanat Ali	———	,,	,,
212.	,,	Hoshdar Khan	———	,,	,,
213.	,,	Karim Baksh	———	,,	,,
214.	,,	Zamin Ali	———	,,	,,
215.	,,	Mahfuz Ali	———	,,	,,
216.	,,	Ghazanfar Ali	———	,,	,,
217.	,,	Bande Ali	———	,,	,,
218.	,,	Jafar Husain	———	,,	,,
219.	,,	Istiaq Husain	———	,,	,,
220.	,,	Anjum Ali	———	,,	,,
221.	,,	Faizdar Khan	———	,,	,,
222.	,,	Asalat Khan	———	,,	,,
223.	,,	Akbar Khan	———	,,	,,
224.	,,	Medu Khan	———	Meo	Hanged
225.	,,	Mozam	———	,,	,,
226.	,,	Zabardast Khan	———	,,	,,
227.	,,	Qutbuddin	———	,,	,,
228.	,,	Chand Khan	———	,,	,,
229.	,,	Mahbub Baksh	———	,,	,,
230.	,,	Peer Khan	———	,,	,,
231.	,,	Rahim Khan	———	,,	,,
232.	,,	Daula	———	,,	,,

233.	,,	———	Mazhar Ali	Muslim, CNK	WPR
234.	,,	———	Matlub Husain	,,	,,
235.	,,	———	Wazirullah Khan	,,	,,
236.	,,	———	Ashraf Husain	,,	,,
237.	,,	———	Abbas Khan	,,	,,
238.	,,	———	Bedar Singh	,,	,,
239.	,,	———	Zabardast Khan	,,	,,
240.	,,	———	Ahsan Ali	,,	,,
241.	,,	———	Ahmad Ali s/o Husain Ali	,,	,,
242.	,,	———	Ghulam Hyder s/o Shaikh Amir	,,	,,
243.	,,	———	Imamuddin s/o Ahmad Khan	,,	,,
244.	,,	———	Ismail s/o Sitab Khan	,,	,,
245.	,,	———	Rahim Khan s/o Hafiz Khan	,,	,,
246.	,,	———	Arshad Ali s/o Awaz Ali	,,	,,
247.	,,	———	Fardand Husain	,,	,,
248.	,,	———	Afzal Ali s/o Midra	,,	,,
249.	Shahpur (Went Underground -18)	———	Mir Javed Ali	,,	,,
250.	,,	———	Asghar Ali s/o Babar Ali	,,	,,
251.	,,	———	Azmat Ali s/o Amanat Ali	,,	,,
252.	,,	———	Yousuf Ali s/o Ashraf Ali	,,	,,

253.	,,	———	Ali Baksh s/o Khairati Ali	,,	,,
254.	,,	———	Walant Ali	,,	,,
255.	,,	———	Allah Husain	,,	,,
256.	,,	———	Asghar Ali	,,	,,
257.	,,	———	Anjum Ali	,,	,,
258.	,,	———	Amir Ali s/o Zawar Ali	,,	,,
259.	,,	———	Munawwar s/o Ghulam Ali	,,	,,
260.	,,	———	Zafar Ali s/o Ghulam Ali	,,	,,
261.	,,	———	Zulfiqar Ali s/o Abdul Ghani	,,	,,
262.	,,	———	Amir Baksh s/o Ilahi Baksh	,,	,,
263.	,,	———	Imam Ali s/o Shujat Ali	,,	,,
264.	Garhi Harsaru (Total Martyrs-2, Went Underground -4)	Zakat Ali s/o Khuda Baksh	———	Sayyed	Hanged in Dec. 1857
265.	,,	Rahim Baksh s/o Najibullah	———	Shaikh	,,
266.	,,	———	Bakhtawar Singh	Rajput	WPR
267.	,,	———	Debi Singh s/o Amir Singh	,,	,,
268.	,,	———	Ram Baksh s/o Fateh Chand	Hindu, CNK	,,

269.	,,	———	Rahimuddin	Muslim, CNK	,,
270.	Balokar (Went Underground -2)	———	Wahid Ali s/o Anjum Ali	,,	,,
271.	,,	———	Imam Baksh s/o Musaib Ali	,,	,,
272.	Barehra Sangata (Total Martyrs-1)	Mohan Singh s/o Ram Kishan	———	Ahir	Hanged in Jan. 1858
273.	Imauli (Went Underground -1)	———	Daulat Ram s/o Bholu Ram	,,	WPR
274.	Naurangpur (Total Martyrs-2, Went Underground -1)	Rajo	———	Shaikh	Hanged in 30.12.1857
275.	,,	Mohammad Khan	———	,,	,,
276.	,,	Gariba s/o Channa	Zuber Khan	Muslim, CNK	WPR

277.	Bagkanki or Kherki (Total Martyrs-3)	Shahlaj	———	Meo	Hanged in Feb. 1858
278.	,,	Nathu	———	,,	,,
279.	,,	Sahza	———	,,	,,
280.	Dhandawas (Went Underground -1)	———	Hyder Khan	Muslim, CNK	WPR
281.	Kadarpur (Total Martyrs-3)	Mohrab	———	Gujar	Hanged in November 1857
282.	,,	Saheba	———	,,	,,
283.	,,	Chhajju Lambardar	———	,,	Hanged in December 1857
283.	Bhora Kalan (Total Martyrs-2)	Abbu	———	Muslim Rajput	,,
284.	,,	Dowla	———	Meo	Hanged in Jan. 1858
285.	Moham-madpur (Total Martyrs-7, Traceable-2)	Razim	———	,,	Shot
286.	,,	Alu	———	Nai	,,

287.	Nunera (Total Martyrs-8)	Rahida	———	Meo	Hanged
288.	,,	Chander	———	,,	,,
289.	,,	Manghu	———	,,	,,
290.	,,	Zhamman	———	,,	,,
291.	,,	Khayali	———	,,	,,
292.	,,	Zhaggar	———	,,	,,
293.	,,	Mujat Khan	———	,,	,,
294.	,,	Khayali	———	,,	,,
295.	Hariahera (Total Martyrs-10, Traceable-3)	Ram Singh	———	,,	Hanged in Dec. 1857
296.	,,	China	———	,,	,,
297.	,,	Redu	———	,,	,,
298.	Shahjahanpur (Total Martyrs-2)	Mehtab	———	,,	Hanged in Jan. 1858
299.	,,	Nahar Kahn s/o Gauhar	———	Ranghar	Hanged in Feb. 1858
300.	Rithoj (Total Martyrs-2)	Ganga	———	Gujar	Hanged on 7.12.1857
301.	,,	Nanda	———	,,	,,
302.	Patli (Total Martyrs-1)	Daya Ram	———	Jat	Hanged in Dec. 1857

303.	Rathiwas (Went Underground -1)	———	Chhatar Singh s/o Bhawani Singh	,,	WPR
304.	Khera (Total Martyrs-1)	Zabardast Khan	———	Shaikh	Hanged in Nov. 1857
305.	Bilaspur (Went Underground -1)	———	Lal Sigh s/o Jodh Singh	Jat	WPR
306.	Miscellaneous (Total Martyrs-5)	Amanat Khan	———	Muslim, CNK	Hanged
307.	,,	Khillu Singh	———	Jat	,,
308.	,,	Matadin	———	,,	,,
309.	,,	Bhik Singh	———	,,	,,
310.	,,	Puran	———	,,	,,

References

1. Yadav, K.C., *Roll of Honour: Haryana's Martyrs of 1857*, Gurgaon, 2008, pp. 23-40.

Annexure-VII

List of the Revolutionaries Martyred and Accused from Faridabad District[1]

Sr. No.	Name of the Village with Details	Name of the Traceable Martyrs	Name of Revolutionaries Accused But went Underground	Caste/ Religion	Punishment
1.	Faridabad (Total Martyrs-7, Traceable-5)	Dhanna Singh	———	Rajput	Hanged in Feb. 1858
2.	,,	Ilahi Baksh	———	Shaikh	,,
3.	,,	Ali Mohammad	———	,,	,,
4.	,,	Khuda Baksh	———	Manihar	,,
5.	,,	Inzmam Ali	———	,,	,,
6.	Ballabhgarh (Total Martyrs-4)	Raja Nahar Singh	———	Jat	Hanged on 9.1.1858
7.	,,	Mohan Singh of Madhopur	———	,,	Hanged in January 1858
8.	,,	Karim Baksh	———	Shaikh	,,
9.	,,	Gulab Singh	———	Saini	,,

10.	Sihi (Went Underground -1)	———	Raj Singh (Great grandfather of Ch. Charan Singh, PM of India)	Jat	WPR
11.	Palwal (Total Martyrs-36, Went Underground -17)	Nabi Baksh	———	Shaikh	Hanged in Dec. 1857
12.	,,	Daula	———	,,	,,
13.	,,	Inayat Ali	———	,,	,,
14.	,,	Niyamat Ali	———	,,	,,
15.	,,	Rahmatullah	———	,,	,,
16.	,,	Sharfuddin Ali	———	,,	,,
17.	,,	Maini	———	,,	,,
18.	,,	Khuda baksh	———	,,	,,
19.	,,	Karimullah	———	,,	,,
20.	,,	Sahmat Ali	———	,,	,,
21.	,,	Imamuddin	———	Meo	Hanged in January 1858
22.	,,	Shamsuddin	———	,,	,,
23.	,,	Nabi Baksh s/o Bakshullah	———	,,	,,
24.	,,	Rahimullah s/o Niamatullah	———	,,	,,

25.	,,	Hayat Ali Thanedar	————	,,	Hanged in Feb. 1858
26.	,,	Sahmat Khan	————	,,	,,
27.	,,	Innan	————	,,	,,
28.	,,	Sadat Khan s/o Jangli	————	,,	Hanged in April 1858
29.	,,	Sarup Lal	————	Bania	,,
30.	,,	Harsukh s/o Radha Kishan	————	,,	,,
31.	,,	Saruplal	————	,,	Hanged in March 1858
32.	,,	Mehta	————	,,	,,
33.	,,	Dhanna Singh	————	Muslim Rajput	,,
34.	,,	Khuda Baksh	————	,,	,,
35.	,,	Mirza Ghafur	————	,,	Hanged in Jan. 1858
36.	,,	Mohammad Yousuf	————	,,	,,
37.	,,	Imam Khan	————	,,	,,
38.	,,	Inayat Ali	————	Sayyed	Hanged in Dec. 1857
39.	,,	Mohammad Khan	————	,,	,,
40.	,,	Nizabat Ali	————	,,	,,
41.	,,	Ramzan Ali	————	,,	,,
42.	,,	Haari s/o Suri	————	,,	Hanged in Jan. 1858
43.	,,	Shahnaz Ali	————	,,	,,
44.	,,	Murtaza Khan	————	,,	,,
45.	,,	Shahadat	————	,,	,,
46.	,,	Daya Ram	————	Jat	Hanged in Dec. 1857

47.	,,	———	Hafizuddin	Muslim, CNK	WPR
48.	,,	———	Mohammad Baksh	,,	,,
49.	,,	———	Mardan s/o Burhan	,,	,,
50.	,,	———	Mir Khan s/o Babar	,,	,,
51.	,,	———	Ilahi Baksh s/o Gunni	,,	,,
52.	,,	———	Iban Ali s/o adil	,,	,,
53.	,,	———	Jodab s/o Kamdar	,,	,,
54.	,,	———	Nabi Baksh s/o Khuda Baksh	,,	,,
55.	,,	———	Alizar Beg s/o Amanat Beg	,,	,,
56.	,,	———	Sadullah Khan s/o Bahadur Khan	,,	,,
57.	,,	———	Mehtab Khan s/o Chand Khan	,,	,,
58.	,,	———	Iradat Beg s/o Amir Beg	,,	,,
59.	,,	———	Mohammad Khan	,,	,,
60.	,,	———	Karim Baksh s/o Khuda Baksh	,,	,,
61.	,,	———	Ilahi Baksh s/o Faiz Baksh	,,	,,
62.	,,	———	Zable Khan	,,	,,
63.	,,	———	Khairat Ali s/o Babar Ali	Shaikh	,,

64.	Rasulpur (Total Martyred-5, Went Underground -5)	Zafar Husain	———	Meo	Hanged in January 1858
65.	,,	Ishtiaq Ali	———	,,	,,
66.	,,	Duam Ali	———	,,	,,
67.	,,	Anjum Ali	———	,,	,,
68.	,,	Imam Baksh	———	,,	,,
69.	,,	———	Hatim Ali	Muslim, CNK	WPR
70.	,,	———	Bisarat Ali	,,	,,
71.	,,	———	Nazma Ali	,,	,,
72.	,,	———	Sorab Khan s/o Dorab Khan	,,	,,
73.	,,	———	Turrebaz Khan s/o Sorab Khan	,,	,,
74.	Khajurka (Total Martyrs-1, Went Underground -7)	Anjum Beg	———	Meo	Hanged on 30.1.1858
75.	,,	———	Musahib Beg s/o Azad Beg	Muslim, CNK	WPR
76.	,,	———	Sarfaraz Beg s/o Mohammad	,,	,,
77.	,,	———	Babar Beg s/o Nek Ali	,,	,,
78.	,,	———	Adil Beg s/o Hamid Beg	,,	,,

79.	,,	———	Rahim Ali Beg s/o Karim Beg	,,	,,
80.	,,	———	Lari Beg s/o Fazal Beg	,,	,,
81.	,,	———	Alimuddin s/o Ghulam Ali	,,	,,
82.	Deeghot (Total Martyrs-6)	AotiyaKallan	———	Meo	Hanged in January 1858
83.	,,	Nanua	———	,,	,,
84.	,,	Hetram	———	Jat	,,
85.	,,	Tulla	———	,,	,,
86.	,,	Nihal Singh	———	,,	,,
87.	Chhajju Nagar (Total Martyrs-11)	Kalua	———	,,	,,
88.	,,	Chena	———	,,	,,
89.	,,	Bijender	———	,,	,,
90.	,,	Hardev	———	,,	,,
91.	,,	Brija	———	,,	,,
92.	,,	Lekha	———	,,	,,
93	,,	Daulat	———	,,	,,
94.	,,	Snehi	———	,,	,,
95.	,,	Harlal	———	,,	,,
96.	,,	Hardayal	———	,,	,,
97.	,,	Lehna	———	,,	,,
98.	Tuppel (Total Martyrs-1)	Sheo Charan	———	,,	Hanged in March 1858
99.	Gudhrana (Total Martyrs-3)	Wazir Khan	———	Meo	Hanged in January 1858

100.	,,	Zafar Khan	———	,,	,,
101.	,,	Fazal Ali	———	,,	Hanged in Feb. 1858
102.	Pahladpur (Total Martyrs-12)	Shiv Sahai	———	Jat	,,
103.	,,	Nain Sukh	———	,,	,,
104.	,,	Shobha Ram	———	,,	,,
105.	,,	Johari	———	,,	,,
106.	,,	Nanda	———	Jat	,,
107.	,,	Sola	———	,,	,,
108.	,,	Sita Ram	———	,,	,,
109.	,,	Hardev	———	,,	,,
110.	,,	Kayali	———	,,	,,
111.	,,	Bhanwara	———	Bania	,,
112.	,,	Bhagwat	———	Kahar	,,
113.	,,	Hardial	———	Brahman	,,
114.	Ahrwan (Total Martyrs-14)	Sadhu	———	Jat	Hanged in Dec. 1857
115.	,,	Chet Ram	———	,,	,,
116.	,,	Dulli	———	,,	,,
117.	,,	Tulsia	———	,,	,,
118.	,,	Siya Ram	———	,,	,,
119.	,,	Bhima s/o Inder	———	,,	,,
120.	,,	Pohop Singh	———	,,	,,
121.	,,	Heta	———	,,	,,
122.	,,	Makhhan Singh	———	,,	,,
123.	,,	Dharma	———	,,	,,
124.	,,	Man Singh s/o Khumu	———	Dhobi	,,
125.	,,	Chetan	———	SC	,,

126.	,,	Harnam	———	,,	,,
127.	,,	Samandar	———	,,	,,
128.	Phulwari (Total Martyrs-3)	Sidhu	———	Rajput	Hanged in January 1858
129.	,,	Sudhir Singh	———	,,	,,
130.	,,	Samandar	———	,,	,,
131.	Bas (Total Martyrs-1)	Imam Baksh s/o Sanwat	———	Meo	,,
132.	Khatela (Went Underground -1)	———	Shadi Khan	Shaikh	WPR
133.	Pingor (Total Martyrs-3)	———	Murtaza Husain	Muslim, CNK	,,
134.	,,	———	Rahim Ali	,,	,,
135.	,,	———	Bhau Ali s/o Jamait Ali	,,	,,
136.	Nagli (Total Martyrs-11)	Bisambhar	———	Meo	Hanged in Feb. 1858
137.	,,	Ilahi Baksh	———	,,	,,
138.	,,	Ananta	———	,,	,,
139.	,,	Laru	———	,,	,,
140.	,,	Lahana	———	,,	,,
141.	,,	Ruza	———	,,	,,
142.	,,	Chena	———	,,	,,
143.	,,	Mangal	———	,,	,,
144.	,,	Chhattar	———	,,	,,

145.	,,	Usta	————	,,	,,
146.	,,	Abdullah	————	,,	,,
147.	Hodal (Total Martyrs-3)	Radha Kishan s/o Bhakta Ram	————	Jat	Hanged in Jan. 1858
148.	,,	Shyamsukh	————	,,	,,
149.	,,	Narain	————	,,	,,
150.	Tuseni (Total Martyrs-3)	Dhiru	————	Meo	Hanged in March 1858
151.	,,	Maluka	————	,,	Hanged in Jan. 1858
152	,,	Murad Baksh Lambardar	————	,,	,,
153.	Mankaka (Total Martyrs-1)	Khuda Baksh	————	Muslim, CNK	Hanged in Feb. 1858
154.	Garhi (Total Martyrs-15)	Kishan Lal	————	Jat	Hanged in Jan. 1858
155.	,,	Rajnandan	————	,,	,,
156.	,,	Lakshman	————	,,	,,
157.	,,	Ram Baksh	————	,,	,,
158.	,,	Hardev	————	,,	,,
159.	,,	Kishan Singh	————	,,	,,
160.	,,	Mansa	————	,,	,,
161.	,,	Hardev Singh	————	,,	Hanged in Feb. 1858

162.	,,	Kishna	———	,,	,,
163.	,,	Bhagirath	———	,,	,,
164.	,,	Shambhu	———	,,	,,
165.	,,	Lachhman	———	,,	,,
166.	,,	Ram baksh	———	,,	,,
167.	,,	Kishan Lal	———	,,	,,
168.	,,	Hardev	———	,,	,,
169.	Kheda (Total Martyrs-1)	Zabardast Khan	———	Muslim, CNK	Hanged in Nov. 1857
170.	Dhamaka Nagli (Total Martyrs-20, Traceable-3, in addition 17 persons were sentenced to life imprisonment in Jan. 1858)	Devi Ram s/o Jagram	———	jat	Hanged in Dec. 1857
171.	,,	Shiv Lal s/o Ram Sahai		———	,, ,,
172.	,,	Prithvi s/o Ram Singh		———	,, ,,
173.	Maroli (Total Martyrs-1)	Gulzari Lal	———	Jat	Hanged in Jan. 1858

References

1. Yadav, K.C., *Roll of Honour: Haryana's Martyrs of 1857*, Gurgaon, 2008, pp. 59-68.

Annexure-VIII

List of the Revolutionaries Martyred and Accused from Rewari District[1]

Sr. No.	Name of the Village with Details	Name of the Traceable Martyrs	Name of Revolutionaries Accused But went Underground	Caste/ Religion	Punishment
1.	Rewari (Total Martyrs-18, Traceable-12, Life Imprisonment -1, Went Underground -13)	Azam Khan	———	Pathan	Hanged on 1.2.1858
2.	,,	Sher Khan	———	,,	,,
3.	,,	Karim Khan	———	,,	,,
4.	,,	Sitab Khan	———	Shaikh	,,
5.	,,	Mir Khan	———	,,	,,
6.	,,	Nizamuddin s/o Imamuddin	———	,,	Hanged in Jan. 1858

7.	,,	Sultan Khan	———	,,	Hanged in March 1858
8.	,,	Bunyad Ali	———	Sayyed	,,
9.	,,	Jahur Beg	———	Mughal	,,
10.	,,	Gomesh Singh	———	Rajput	Hanged in Dec. 1857
11.	,,	Sidhu	———	,,	Hanged in Jan. 1858
12.	,,	Ganeshi	———	Koli	,,
13.	,,	Aslam s/o Amir Beg	———	Mughal	Life Imprisonment
14.	,,	———	Rao Tula Ram	Ahir	Died in Kabul, 23.9.1863
15.	,,	———	Rao Gopal Dev s/o Rao Nathu Singh	,,	WPR
16.	,,	———	Sheo Prashad	Bania	,,
17.	,,	———	Umrao Singh	,,	,,
18.	,,	———	Babar Ali s/o Majid Husain	Shaikh	,,
19.	,,	———	Murad Ali s/o Hisamuddin	,,	,,
20.	,,	———	Mohammad Amir Khan	,,	,,
21.	,,	———	Amjad Ali	,,	,,
22.	,,	———	Munawwar Ali	,,	,,
23.	,,	———	Amin Ali	,,	,,

24.	,,	———	Fateh Husain s/o Ghulam Husain	,,	,,
25.	,,	———	Aman Ali s/o Wazir Ali	,,	,,
26.	,,	———	Ahmad Baksh s/o Amirullah	,,	,,
27.	Nahar (Total Martyrs-40 untraceable)	40 Sepoys of Jhajjar and Delhi lost their lives while fighting against Showers	———	———	———
28.	Jatusana (Total Martyrs-6, Traceable-1, Went Underground -1)	Bajid Ali s/o Maru	———	Muslim Rajput	Hanged in August 1857

29.	,,	———	Mir Khan	Shaikh	WPR
30.	Nangal Pathani (Total Martyrs-2, Went Underground -2)	Kishan Singh	———	Ahir	Killed at Narnaul, 16.11. 1857
31.	,,	Ram Lal	———	,,	,,
32.	,,	———	Ram Sukh s/o Jiwa Ram	,,	WPR
33.	,,	———	Hira Singh	,,	,,
34.	Lisan (Went Underground -3)	———	Brijlal s/o Najib Singh	,,	,,
35.	,,	———	Tara Singh s/o Radha Kishan	,,	,,
36.	,,	———	Chhajju Ram s/o Rup Ram	,,	,,
37.	Asiaki (Went Underground -7)	———	Bhanu Pratap s/o Sawai Singh	,,	,,

38.	,,	———	Har Sewak s/o Sawai Singh	,,	,,
39.	,,	———	Man Singh s/o Bhanu Pratap	,,	,,
40.	,,	———	Tula Ram s/o Khushal Singh	,,	,,
41.	,,	———	Salig Ram s/o Khushal Singh	,,	,,
42.	,,	———	Sampat Singh s/o Sadhu Singh	,,	,,
43.	Jaitpur (Went Underground -1)	———	Bal Mukund s/o Hukum Singh	,,	,,
44.	Dharuhera (Went Underground -1)	———	Jagat Singh Ram s/o Kripa ram	,,	,,
45.	Bolni (Went Underground -1)	———	Hem Karan s/o Rura Ram	,,	,,

46.	Gurawara (Went Underground -1)	———	Baldev s/o Khub Ram	,,	,,
47.	Usadpur (Went Underground -1)	———	Daulat Ram s/o Hari Ram	,,	,,
48.	Palhawas (Went Underground -5)	———	Sewa Ram s/o Zahri Singh	,,	,,
49.	,,	———	Kanhi Ram s/o Sewa Ram	,,	,,
50.	,,	———	Ram Ratan s/o Zahri Singh	,,	,,
51.	,,	———	Sadi Ram s/o Gulab Singh	,,	,,
52.	,,	———	Har Sahai s/o Daulat Singh	,,	,,
53.	Guriani (Went Underground -6)	———	Salim Khan	Sayyed	,,
54.	,,	———	Khwaja Khan s/o Mehrab Khan	,,	,,

55.	,,	———	Mohammad Khan s/o Daulat Khan	Pathan	,,	
56.	,,	———	Bakshullah Khan s/o Nijat Khan	,,	,,	
57.	,,	———	Phool Mohammad s/o Salim Khan	,,	,,	
58.	,,	———	Najibuddaulah s/o Ghulam Mohd		,,	,,
59.	Kosli (Went Underground -2)	———	Prem Sukh s/o Khushal Singh	Ahir	,,	
60.	,,	———	Ramdhan s/o Kishan Sahai	,,	,,	
61.	Turkiawas (Total Martyrs-1, Went Underground -10)	Sadat Ali		Shaikh	Hanged in January 1858	
62.	,,	———	Najaf Ali	Muslim, CNK	WPR	
63.	,,	———	Haidar Ali	,,	,,	
64.	,,	———	Ahsan Ali	,,	,,	
65.	,,	———	Murad Baksh s/o Karim Beg	,,	,,	

66.	,,	———	Gulab Ali s/o Turrab Ali	,,	,,
67.	,,	———	Babar Ali s/o Nizam Ali	,,	,,
68.	,,	———	Talib Ali s/o Tayyab Ali	,,	,,
69.	,,	———	Baqar Ali s/o Qurban Ali	,,	,,
70.	,,	———	Nazar Ali s/o Najaf Ali	,,	,,

References

1. Yadav, K.C., *Roll of Honour: Haryana's Martyrs of 1857*, Gurgaon, 2008, pp. 69-74.

Annexure-IX

List of the Revolutionaries Martyred and Accused from Mahendragarh District[1]

Sr. No.	Name of the Village with Details	Name of the Traceable Martyrs	Name of Revolutionaries Accused But went Underground	Caste/ Religion	Punishment
1.	Mahendragarh or Kanaud (Total Martyrs-25)	Purdil Khan	———	Muslim, CNK	Hanged
2.	,,	Jummal	———	,,	,,
3.	,,	Ramju	———	,,	,,
4.	,,	Soman	———	,,	,,
5.	,,	Karim Khan	———	,,	,,
6.	,,	Nanu Ghazi	———	,,	,,
7.	,,	Kadi Ghazi	———	,,	,,
8.	,,	Abdul Khan	———	,,	,,
9.	,,	Tibbar Khan	———	,,	,,
10.	,,	Duggal Khan	———	,,	,,
11.	,,	Shahbaz Khan	———	,,	,,
12.	,,	Fayaz Mohammad	———	,,	,,

13.	,,	Shalut Khan	———	,,	,,
14.	,,	Duleh Khan	———	,,	,,
15.	,,	Sadur Khan	———	,,	,,
16.	,,	Hasu Khan	———	,,	,,
17.	,,	Sikandar Khan	———	,,	,,
18.	,,	Rahmat Khan	———	,,	,,
19.	,,	Gulab Khan	———	,,	,,
20.	,,	Kurum Khan	———	,,	,,
21.	,,	Bagga Khan	———	,,	,,
22.	,,	Baja Khan	———	,,	,,
23.	,,	Fayaz Khan	———	,,	,,
24.	,,	Nanak	———	,,	,,
25.	,,	Imam Khan	———	Muslim Rajput	Hanged in Jan. 1858
26.	Narnaul (Total Martyrs-460: 4 from Narnaul and 456 from different places died in the battle of Narnaul or Nasibpur; the most prominent were Rao Kishan Singh, Rao Ram Lal, Ghaus Mohammad Khan)	Afzal Khan	———	Muslim CNK	Hanged

27.	,,	Musharraf Khan	———	,,	,,
28.	,,	Khwaja Baksh	———	,,	Hanged in August 1857
29.	,,	Khairati	———	Shaikh	Hanged in Jan. 1858

References

1. Yadav, K.C., *Roll of Honour: Haryana's Martyrs of 1857*, Gurgaon, 2008, pp. 75-76.

Annexure-X

List of the Mewati Revolutionaries of Mewat Region, who faced Imprisonment and Property Confiscation[1]

Sr. No.	Name	Father's Name	Place	Punishment
1.	Ali Khan	Ishaq Khan	Jhajjar	Three Years Imprisonment
2.	(——)Baloch Pathan	——-	Gurabowani, Gurgaon	Terminated from Service of 3rd Regiment Punjab Cavalry
3.	Faijuddin Khan, Risaldar	Afzal Khan	Ghareni, Jhajjar	——-
4.	Ahmad Ali Khan, Naib Risaldar	Peer Khan	-do-	——-
5.	Azimullah Khan, Jamadar	Saadat Khan	-do-	-do-
6.	Moinuddin Khan, Dafadar	Peer Khan	-do-	-do-
7.	Hinjan Khan, Dafadar	Nawaz Khan	-do-	-do-
8.	Wali Mohammad Khan, Dafadar	Fazal Khan	-do-	-do-

9.	Risalat Khan, Dafadar	Fazal Khan	-do-	-do-
10.	Niyaz Mohammad Khan, Dafadar	Kunjeet Khan	Gherni	-do-
11.	Ghaus Mohammad Khan, Dafadar	Fateh Mohammad Khan	-do-	-do-
12.	Fazal Mohammad Khan, Dafadar	Ghulam Mohammad Khan	-do-	-do-
13.	Fateh Ahmad Khan, Nishanbardar	Jeevan Khan	———	——-
14.	Shaikh Wazir, Trumpeter	Shaikh Amanullah	Badashahpur	-do-
15.	Shaikh Naib Ali, Sawar	Shaikh Ameerullah	——-	-do-
16.	Shamsher Khan	———-	Dhareena, Jhajjar	-do-
17.	Niyaz Mohammad Khan	Fazal Khan	Burenis, Jhajjar	-do-
18.	Ismail Khan	Fateh Ali Khan	Dhareena, Jhajjar	-do-
19.	Husain Ali Khan	Sadullah Khan	——-	———

20.	Mahmood Khan	Meraj Khan	-do-	———
21.	Khudadad Khan	Jeevan Khan	-do-	-do-
22.	Faiyaz Ali Khan	Peer Khan	-do-	-do-
23.	Mohammad Yaar Khan	Noor Khan	-do-	-do-
24.	Izzat Khan	Fazal Khan	Burenis, Jhajjar	-do-
25.	Inam Ali Khan	Abdullah Khan	Dhareena, Jhajjar	-do-
26.	Mohammad Yaar Khan	Fazal Khan	Burenis, Jhajjar	-do-
27.	Shaikh Khuda Baksh	Shaikh Husain Baksh	Bhoorpur, Jhajjar	-do-
28.	Nabi Baksh Khan	Niyaz Mohammad Khan	Burenis, Jhajjar	-do-
29.	Ratan Singh	Khusral Singh	Firozabad, Jhajjar	-do-
30.	Jangbaz Khan	Samad Khan	Dhareena, Jhajjar	-do-
31.	Hameera Meo	———	Punhana, Gurgaon	———
32.	Bakhtawar Singh	———	Jhajjar	Property confiscated
33.	Ilahi baksh	———	Badshahpur	-do-

34.	Meer Khan	———	Naurangpur	-do-
35.	Raja Ballabhgarh	———	Ballabhgarh	-do-
36.	Sewa Ram	———	Paharjabas	-do-
37.	Harsahai	———	Nandrampurbas	-do-
38.	Mehtab	———	Shajahanpur, Palwal	-do-
39.	Brijnandan	———	Palwal	-do-
40.	Ramjas urf Zia	———	Rasulpur, Palwal	-do-
41.	Jafar	———	-do-	-do-
42.	Noor Khan	———	Shikrawa, Nuh	-do-
43,	Ghareeba Tilanga	———	Firozpur Jhirka	-do-
44.	(——)Mewati	———	Khora, Jharsa	-do-
45.	(——)Mewati	———	Khubri, Jharsa	-do-
46.	(——)Mewati	———	Jalalpur, Muari Jataula	-do-
47.	Paghambar Baksh, Sadar Ameen	———	Gurgaon	-do-
48.	Imdad Ali, Sarishtadar	———	-do-	-do-
49.	Ameer Ali, Munshi Sikh Regiment	———	-do-	Firstly imprisoned but freed later on
5C.	Abdul Ghafoor, Sikh Regiment	———	———	-do-

51.	Kunde Khan, Dafadar, II Punjab Cavalry	———	———-	-do-
52.	Sayed Ataul haq, kotwal Agra	———	Khajeenawara, Palwal	Imprisoned
53.	Fateh Khan	——-	——-	-do-
54.	Yaqub Ali Khan	———	———	Property confiscated
55.	Abdullah, Peon	——-	———	-do-
56.	Ram Gopal Dev	——-	———-	———-
57.	Nawab Farrukhnagar	——-	———	-do-
58.	Hamza Ali	———-	Rasulpur Palwal	-do-
59.	Ahsan Beg Mughal	Ameer Beg	Rewari	Imprisoned for 14 yrs but later freed
60.	Musahib Beg Mughal	Ameer Beg	Rewari	-do-
61.	Baba Goojar	——	Bhagoni	Imprisoned for 14 yrs
62.	Chandra Meo	Nandu	Tekri	Imprisoned for 7 yrs
63.	Mutru Meo	Chhotu	Tekri	-do-
64.	Peer Baksh	——-	———	Imprisoned for 3 yrs

65.	Chaina Goojar	Zalim	Bhango	Imprisoned for 14 yrs but later freed
66.	Hukum Singh Ahir	Fateh Singh	Rewari	Imprisoned for 7 yrs but later freed
67.	Dilawar Khan	Islam Khan	Farrukhnagar	Imprisoned for 11 yrs and fined with Rs. 50
68.	Rahim Baksh	Ilahi Baksh	Hasanpur	Life Imprisonment
69.	Mahmud Khan	Ghazi Khan	Kanpur	Imprisoned for 14 yrs
70.	Abdullah	Madara	Bhogipur	Imprisoned for 7 yrs
71.	Ali Khan	Isa Khan	Jhajjar	Imprisoned for 3 yrs but later freed with 50 Rs. fine
72.	Maula Baksh	Ghazi	Bahadurgarh	Imprisoned for 14 yrs
73.	Kewal Jat	Ramsukh	Chundhibas	Imprisoned for 5 yrs and fined with Rs. 1000
74.	Sewaram Jauhari	——-	Pulabas	Imprisoned for 3 yrs and fined with Rs. 2000
75.	Maulabaksh	Ghasi	Bahadurgarh	Imprisoned for 14 yrs

76.	Sewaram Jauhari	———	Rewari	Imprisoned for 4 yrs
77.	Ahsan Beg	Ameer Beg	Rewari	Imprisoned for 14 yrs
78.	Musahib Beg	Zameer Beg	Rewari	Imprisoned for 14 yrs
79.	Rahim Baksh	Ilahi Baksh	Hasanpur	Life Imprisonment
80.	Kewal	——-	Changhut	Imprisoned for 5 yrs

References

1. *File No. R/189, 194 Part-2, & 192*, Deputy Commissioner's office, Gurgaon, see also Yadav, K.C., *Revolt of 1857 in Haryana*, New Delhi, 1977, p. 140 and Husain, Iqbal, *1857 Ke Swatantra Sangram Me Mewatiyon Ka Balidan*, (Unpublished) AMU Aligarh, pp. 157-160.

Annexure-XI

List of the Mewati People Prized for their Loyalty[1]

Sr. No.	Name	Father's Name	Place	Prize
1.	Nanda Singh Sawar	———	———	Rupees 150/-
2.	Rampath	Todarmal	Rewari	Occupation of a confiscated village
3.	Shaikh Ghulam Nazar	Ghulam Husain	Rango	Rs. 200/- and land of three Beegha
4.	Ilahi Baksh	Husain Baksh	Gohana	-do-
5.	Meer Hidayat Ali	Tafazzul Ali	Mohna	Occupation of Mohna village
6.	Meer Farhat Ali	Husain Ali	Rasulpur	Pension of Sikri Jagirdar
7.	Harjeewan Lal Kayasth	Bahadur Singh	Sonali	Occupation of a confiscated village
8.	Harbaksh Kayasth	Nathumal	Sonali	Occupation of 22 Beegha in Sonali village

9.	Rasul Husain	Asghar Husain	Rasulpur	Rs. 120/- and land of 200 Beegha
10.	Shiv Sahai	Bhagwandas	Muradabad	Rs. 250/-
11.	Dhurwa Koiri	Bakshram	Matad	Rs. 30/-
12.	Mohammad Najaf Khan Tahsildar	Mohammad Mujeeb Khan	Narnaul	Rs. 1200/-
13.	Shankar Sahai Kayasth	Bhagwan Das	Muradabad	Rs. 250/-
14.	Jamuna Jat	Moti	Gurgaon	Rs. 200/- and land of 200 Beegha
15.	Lakshman Singh	Bhishm Singh	Nanu	Rs. 600/- and occupation of Mohammadpur village
16.	Sahab Singh	Bhishm Singh	Nanu	Rs. 120/-
17.	Govind Ram	Gyan Singh	-do-	-do-
18.	Sadiq Ali Sayed	Mohammad Shah	Shahpur	-do-
19.	Shahadat Ali	———	Shahpur	-do-
20.	Bajjar Singh	———-	Bhondsi	-do-
21.	Ahmad Khan Ranger	———	Alwar	-do-
22.	Bakshi Ram Rajput	———-	Shamshali, Alwar	-do-
23.	Jesu Dafadar	Chaturbhuj	Dola, Sonali	Rs. 68/- and occupation of a village

24.	Mohan Singh Sawar	Rambaksh	Sonali	Rs. 120/-
25.	Bhwani Singh Jamadar	Lal Singh	Kunti	Rs. 270/-
26.	Harphool Dafadar	Dheeraj Singh	Jharsa	Rs. 168/-
27.	Balwant Singh Sawar	Chaturbhuj	Dola	Rs. 120/-
28.	Baldev Singh Sawar	Fatha	Kote	-do-
29.	Durab Singh Sawar	Chaturbhuj	Bhondsi	-do-
30.	Guna Singh Sawar	Mankam Singh	Hirmithla	-do-
31.	Bhujan Singh Sawar	Kundan Singh	Bhaliali	Rs. 168/- and Rs. 30 per month for his two wives
32.	Suraj Singh Sawar	Pratap Singh	Rajgarh	Rs. 120/-
33.	Gulab Singh Sawar	Sewa Ram	Bhondsi	-do-
34.	Ratan Singh Sawar	Sumeet Singh	Bhondsi	-do-
35.	Vijayram Sawar	Najeeb Ram	Bhaliali	-do-
36.	Dode Ram Sawar	Hundan Singh	Bhaliali	-do-
37.	Umar Singh Sawar	Chharra Singh	Ballabhgarh	-do-
38.	Jairam Sawar	Anandan Singh	Bhondsi	-do-
39.	Asadullah Khan Sawar	Sadullah Khan	Basai	-do-

40.	Murtaza Khan Sawar	Shakirullah Khan	Basai	-do-
41.	Chetram Sawar	Kundu	Daula	-do-
42.	Khudabaksh	——-	Jhajjar	-do-
43.	Shaikh Zaheeruddin Sawar	Ameeruddin	Rasulpur	-do-
44.	Tafazzul Husain Sawar	Akbar Husain	Rasulpur	-do-
45.	Ameechand Sipahi	Juha	Gharang	Rs. 24/-
46.	Shiv Singh Sawar	Nangu Singh	Bhondsi	Rs. 120/-
47.	Kabeer Singh Sipahi	Sujja Singh	Bhondsi	Rs. 24/-
48.	Sandal Singh Sipahi	Ram Sahai	Bhondsi	-do-
49.	Jorawar Singh Sipahi	Pratap Singh	Mohammadpur	-do-
50.	Ilahi Baksh Sawar	Nabi Baksh	Rasulpur	Rs. 120/-
51.	Jamshed Khan Sawar	Jamiyat Khan	Kanpur	-do-
52.	Shaikh Zaheeruddin	Ameenuddin	Rasulpur	-do-
53.	Madde Khan	Islam Khan	Rasulpur	-do-
54.	Nathura	Tajo	Rasulpur	-do-
55.	Mehdi Khan	Shamat Khan	Rasulpur	-do-
56.	Lambardar, Geelah	——-	Geelah	Rs. 200/- and occupation of Bhinguri village

57	Lambardar, Kulsadah	——-	Kulsadah	Rs. 200/-
58.	Chainsukh Bania	———	Badshahpur	Occupation of Tekri village
59.	Jawahir Bhishti	——-	Muradabad	Rs. 100/-
60.	Karimuddin	——-	Gurgaon	Rs. 24/- and land of 100 Beegha
61.	Jumman Khan	——-	Ludhiana	Rs. 50/-
62.	Husain Baksh	——-	Bangli	-do-
63.	Jan Mohammad	——-	Banaras	-do-
64.	Jhunga	——-	Barnala	-do-
65.	Sadul	——-	Uchhlipur	-do-
66.	Jhungru	——-	Barnala	-do-
67.	Nanku	——-	Musadis	-do-
68.	Soodil	——-	Hoak	-do-
69.	Nanu	——-	Amipur	-do-
70.	Bhugoli	——-	Numles	-do-
71.	Ameenuddin Lambardar	——-	Harsau	No Prize
72.	Hayat Khan	——-	——-	Occupation of a village
73.	Mansukh	——-	——-	-do-
74.	Nasrullah Khan	——-	——-	Rs. 200/-
75.	Ashraf Khan	——-	——-	-do-
76.	Lala Kishori Lal	——-	Delhi	——-
77.	Karim Khan Dafadar	——-	——-	——-
78.	Pawanda Khan Chaukidar	——-	Shikarpur	——-

79.	Munna Lal	——-	———	——-
80.	Mehrab Khan Mewati, Peon	——-	Sohna	——-
81.	Tej Singh Jamadar	——-	———	——-
82.	Mohan Singh Sawar	——-	———	——-
83.	Ramdhan Jamadar	——-	Shahjahanpur	Rs. 400/- and assured for robe of honour

References

1. *File No. R/169*, Deputy Commissioner's office, Gurgaon, see also Husain, Iqbal, *1857 Ke Swatantra Sangram Me Mewatiyon Ka Balidan*, (Unpublished) AMU Aligarh, pp. 181-189.

Bibliography

Confidential Files, Journals, Magazines, and Newspapers

1. *Aaj Kal* (Magazine), New Delhi, 2007.
2. *Akhbar-uz-Zafar*, Delhi, 13th September, 1857.
3. *Akhbar-uz-Zafar*, Delhi, 19th July, 1857.
4. *Akhbar-uz-Zafar*, Delhi, 23 August, 1857.
5. *Arzdast, Mujahideene Mewat*, NAI, New Delhi.
6. *Dehli Urdu Akhbar*, Delhi, 24 May, 1857.
7. *Dehli Urdu Akhbar*, Delhi, 5th July, 1857.
8. *ELTWeekly*, Vol. 5, Issue-16, 13 May, 2013.
9. *File No. R/1, 8, 143, 168, 169, 184, R/189, 192, 193, 194 Part-2*, and *R/194*, Deputy Commissioner's Office, Gurgaon.
10. *Frontline*, Vol. 24, Issue 12, June 16-29, 2007.
11. *Journal of the Research Society of Pakistan*, (*History of Mewat: An Outline*, Shahabuddin Khan Meo) Vol. 48, No. 1, University of the Punjab, Lahore, 2011.
12. *Meo Darpan*, August, 1997.
13. *People's Democracy*, Vol. XXXI, No. 14, April, 8, 2007.
14. *People's Democracy*, Vol. XXXI, No. 21, May 27, 2007.
15. *Research Paper*, Shamsul Islam, *Hindus and Muslims in the First War of Independence of 1857 & Emergence of Two-Nation Theory* (Paper presented in a conference at Trivandrum, Kerala, on May 19, 2007).
16. *Shodh Samiksha Aur Mulyankan*, International Referred Research Journal, Jaipur, July, 2011 Vol. III, Issue- 30.

17. *Social Scientist*. Vol. 26, No. 1-4 (Jan-April 1998), New Delhi.

18. *The Dawn*, Magazine, July 30, 2006.

19. *The Panjab Past and Present*, Vol. XXXVIII, Patiala, April 2007.

20. *World Policy Journal*, (*The Hidden Roots of Wahhabism in British India*- Charles Allen), Vol. 22, No. 2, Massachusetts, USA, Summer 2005.

Gazetteers

1. *A Gazetteer of the Territories under the Government of the East India Company*, Thornton, Edward, Vol. II, London, 1854.

2. *Gazetteer of Ulwur*, Powlett, W., London, 1878.

3. *Gurgaon District Gazetteer*, Chandigarh, 1983.

4. *Haryana District Gazetteer, Hisar*, Chandigarh, 1987.

5. *Haryana District Gazetteer, Mahendragarh*, Chandigarh, 1988.

6. *Haryana District Gazetteers, Faridabad*, Chandigarh, 1993.

7. *Haryana State Gazetteer*, Volume I, Chandigarh, 2001.

8. *Haryana State Gazetteer*, Volume II, Chandigarh, 2005.

9. *Imperial Gazetteer of India*, Frowde, Henry, Vol. XVI, London, 1908.

10. *Imperial Gazetteer of India*, Horace, W. Carpentier, Provincial Series, Vol. II, Calcutta, 1908.

11. *Imperial Gazetteer of India*, Hunter, William Wilson, Vol. V, London 1885.

12. *Punjab District Gazetteer*, Vol. IV-A, Lahore, 1911.

13. *Punjab Gazetteer, Gurgaon District, 1883-84*, Lahore, 1884.

Books

1. Abdul Shakoor, Hakim, *Tarikh Meo Kshatri*, Shikrawa, 2010.

2. Abul Fazal, *Ain-i-Akbari*, Eng. Trans., H. Blochmann, Vol. I, Calcutta, 1873.

3. Ahmad, Aijaz, *Mewat: A Retrospective*, Ghaziabad, 2013.

4. Ahmad, Iqbal, *Nawab Shamsuddin Khan Aur Karim Khan Meo*, Lahore, 2010.

5. Aitchison, Charles, *Rulers of India: Lord Lawrence*, Oxford, 1892.

6. Alexander Smith, Faulkner, *An Historical Sketch of the Naruka State of Ulwar in Rajputana*, Calcutta, 1895.

7. Athar, Mohammad Swaleh Khan, *Tarikh Meo Mehar*, Firozpur Jhirka, 2009.

8. Atkinson, Edwin Thomas, *Statistical Descriptive and Historical Account of the North Western Provinces of India*, Vol. II, Allahabad, 1875.

9. Babar, Zaheeruddin Mohammad, *Tuzuk-i-Babari*, (Eng. Trans. John Leyden and William Erskine, *Memoirs of Zaheeruddin Mohammad Babar*), London, 1826.

10. Ball, Charles, *History of the Indian Mutiny*, Vol. II, London, 1863.

11. Barani, Ziauddin, *Tarikh-i-Firoz Shahi*, (Urdu Trans. Sayed Muinul Haque), Lahore, 2004.

12. Beale, Thomas William, (Revised by Henery George Jeene), *An Oriental Biographical Dictionary*, London, 1894.

13. Budh Prakash, *Glimpses of Haryana*, Kurukshetra, 1967.

14. Cave-Browne, John, *The Punjab and Delhi in 1857*, Vol. II, Edinburgh, 1861.

15. Channing, F.C., *Land Revenue Settlement of Gurgaon District*, Lahore, 1882.

16. Chick, N.A., *Annals of the Indian Rebellion, 1857-58*, London, 1874.

17. Cunningham, Alexander, *Reports of the Tour in Eastern Rajputana in 1882-83*, Vol. XX, Calcutta, 1885.

18. Elliot, H.M. and Dowson, John, *History of India, as told by its own Historians, The Mohammadan Period*, Vol. III, London, 1871.

19. Elliot, H.M. and Dowson, John, *History of India, as told by its own Historians, The Mohammadan Period*, Vol. II, London, 1869.

20. Elliot, H.M. and Dowson, John, *The History of India as told by its own Historians, The Mohammadan Period*, Vol. V, London, 1873.

21. Elliot, H.M. and Dowson, John, *The History of India, as told by its own Historians, The Mohammadan Period*, Vol. IV, London, 1872.

22. Firishta, Mohammad Qasim Hindu Shah, *Tarikh-i-Firishta*, (Eng. Trans., John Briggs, *History of the Rise of the Mohammadan Power in India, Till the Year 1612*, Vol. II), London, 1829.

23. Firishta, Mohammad Qasim Hindu Shah, *Tarikh-i-Firishta*, (Eng. Trans., John Briggs, *History of the Rise of the Mohammadan Power in India, Till the Year 1612*, Vol. I), London, 1829.

24. Growse, F. S., *Mathura: A District Memoire; With Numerous Illustrations*, Third Edition, North-Western Province And Oudh Government Press, 1883.

25. Gubbins, Martin Richard, *An Account of the Mutinies of Oudh and of the siege of the Lucknow Residency; With some Observation on the Condition of the Province of Oudh and of the Causes of the Mutiny of the Bengal Army*, London, 1858.

26. Haig, Sir Wolseley, *The Cambridge History of India, Volume III, Turks and Afghans*, Cambridge, 1928.

27. Handcock, Arthur Gore, *The Siege of Delhi in 1857: A Short Account*, Allahabad, 1897.

28. Hashim, Amir Ali, *The Meos of Mewat: Old Neighbours of New Delhi*, New Delhi, 1970.

29. Hodson, William Stephen Raikes, *Twelve Years of a Soldiers Life in India: Being Extracts from the Letters of the Late Major W. S. R. Hodson*, (edited by George H. Hodson), Boston, 1860.

30. Hunter, William Wilson, *The Indian Musalmans*, London, 1876.

31. Husain, Iqbal, *1857 Ke Swatantra Sangram Me Mewatiyon Ka Balidan*, (Unpublished) AMU Aligarh.

32. Ibbetson, Denzil, *Panjab Castes*, Lahore, 1916.

33. Innes, P.R., *History of the Bengal European Regiment, now the Royal Munster Fusiliers and How It Helped to Win India*, London, 1886.

34. James Burgess, *The Chronology of Modern India, for Four Hundred Years from the Close of the Fifteenth Century, A.D. 1494-1894*, Edinburg, 1913.

35. Jaques, Tony, *Dictionary of the Battles and Seiges*, Connecticut, USA, 2007.

36. Karl Marx and Angels, *Collected Works*, Part-39, Moscow, 1986.

37. Khan, Habibur Rahman, *Tazkira Sufia-i-Mewat*, Delhi 1985.

38. Khan, Mohammad Ashraf, *Meo Qaum Aur Mewat*, Nuh, (ND).

39. Khan, Syed Ahmad, *Asbab-e-Baghawat-e-Hind*, Patna, 1999.

40. Lane-Poole, Stanley, *Babar*, Oxford, (ND).

41. Lowe, Thomas, *Central India During the Rebellion of 1857 and 1858, London, 1860.*

42. Malleson, George Bruce, *The Indian Mutiny of 1857*, New York, 1891.

43. Malleson, George Bruce, *History of the Indian Mutiny, 1857-59*, Vol. III, London, 1880.

44. Malleson, George Bruce, *Indian Mutiny of 1857*, London, 1912.

45. Malleson, George Bruce, *Kaye's and Malleson's History of the Indian Mutiny of 1857-8*, Vol. V, London, 1896.

46. Malleson, George Bruce, *Kaye's and Malleson's History of the Indian Mutiny of 1857-8*, Vol. IV, London, 1911.

47. Malleson, George Bruce, *Kaye's and Malleson's History of the Indian Mutiny of 1857-8*, Vol. VI, London, 1914.

48. Mayaram, Shail, *Against History Against State: Counterperspectives from the Margins*, New Delhi, 2004.

49. Mead, Henry, *The Sepoy Revolt: Its Causes and its Consequences*, London, 1858.

50. Meo, Siddiq Ahmad, *Sangram 1857: Mewatiyon Ka Yogdan*, Nuh, 2006.

51. Metcalfe, Charles Theophilus, *Two Native Narratives of the Mutiny in Delhi*, (Eng. Trans. of *Roznamcha Mainudin Hasan Khan* and *Munshi Jeewan Lal*), London, 1898.

52. Mirza Asadullah Khan Ghalib, *Dastamboo*, Urdu Trans. Khwaja Ahmad Faruqi, New Delhi, 2000.

53. Muir, Sir William, *Records of the Intelligence Department of the Government of the North-West Provinces of India During the Mutiny of 1857*, Vol. I, Edinburgh, 1902.

54. Muir, Sir William, *Records of the Intelligence Department of the Government of the North-West Provinces of India during the Mutiny of 1857*, Vol. II, Edinburgh, 1902.

55. Nawab Server-ul-Mulk Bahadur, *My Life, Being the Autobiography*, Eng. Trans. Nawab Jiwan Yar Jung Bahadur, London, (ND).

56. Noorani, Khushtar, *Allama Fazle Haq Khairabadi: Chand Unwanat*, Idara-e-Fikre Islami, Delhi, 2011.

57. Qasmi, Ataur Rahman, *1857 Aur Haryana*, New Delhi, 2011, p. 70.

58. Raikes, Charles, *Notes on the Revolt in the North-Western Provinces of India*, London, 1858.

59. Reginald, George Burton, *The Revolt in Central India 1857-59*, Simla, 1908.

60. Rice Holmes, T., *A History of the Indian Mutiny and of the Disturbances which Accompanied it among the Civil Population*, New York, 1898.

61. Roberts, P.E., *A Historical Geography of the British Dependencies: India*, Vol. VII, London, 1914.

62. Rose, H.A., *A Glossary of the Tribes and Castes of the Punjab and North-West Frontier Province*, Vol. III, New Delhi, 1977.

63. Sahai, Jwala, *History of Bharatpur*, Agra, 1912.

64. Shamsh, Shamsuddin, *Meos of India: Their Customs and Laws*, Delhi, 1983.

65. Sharma, S.R., *Mughal Empire in India, 1526-1761*, Part-I, Bombay, 1934.

66. Showers, Charles Lionel, *A Missing Chapter of the Indian Mutiny*, New York, 1888.

67. Shrivastawa, M.P., *The Indian Mutiny of 1857*, Allahabad, 1979.

68. Siraj, Minhaj, *Tabaqat-i-Nasiri*, Urdu Trans. Ghulam Rasul Mehar, Vol. II Lahore, 2004.

69. Verma, D.C. & Sukhbir Singh, *Haryana*, New Delhi, 2009.

70. Vibart, H.M., *Richard Baird Smith: The Leader of the Delhi Heroes in 1857*, Westminster, 1897.

71. Williams, Rushbrook, *An Empire Builder of the 16th century*, London, 1918.

72. Yadav, K.C., *Haryana, Itihas Avam Sanskriti*, part-2, New Delhi, 1992.

73. Yadav, K.C., *Revolt of 1857 in Haryana*, New Delhi, 1977.

74. Yadav, K.C., *Roll of Honour: Haryana's Martyrs of 1857*, Gurgaon, 2008.

75. Yadav, K.C., *1857: The Role of Punjab Haryana and Himachal Pradesh*, New Delhi, 2013.

76. Yadava, S.D.S., *Followers of Krishna: Yadavas of India*, New Delhi, 2006.

77. Zakir, Kashmiri Lal, *Tahrik-e-Azadi Aur Mewat*, Panchkula, 2008.